INTERNATIONAL POLITICAL ECONOMY SERIES

General Editor: Timothy M. Shaw, Professor of Political Science and International Development Studies, and Director of the Centre for Foreign Policy Studies, Dalhousie University, Nova Scotia, Canada

Recent titles include:

Pradeep Agrawal, Subir V. Gokarn, Veena Mishra, Kirit S. Parikh and Kunal Sen
ECONOMIC RESTRUCTURING IN EAST ASIA AND INDIA : Perspectives on Policy Reform

Solon L. Barraclough and Krishna B. Ghimire
FORESTS AND LIVELIHOODS: The Social Dynamics of Deforestation in Developing Countries

Jerker Carlsson, Gunnar Köhlin and Anders Ekbom
THE POLITICAL ECONOMY OF EVALUATION: International Aid Agencies and the Effectiveness of Aid

Edward A. Comor (*editor*)
THE GLOBAL POLITICAL ECONOMY OF COMMUNICATION

Paul Cook and Frederick Nixson (*editors*)
THE MOVE TO THE MARKET?: Trade and Industry Policy Reform in Transitional Economies

O. P. Dwivedi
DEVELOPMENT ADMINISTRATION: From Underdevelopment to Sustainable Development

John Healey and William Tordoff (*editors*)
VOTES AND BUDGETS: Comparative Studies in Accountable Governance in the South

Noeleen Heyzer, James V. Riker and Antonio B. Quizon (*editors*)
GOVERNMENT–NGO RELATIONS IN ASIA: Prospects and Challenges for People-Centred Development

George Kent
CHILDREN IN THE INTERNATIONAL POLITICAL ECONOMY

Laura Macdonald
SUPPORTING CIVIL SOCIETY: The Political Role of Non-Governmental Organizations in Central America

Gary McMahon (*editor*)
LESSONS IN ECONOMIC POLICY FOR EASTERN EUROPE FROM
LATIN AMERICA

Juan Antonio Morales and Gary McMahon (*editors*)
ECONOMIC POLICY AND THE TRANSITION TO DEMOCRACY: The Latin
American Experience

Paul J. Nelson
THE WORLD BANK AND NON-GOVERNMENTAL ORGANIZATIONS
The Limits of Apolitical Development

Archibald R. M. Ritter and John M. Kirk (*editors*)
CUBA IN THE INTERNATIONAL SYSTEM: Normalization and Integration

Ann Seidman and Robert B. Seidman
STATE AND LAW IN THE DEVELOPMENT PROCESS: Problem-Solving and
Institutional Change in the Third World

Tor Skålnes
THE POLITICS OF ECONOMIC REFORM IN ZIMBABWE: Continuity and
Change in Development

John Sorenson (*editor*)
DISASTER AND DEVELOPMENT IN THE HORN OF AFRICA

Howard Stein (*editor*)
ASIAN INDUSTRIALIZATION AND AFRICA : Studies in Policy Alternatives
to Structural Adjustment

Deborah Stienstra
WOMEN'S MOVEMENTS AND INTERNATIONAL ORGANIZATIONS

Larry A. Swatuk and Timothy M. Shaw (*editors*)
THE SOUTH AT THE END OF THE TWENTIETH CENTURY: Rethinking the
Political Economy of Foreign Policy in Africa, Asia, the Caribbean and Latin
America

Sandra Whitworth
FEMINISM AND INTERNATIONAL RELATIONS

Children in the
International Political
Economy

George Kent
Professor of Political Science
University of Hawaii, Honolulu

First published in Great Britain 1995 by
MACMILLAN PRESS LTD
Houndmills, Basingstoke, Hampshire RG21 6XS
and London
Companies and representatives
throughout the world

A catalogue record for this book is available
from the British Library.

ISBN 0–333–59897–0

First published in the United States of America 1995 by
ST. MARTIN'S PRESS, INC.,
Scholarly and Reference Division,
175 Fifth Avenue,
New York, N.Y. 10010

ISBN 0–312–12870–3

Library of Congress Cataloging-in-Publication Data
Kent, George, 1939–
Children in the international political economy / George Kent.
p.   cm. — (International political economy series)
Includes bibliographical references and index.
ISBN 0–312–12870–3 (cloth)
1. Children—Economic conditions.   2. Children—Social conditions.
3. Children's rights.   I. Title.   II. Series.
HQ767.9.K46   1995
305.23—dc20   95–17960
                                                              CIP

10   9   8   7   6   5   4   3   2   1
04   03   02   01   00   99   98   97   96   95

Printed and bound in Great Britain by
Ipswich Book Co Ltd
Ipswich, Suffolk

Contents

List of Tables and Figures   ix

Preface   xi

List of Abbreviations   xiii

PART I   FRAMEWORK AND SETTING

1 Responsibility   **3**
Children's Conditions   3
Children in Civil Society   5
Children in Global Civil Society   8
Overview   10

2 The Global Economy   **13**
Division of Labor   13
Debt and Structural Adjustment   16
The Roots of Poverty   18
Population and the Economy   20
International Obligations   27

PART II   CHILDREN'S PROBLEMS

3 Mortality   **31**
Priorities, Not Poverty   34
Denial   36
Intentionality   37
Hatred?   39
Genocide?   41

4 Child Labor   **45**
Remedies   47
Business-Like Schooling   51

5 Child Prostitution   **57**
Trafficking   58
Traveling Customers   62
Economic Pressures   71
Domestic Law   74
International Control   76

6 Armed Conflict **83**
Trade Guns for Butter? 90
International Humanitarian Law 92
Implementation 96
Implementing Article 38 97
The Question of Agency 98

7 Malnutrition **103**
Causes of Malnutrition 103
Malnutrition and Mortality 106
Growth Measurement 107
Numbers of People Malnourished 109

PART III   THE HUMAN RIGHTS RESPONSE

8 Nutrition Rights **117**
History of Nutrition Rights 117
Why Children? 120
The Principle 121
Multi-Layering 125
Carrots, Not Sticks 127
Funding 128
Capping Entitlements 129
Using Existing Programs 130
Goals as Rights 133
Nutrition Rights Advocacy 137

9 Children's Rights **141**
Soft vs. Hard Rights 142
Rights Require Accountability 145
Monitoring and Reporting on Rights 148
International Nutrition Monitoring 155

10 International Children's Rights **157**
Rights to Assistance 158
The Question of Consent 159
Progressive Realization 163
Chronic Conditions 166
Development Assistance vs. Humanitarian Assistance 167
The Principle Internationally 169
International Nutrition Rights 171
Implementation Internationally 173

Contents

A Global Action Plan   174
Sovereignty and Civilization   176

Appendix: Data on Children   179

Notes and References   213

Select Bibliography   239

Index   249

List of Tables and Figures

Tables
3.1 Estimated annual deaths of children under 5 by
cause, 1986   33
7.1 Malnutrition in developing countries, 1975–90   110
7.2 Prevalence of underweight children under 5 years in
developing countries, 1975–90   111

Figures
7.1 Prevalence of underweight children in developing
countries, 1975–90   112
7.2 Percentage underweight preschool children vs. GNP
per capita   113

Appendix Tables
A1 Basic indicators   182
A2 Nutrition   190
A3 Health   198
A4 Education   206

Preface

The sorry condition of children throughout the world is well documented, showing up in an endless stream of documentation from the United Nations agencies, Defense for Children International, Amnesty International, and many other organizations. We have a great deal of information about their plight. The real puzzles are how should we understand that plight and what can we do about it? How do we get past the horror stories?

Echoing the *Declaration of the Rights of the Child of* 1924, the *Declaration of the Rights of the Child* of 1959 said 'mankind owes to the child the best it has to give.' In this study I explore the nature of our obligations to children and suggest ways in which those obligations could be fulfilled more effectively. In particular, if children are to have clear rights, it is also necessary to spell out the duties that individuals and agencies must carry out to honor those rights. Only then will we know who owes what, and only then will we be able to hold anyone accountable for fulfilling these duties.

Our obligations are not only to children within the borders of our separate nations. Where there are large-scale failures to look after the needs of children, and national governments will not or cannot do what needs to be done, the international community has a positive obligation to act to assure that the quality of children's lives comes up at least to some minimum level of decency.

As the select bibliography suggests, this book builds on the work of many others, including many specialists on children issues, nutrition, and human rights. I am also indebted to the publishers of my earlier writing for allowing me to re-use some of that material here. An earlier version of Chapter 5 appeared as 'Little Foreign Bodies: International Dimensions of Child Prostitution,' in Michael Freeman and Philip Veerman, eds., *The Ideologies of Children's Rights* (Dordrecht, The Netherlands: Martinus Nijhoff, 1992), pp. 323–46. Most of Chapter 8 appeared as 'Children's Right to Adequate Nutrition,' in the *International Journal of Children's Rights*, Vol. 1, No. 2 (1993), pp. 133–54. Material from both of these articles is reprinted by permission of Kluwer Academic Publishers. A version of Chapter 2 originally appeared as 'The Massive Mortality of Children,' in Israel W. Charny, ed., *The Widening Circle of Genocide* (New Brunswick, New Jersey: Transaction Books, 1994), which is

Volume 3 in the series, *Genocide: A Critical Bibliographic Review*. Chapter 2 also draws from my brief essay, 'The Denial of Children's Mortality,' *Internet on the Holocaust and Genocide*, No. 44–6 (September 1993), pp. 18, 20.

Much of the material in Chapter 6 appeared in a monograph on *War and Children's Survival* and a working paper on *Implementing the Rights of Children in Armed Conflict*, both published by the Spark Matsunaga Institute for Peace at the University of Hawaii. I like to think that putting these various analyses into this larger framework makes them more meaningful.

I also want to thank the United Nations Administrative Committee on Coordination/Subcommittee on Nutrition for permission to republish some of their tables and figures, and the United Nations Children's Fund for permission to republish their data on children in the appendix.

Tim Shaw of Dalhousie University, general editor of the series on International Political Economy, and Clare Andrews and Gráinne Twomey, editors of the series for Macmillan, deserve special gratitude for their support and encouragement. Also Jeffrey Owens, Michael Owens, Rudy Rummel, Mike Shapiro, and Bob Stauffer have been generous with their comments and advice on the manuscript, and I thank them for that.

I want to thank my wife, Joan, and our children, Greg and Jeff, for their tolerance for my sustained attention to this project. They should know that even while I worry about all the world's children, the three of them are there in the very center of my personal rings of responsibility, and I am concerned with them first.

Finally, I want to dedicate this book to the memory of James P. Grant, in gratitude for his extraordinary leadership of the United Nations Children's Fund from 1980 until early 1995. He helped to save and improve the lives of millions of children around the world, and he inspired all who knew of his work and his vision.

GEORGE KENT

List of Abbreviations

ACC/SCN	Administrative Committee on Coordination, Subcommittee on Nutrition of the United Nations
AFDC	Aid to Families with Dependent Children
CDF	Children's Defense Fund
CESCR	Committee on Economic, Social, and Cultural Rights of the United Nations
CMR	children's mortality rate (number of children dying before their fifth birthdays for every thousand born alive)
CRC	Committee on the Rights of the Child
DCI	Defence for Children International
DHA	Department of Humanitarian Affairs of the United Nations
ECOSOC	Economic and Social Council of the United Nations
ECPAT	End Child Prostitution in Asian Tourism
FAO	Food and Agriculture Organization of the United Nations
FIAN	Foodfirst Information and Action Network
ICESCR	International Covenant on Economic, Social, and Cultural Rights
ICRC	International Committee for the Red Cross
IDNDR	International Decade for Natural Disaster Reduction
IEFR	International Emergency Food Reserve
IFAD	International Fund for Agricultural Development of the United Nations
IGO	international governmental organization
ILO	International Labour Office
IMR	infant mortality rate (number of children dying before their first birthdays for every thousand born alive)
INGO	international nongovernmental organization
OFDA	Office of Foreign Disaster Assistance of USAID
PEM	protein-energy malnutrition
SIDA	Swedish International Development Authority
TFCNR	Task Force on Children's Nutrition Rights
TINP	Tamilnadu Integrated Nutrition Program
UNDP	United Nations Development Programme
UNDRO	United Nations Disaster Relief Office
UNHCR	United Nations High Commissioner for Refugees
UNICEF	United Nations Children's Fund
USAID	United States Agency for International Development

WANAHR   World Alliance for Nutrition and Human Rights
WFC   World Food Council of the United Nations
WFP   World Food Programme of the United Nations
WHO   World Health Organization of the United Nations

Part I
Framework and Setting

1 Responsibility

Much of our understanding of the plight of the world's children is based on individual horror stories coming from distant countries in Africa and Asia or nearby inner cities. News magazines and television carry those haunting images of three-year olds carrying bricks, children brutalized in warfare, physically and sexually abused children, and hollow-eyed toddlers starving to death. We need to get at the larger dimensions of the situation of children, however, if we are to understand and respond efficiently and effectively to these issues.

CHILDREN'S CONDITIONS

Worldwide, more than twelve million children die before their fifth birthdays each year. Over 180 million children in developing countries are seriously underweight. Many millions are seriously ill. Many live on the streets. Many are subjected to abusive working conditions. Detailed information on children worldwide is assembled every year in the United Nations Children's Fund's *The State of the World's Children*. Selected data from the 1994 edition are provided in the appendix. The striking thing shown in these data is the enormous variation in the quality of children's lives, from the worst to the best. For example, Table A.1 in the appendix shows that in 1992, in Niger 320 children died before their fifth birthdays for every thousand born. In contrast, in Japan and Ireland only six died for every thousand born. Table A.2 indicates that in Niger forty nine percent of the children under five were moderately or severely underweight. In many poor nations twenty percent or more of the newborns have low birth weights, while in several developed nations only four percent had low birth weights. In many poor nations less than half the children are enrolled in primary school. Consistently, children of poor nations, and particularly children of non-white poor nations, are the worst off. In the aggregate, the largest numbers of miserable children are in South Asia.

Money isn't everything. In some places such as Costa Rica, children are much better off than would be expected on the basis of the nation's economic level. Similarly, there are some high income nations in which children do much worse than would be expected on the basis of income considerations alone. In some of these nations much of the income is from oil, with the proceeds benefiting only a narrow elite. Apart from considerations of wealth totals and distribution, there also seems to be a strong cultural factor at work. With regard to children's well-being, Scandinavian nations do especially well, and Muslim nations do poorly.

Aggregate data for entire nations of the sort shown in the tables mask important variations within nations. For example, Table A.2 in the appendix shows that most poor nations have close to one hundred percent of the daily per capita calorie supply that is required, but these data describe national averages. Some people get more than they need, and many others get less than they need. Just as resources and well-being are not distributed uniformly across the world, they also tend to be skewed in favor of particular areas and particular groups within nations.

In industrialized nations, most children do well, but some are severely disadvantaged. In the United States, for example, fully one-fifth of the nation's children live below the official poverty line, and immunization rates are worse than those of any other developed nation. In the United States and the United Kingdom, children were estimated to have been worse off in 1989 than they were two decades earlier.[1]

Of course, many of the problems faced by children are not counted and coded in ways that can be presented in neat tables. Several of these problems are reviewed in Part II of this book.

There has been real progress in the quality of children's lives, regularly documented in UNICEF's *State of the World's Children* reports and also in its new annual series, *The Progress of Nations*:

> In little more than one generation, average real incomes have more than doubled; child death rates have been more than halved; malnutrition rates been reduced by about 30%; life expectancy has increased by about a third; the proportion of children enrolled in primary school has risen from less than half to more than three quarters; and the percentage of rural families with access to safe water has risen from less than 10% to more than 60%.[2]

However, satisfaction with successes to date must be tempered with appreciation of the great distance still to be traveled if all children are to live a life of decency. Measles, for example, 'is being forced to relinquish its grip,' but it 'still kills more children every year than all the world's wars and famines put together.'[3]

One clear lesson learned is that significant gains in children's well-being do not result from economic growth alone. They also require progressive social policy based on a sustained commitment to improvements in the well-being of the poor. Much larger commitments need to be made in areas such as nutrition, primary health care, basic education, safe water supply, and family planning.[4] Progressive social policy is one of the key defining features of what civil society ought to be.

CHILDREN IN CIVIL SOCIETY

Scholars who study *civil society* explore not how societies are organized but how they ought to be organized. What forms of social organization best lead to human fulfillment? Is the good society one that emphasizes democracy and public participation in decision-making? Is it one that emphasizes the virtues of creative work? Should it be based on production and consumption based on a free market? Is it one centered on nationalism? Or should civil society be a combination of these, accommodating diversity among individuals and encouraging many forms of free social association at local, national, regional, and global levels?[5] In this scholarly discussion, as in so many other contexts, children are neglected.

What is the place of children in civil society? What does it mean to be a child? As one observer put it, the child

> ... is to be shielded from the *direct* demands of economic, political, and sexual forces. Children have a claim on their parents, and they have a right to receive support from their families and their communities, regardless of their economic value in accounting terms. Usually families want to provide this support and will do so if at all possible. But when parents cannot provide for their children, society must acknowledge some responsibility in helping them.[6]

This can be said more systematically. Between birth and adulthood, children start out in high dependency and low competence and then normally grow to the opposite, low dependency and high competence, to become fully active participant-citizens in society. The focus here is on the beginning of that continuum, the role of highly dependent small children in society.

Our principal obligation toward children is to promote their development, understood as empowerment or increasing self-reliance. The task is to help increase children's capacity to define, analyze, and act on their own problems until they can become independent, full participants in civil society.

Who is responsible for children? As highly dependent creatures, small children need to have others take care of them. The first line of responsibility is with the parents, of course, but others have a role as well. In asking who is responsible for children, the question is not whose fault is it that children suffer so much (who caused the problems?) but who should take action to remedy the problems? Many different social agencies may have some role in looking after children, but what should be the interrelationships among them? What should be the roles of churches, fraternal societies, local and national governments and other agencies?

Most children have two vigorous advocates from the moment they are born, and even before they are born. Their parents devote enormous resources to serving their interests. These are not sacrifices. The best parents do not support their children out of a sense of obligation or as investments. Rather, they support their children as extensions of themselves, as part of their wholeness.

In many cases, however, that bond is broken or is never created. Fathers disappear. Many mothers disappear as well. In some cities hundreds of children are abandoned each month in the hospitals in which they are born. Bands of children live in the streets by their wits, preyed upon by others. Frequently children end up alone as a result of warfare or other political crises. Many children are abandoned because they are physically or mentally handicapped. Some parents become so disabled by drugs or alcohol that they cannot care for their children.

In some cases children who cannot be cared for by their biological parents are looked after by others. In many cultures children belong not only to their biological parents but to the community as a whole. The responsibility and the joy of raising children are widely shared.

In many places, especially in 'developed' nations, that option of community-based care is no longer available because of the collapse of the idea and the practice of community. Many of us live in nice neighborhoods in well-ordered societies, but the sense of community – of love and responsibility and commitment to one another – has vanished. In such cases the remaining hope of the abandoned child is the government, the modern substitute for community. People look to government to provide human services that the local community no longer provides.

As children mature the first priority is to help them become responsible for themselves. So long as they are not mature, however, children ought to get their nurturance from their parents. Failing that, they ought to get it from their local communities. Failing that, they ought to get it from the local governments. Failing that, it should come from their national governments. Failing that, they ought to get it from the international community. The responsibility hierarchy looks like this:

child
family
community
local government
state government
national government
international nongovernmental organizations
international governmental organizations

This can be pictured as a set of nested circles, with the child in the center of the nest, surrounded, supported, and nurtured by family, community, government, and ultimately, international organizations.

This is straightforward. The idea that needs to be added is that in cases of failure, agents more distant from the child should not simply substitute for those closer to the child. Instead, those who are more distant should try to *work with and strengthen* those who are closer to help them become more capable of fulfilling their responsibilities toward children. To the extent possible, local communities should not take children away from inadequate parents but rather should help them in their parenting role. State governments should not replace local governments, but instead should support local governments in their work with children. The international community should help national governments in their work with children. The same reasoning should apply to care for others who cannot care for themselves such as the physically disabled and the mentally ill.

Agencies in the outer rings should help to overcome, not punish, failures in the inner rings. They should try to respond to failures in empowering, positive ways.

So far I have been talking about responsibility in the moral sense. However, there is a distinctive role for national governments in the rings of responsibility arising from the fact that the state is the keeper of the law. With the rise of civil society and the increasing importance of rules over rulers, some responsibilities become enshrined as legal responsibilities, that is, *obligations*. Through democratic processes the state may decide that citizens and other entities have specific legal *obligations* as well as legal rights.

Moreover, in civil society the state itself has obligations and rights. Just as the rights and obligations of citizens should be spelled out in the law, the rights and obligations of the state should be spelled out as well.

With the emergence of civil society, citizens come to be recognized as` the source of political authority. From this there has evolved a broad consensus that the state has some responsibility for the well-being of its citizens. In particular, there is a responsibility to provide a social safety net for the weakest members of society, a responsibility of government that becomes a part of the state's specific obligations. This is implicitly acknowledged in advanced industrial nations in the fact that all of them have extensive social service programs. About 25% of their national incomes are channeled through their public budgets to social services, unemployment benefits and welfare payments.[7] They see the need for having such programs, recognizing that relying on charity alone is not enough. These services are often confused, inept, corrupt, inadequate, and badly targeted, but there is recognition of real obligations, beyond charity, to the poor and the weak.

The problem is that the state's responsibilities frequently are ill-defined. Many social services are provided inconsistently and reach only a fraction of the population groups that ought to get them. Often people who fail to get the services they ought to get have no legal basis and no effective mechanism for complaining. In my view, there should be a recognized *legal obligation* of the state to look after the weakest members of society that is clearly articulated in the law. Civil society should provide legal assurance of at least some minimal quality of life, some form of social security, at least for those who cannot take care of themselves.

CHILDREN IN GLOBAL CIVIL SOCIETY

The responsibility to look after the weakest members of society that is widely accepted within nations has an international counterpart. The rapid development of human rights law since World War II makes it clear that the well-being of people within each nation's borders is at least in some measure the legitimate concern of all people everywhere. There are large programs of international humanitarian assistance. It is increasingly accepted that there is both a right and an obligation for nations to act in behalf of the citizens of other nations, at least in extreme circumstances.

There are many international organizations, both governmental and nongovernmental, that work to alleviate suffering. Development and foreign aid programs do a good deal to lift the quality of life, but they remain a matter of politics and charity. There may be a sense of moral responsibility, but there is no sense of legal duty, no sense that those who receive assistance are entitled to it, and those who provide it owe it. Historically, the idea of a duty to provide social services and to look after the weakest elements in society has been understood as something undertaken at the national and local levels, not as something that ought to be undertaken globally.

Within nations, citizens may grumble when they are taxed to pay for food stamps for their poor compatriots, but they pay nevertheless. Globally, there is nothing like a regular tax obligation through which the rich provide sustenance to the poor in other nations. The humanitarian instinct and sense of responsibility is extending worldwide, but there is still little clarity as to where duties lie.[8] There is international assistance, but there is as yet no broad consensus on what norms ought to guide it. There is no clear and firm sense of sustained obligation at the global level.

The lack of clear policy has been evident in the slow and clumsy global responses to the post-Cold War crises. In mid-1994 the world's attention was on former Yugoslavia and Rwanda, while other comparable humanitarian crises, in places such as Southern Sudan, Angola, Liberia, and Ethiopia, were all but forgotten. It seems assistance is provided not where the needs are greatest but where the television coverage is greatest. Television coverage tends to go to the areas of most intense violence, not the areas of most intense need.

There is increasing discussion of global civil society and global governance.[9] Unfortunately, the discussion has focused on security issues, the major preoccupation of the powerful, and gives too little attention to the well-being of ordinary people. In my view, just as there are duties to assist the weak in civil society at the local and national levels, such duties should be recognized at the global level as well. If there is to be a global civil society, international humanitarian assistance will need to be regularized. Discussion of that idea has begun in the United Nations, but just barely.

In the image proposed here, the international community is the last resort, the outer ring of responsibility. The very outermost ring includes international governmental organizations (IGOs) such as UNICEF, the Food and Agriculture Organization of the United Nations, the World Health Organization, and the United Nations Committee on Human Rights. Just inside that ring is another representing international nongovernmental organizations (INGOs). In the pattern of concentric rings of responsibility, the international bodies' task is not to deliver services to children directly but, to the extent possible, to empower agencies in the inner rings.

Tracing back to the Latin roots of the term, it can be argued that the essence of civil society is a distinctive legal code.[10] Some responsibilities become encoded as legal duties. In global civil society, in the New World Order that needs to be designed and implemented, there should be clear global duties, codified in explicit law, for the sustenance of those who are worst off. The exact nature of those obligations and their magnitude and form will have to be debated, but the debate must begin with the question of principle. The core argument of this book is that *international humanitarian assistance should be regularized through the systematic articulation of international rights and duties regarding assistance.* In the closing chapters I suggest how those rules might be developed, both within states and internationally, for helping to care for the world's children, especially with regard to their nutrition.

OVERVIEW

The normative concept of *civil society* provides the framework for this book. In considering how societies ought to be structured and governed it is important to give attention to the role of children. The first line of responsibility for children rests with the parents, but if they fail others have responsibilities as well. The state has a special role because it is the keeper of the law and because of its responsibility for the well-being of its citizens. Through democratic processes managed by the state, some moral responsibilities become legal duties.

The reasoning should be extended to global civil society. When all others have failed them, children should be able to look to the international community to do what needs to be done, not only as a matter of moral responsibility but also as a matter of duty in the law. The international community is their last resort.

Chapter 2 will sketch the pattern of global economic, political, and social relations in which children's lives are embedded. Of course children are only one among many different groups or categories of people affected by the global economy. Children are distinguished by the fact that they are more powerless than most. Children also are distinctive in that they normally grow out of that status.

Part II provides details on some of the major problems faced by children throughout the world. Chapter 3 surveys the pattern of their deaths. The objective there is not simply to recite numbers, but to extend the discussion of the question of responsibility. We tend to ignore these deaths, finding solace in the thought that they are not our fault. But is that so? What does such a disclaimer mean? There is a need to move beyond the simplistic notion that these are natural and necessary deaths, wholly beyond our control.

Chapters 4 through 7 describe miseries of different kinds. Many children suffer from highly exploitative working conditions, and some are sexually abused for profit. Many are victimized by armed conflict. Some are pressed to serve as soldiers. Many suffer from serious malnutrition.

There are many ways to address these problems, but this study centers on the idea of strengthening human rights law, an essential element of civil society. In Part III, Chapters 8 and 9 look at the nature of children's rights, and argue that the human rights approach can help bring about improvements in the ways children are treated. In these two chapters the focus is on use of the law within nations. Finally, Chapter 10 argues that the international community should take seriously the notion that children have *international* rights. If there is to be a new and better world order as we go into the next millennium, a civil society at the global level, there will have to be a great improvement in the way all the world's children are treated.

2 The Global Economy

The global economic system, like the systems within advanced industrial nations, does a lot of people a lot of good. Many people benefit from the international division of labor which calls for certain kinds of products and services to be produced in some places while others are produced in other places. Likewise, many people benefit from international trade. International lending programs, both official and private, have helped many industries and programs, and thus have benefited many people. There is hope that the structural adjustment programs pressed on developing nations by the international financial institutions since the early 1980s will, after a difficult transition period, help to modernize stagnant economies and integrate them into the global economic system, and thus help to pull people up out of their abject poverty.

However, while the global economic system benefits some, at the same time it does harm to others. My purpose in this chapter is to throw some light on this dark side of the global economy. Children, along with other weak groups, are often hurt by patterns of trade, debt servicing, and structural adjustment. They are hurt not by directly inflicted harms, but indirectly, through the accompanying social structure. They are hurt not so much by what is done as by what could be done and isn't.

Current patterns and policies that disadvantage the weak operate in a system that is already highly skewed. In 1989 the nations with the richest 20% of the world's population received about 82.7% of total global income, while the nations with the poorest 20% of the population received only 1.4%, a ratio of 59 to 1. Moreover, between 1960 and 1989, economic growth in the richest nations was 2.7 times as fast as in the poorest nations. The already wide gap between the rich and the poor, the 'North-South gap,' is widening even further.[1]

Of course the divide between rich and poor is wide not only between nations but also within nations. In one of the more extreme cases, Brazil, the top fifth of the population receives 26 times the income of the bottom fifth.[2]

DIVISION OF LABOR

Just as unskilled people frequently become unemployed, poor nations are learning that their services are no longer required in the post-industrial, service-oriented global economy. Industrialized nations

13

... find that they can now meet an increasing share of consumer demand with skill-intensive production within their own nations and that they need to import less from the developing world. The developing nations' share of world trade fell from 24.8% in 1980 to 19.3% in 1989.[3]

This could be viewed as a blessing in that it reduces poor nations' exposure to possibly unfair trade relationships and increases their incentives for pursuing strategies of self-reliance. In many cases, however, they are firmly structured as export-oriented economies. The international agencies continue to promote that orientation by insisting on structural adjustment policies even as the markets for their products decline.

The increasing 'unemployment' of poor nations increases pressures on many of their workers to leave, either permanently as immigrants, or as temporary 'guest workers' in developed nations. Many skilled workers and professionals, including much-needed doctors, leave as part of the massive brain drain. This constitutes still another form of transfer of value from poor to rich nations.[4] Thus there is a clear division of labor, with poor nations, and the poor in rich nations, carrying out mundane, repetitive, physical tasks in fields and factories, or remaining unemployed, and the rich specializing in high technology, high capital, high knowledge industries, and doing no physical labor at all. The Third World's specializing in tedious labor with low knowledge requirements reinforces the tendency for their children to go without schooling and to be employed under abusive, exploitative working conditions, as described in Chapters 4 and 5.

The global division of labor is apparent not only in the ways in which different countries specialize in different kinds of work but also in the ways in which they specialize in different kinds of products. These differences are the basis for international trade.

Most world trade is concentrated among the richer nations of the world. Only a small percentage is among poorer nations. There is, however, a substantial amount of trade between poor nations and rich nations. The character of that trade is illustrated by the pattern in food trade where, on balance, the net flow of food is from the poor nations to the rich. In 1986, for example, developed countries received over 75% by value and over 62% by weight of all food imports, while developing countries took no more than 25% and 38% respectively.[5] The poor feed the rich.[6]

This pattern is not necessarily bad. As advocates of the free market would point out, the poor nations are paid for this food, and they would not engage in this production and export of food unless they saw it as advantageous. There are three reasons for concern about this argument, however. First, on the face of it, in a world with widespread hunger it simply does not make sense to export major food supplies away from those who do not have enough. Second, while earnings from exports might be used to import cheap food for those most in need, often they are not. The poor are not the ones who decide how the foreign exchange earnings are to be spent. Third, as discussed later in this chapter, the benefits of trade between partners of uneven power will be distributed unevenly, with the result that the gap between them widens steadily.

One clear indicator of the lower bargaining power of people in poor nations is that they are paid much less than people in rich nations for the same labor. Pineapple plantations move away from high wage areas such as Hawaii to places like Costa Rica and Thailand precisely because of these differences. The comparative advantage of poor nations is their disadvantage; that is, their inability to demand high wages.

Another clear indicator of the lower bargaining power of weak nations is that they get paid much less for the same products. Elsewhere I have illustrated the pattern for skipjack tuna, showing that fishing vessels that bring the product into Palau in Micronesia are regularly paid less than half the rate that skipjack draws in California ports.[7] Similarly, farmers of the Third World receive much less in real terms for a bushel of grain than farmers of the first world receive for the same product. The *Human Development Report* also observes that rich producers are paid more than poor ones for identical goods.[8] Producers from poor nations selling the same products ending up on the same markets regularly get less for their efforts, in wages or in commodity prices, than producers in rich nations. In not receiving a fuller share of the benefits produced by their labor, workers producing food and other commodities for export in effect subsidize the rich.

The increased profits resulting from the lower production costs may in part go to the rich in the poorer countries, but increasingly these profits will go to outsiders who own these Third World production facilities. For example, it is primarily the stockholders of the Dole Foods Corporation who benefit from finding cheaper labor in Third World nations to produce their pineapples. Even apart from the repatriated profits, such export-oriented operations benefit rich nations because they provide them with inexpensive food, inexpensive because it is produced with cheap labor. Thus the international trading system allows – indeed, encourages – displaced effects or 'externalities' whereby the costs of enterprises fall more heavily on poor nations (not only low wages but also resource depletion and pollution) while the benefits fall more heavily on rich nations.

DEBT AND STRUCTURAL ADJUSTMENT

Just as international trade has the net effect of shifting value from poor to rich, debt servicing is another means through which value flows from poor nations to rich nations. 'In 1983–89, rich creditors received a staggering 242 billion in net transfers on long term lending from indebted developing nations.'[9] The greatest impact is in sub-Saharan Africa where the debt load is now approximately equal to the region's cumulative gross national product. This site of enormous human tragedy is also the supplier of the greatest per capita income flows back to the North!

Within poor nations, international loans are likely to be of greatest benefit to their middle and upper classes. Debt servicing, however, is likely to have especially heavy negative impacts on the poor and their children, obliging them to do without food subsidies and health and other services, and often pressing them into exploitative working conditions in export-oriented industries.

The amount of money going from South to North for debt servicing greatly exceeds the current amounts of official development assistance going from North to South. Moreover, official development assistance is likely to benefit the rich and middle class rather than the poor in poor nations. Despite rhetoric to the contrary, official development aid does not concentrate on the most needy either within nations or among nations. Overall, 'the richest 40% of the developing world population receives more than twice as much aid per capita as the poorest 40%.'[10]

To deal with the economic pressures on them resulting from their heavy debt load in combination with the global recession of the 1980s, many poor nations have had to make substantial policy adjustments. Structural adjustment programs have been pressed on debtor nations by the international financial institutions. These nations have had to reduce their imports, devalue their currencies, and cut government expenditures. In many cases the adjustments have resulted in higher unemployment and lower wages. The attempts to restore the basis for long-term economic growth have had real short-term costs.[11] The burdens have fallen especially on the poor:

Services which are of concern to the richer and more powerful sections of society – such as the major hospitals, universities, national airlines, prestige development projects, and the military – have not borne a proportional share of the cuts in public spending. With some honourable exceptions, the services which have been most radically pruned are health services, free primary education, and food and fuel subsidies –

the services on which the poor are most dependent and which they have least opportunity to replace by any other, private, means … Meanwhile, the proportion of national budgets devoted to the military is approximately 30 percent higher than total spending on health and education combined.[12]

African nations are poor largely because they are weak players in the global economy, forced to accept prices and other terms that are imposed on them. To be sure, some of them also have corrupt governments that exploit their own people as viciously as any outsiders have ever done. The ongoing ethnic and tribal wars have been enormously destructive. Nevertheless, in many cases the economic adjustments have only made things worse. The deterioration is most evident in the decline of already miserable social services. 12 out of 22 African nations experienced a fall in central government health expenditures per capita between 1975 and 1985.[13] Average health care expenditure declined from $5.16 per person in 1975 to $4.70 in 1985 (both in 1980 dollars).

While structural adjustment policies are justified on the grounds that they will yield economic benefits in the long run, poor people rarely get much of a share of those benefits. Growth- and export-oriented development policy is of greatest benefit to the rich and powerful. UNICEF has been pressing for an alternative, 'adjustment with a human face.' Such adjustment policies would not be carried out at the expense of the poor but would call for a kind of economic growth in which smaller and poorer producers were full participants.[14]

In response to widespread criticism, the international agencies have made provisions to protect or compensate those who were hurt most by structural adjustment programs. Attention has been given to the design of socially-oriented adjustment programs.[15] The initial attempts at stabilization of economies in the early 1980s were followed by structural adjustment policies into the 1990s, but neither gave enough consideration to social consequences. As a result, new attention has been given to the management of social programs while undertaking structural adjustment, especially in the World Bank's Social Dimensions of Adjustment initiative. New socially-sensitive adjustment and development programs have been proposed, particularly for Africa, but they have not been fully implemented.[16] While the international financial institutions now express concern for the social impacts of economic adjustment policies, their primary commitment remains the promotion of externally-oriented market economies.

A number of nations have been making profound changes in the 1990s as they make the transition from socialist to market economies. With very tight budgets, and high priority being placed on economic efficiency, some social services in these new market economies are being weakened or dismantled altogether. There is recognition of the need for maintaining services as compensation for the negative effects of the market system, but

> By and large, social policy and distributive issues have been marginal topics in the debate on the transition to the market economy ... it has not been uncommon for new social policy to pay only little more than token attention on how to prevent poverty, unemployment and homelessness, or to the preservation of the health and general well-being of poor children and other marginal groups.[17]

Increasing poverty in the former socialist countries has affected children in many ways, in the general tightening of food supplies and health services and also in the deterioration of services specifically for children, such as child care and schooling.[18] It may turn out that these negative impacts are only transitional, but in several Eastern European countries the optimism of the early 1990s has evaporated.

THE ROOTS OF POVERTY

Analysts concerned with poverty tend to focus on recent events and policies: the last recession, structural adjustment programs, the stance of the current president or secretary general. This approach helps to explain recent changes, but it does not account for – indeed it hardly even sees – the steady-state background situation in which these changes take place. To be sure, we should be concerned about recent declines in the quality of life in Africa, but we should also ask what accounts for the continuing misery of so much of that continent. Similarly, while it is important to know that the proportion of children in poverty in the United States increased sharply during the Reagan administration, we also should ask why more than ten percent of the children in the United States have lived in poverty throughout this century. More generally, we should face the question: why is there so much persistent poverty in the world?

Nations may be poor for several different reasons. Some have very meager endowments of natural resources. Some have natural resources but lack the capacity for exploiting them. In some cases, nations produce large amounts of wealth, but do so in a way that results in a very skewed distribution of benefits, as in Brazil, Venezuela, or Saudi Arabia. A great deal of poverty 'results from socio-economic development patterns which in most of the poorer nations have been characterized by a high degree of concentration of power, wealth and incomes in the hands of relatively small elites of national or foreign individuals or groups.'[19]

What causes this concentration? The ordinary, normal working of the market system creates wealth, but it also leads to poverty, and thus to concentration and to steadily widening gaps. The way in which the market system concentrates wealth and power in the hands of some and impoverishes others is very straightforward. The elementary transaction of the market system is the bargain, the negotiated exchange. One's bargaining strength depends on the quality of one's alternatives. Some people (or companies, or nations) are stronger than others because they have better options.

Those who have greater bargaining strength tend to gain more out of each transaction than those who have lesser bargaining strength. Thus, over repeated transactions, stronger parties systematically enlarge their advantages over weaker parties. Bargainers do not move to an equilibrium at which the benefits are equally distributed, but instead move apart, with the gap between them steadily widening. Asymmetrical exchange feeds on itself, making the situation more and more asymmetrical.

This pattern of cumulative divergence is visible in the growth of nations. Those that start with higher gross national products rise faster, while those that start lower rise more slowly. For example, in the 1965–84 period the low-income economies had an average annual growth rate in their GNP per capita of 2.8 percent; the lower middle-income economies grew at 3.1 percent; the upper middle-income economies grew at 3.3 percent; and the industrial market economies grew at 2.4 percent.

Expressed in these terms, it may appear that the growth rates were more or less comparable, with the industrial economies growing at a slightly lower rate than the low-income nations. However, these figures are percentages of very different baseline levels of GNP per capita. In 1984, for example, the low-income economies had average per capita income gains of $7.28, while the industrial market economies had average per capita income gains of $274.32. The gains in industrial market economies were more than 37 times those in low-income nations![20]

In voluntary transactions both parties must get some benefit, for any party that did not benefit could refuse to trade. Both parties benefit in the exchange process, *but unequally*. The rich get richer and the poor get richer too, but more slowly.

When the exchange process is accompanied by inflation, however, the real gains to both parties are diminished. The gains to the poorer, weaker party, being smaller, may as a result become negative. This is especially likely because inflation rates are much higher for poor nations than for rich nations. Thus with the combination of trade plus inflation it is likely that the rich get richer and the poor get poorer. The apparent gains from trade for the poor are likely to be wiped out by inflation.

The gap between rich and poor widens partly because the economic transactions between them tend to be of greater benefit to the rich. However, the gap would widen even without those direct transactions. Those with larger amounts to invest always can get higher rates of return on their money. In a market system, the rich always have more and better alternatives, and thus enjoy faster economic growth than the poor.

Poverty is endlessly recreated. It is a product of an ongoing process, not a static condition. If it were not, then surely, with all the development programs that have been undertaken, it would have been eradicated by now. The important forces that cause the persistence of poverty are not only economic but also political, social, and cultural. Those with low bargaining power are destined to remain marginalized because those with whom they interrelate have greater bargaining power.

POPULATION AND THE ECONOMY

Many people worry that saving children on a large scale would aggravate the problem of worldwide population growth in a Malthusian cycle. They believe that hunger and poverty persist mainly because of excessive population growth rates in Third World countries. Apparently premature deaths, while tragic, are nature's way of keeping population growth in check. However, it is important to understand that poverty is not created and recreated simply because of population growth.

Poor, less developed countries have high birth rates and high death rates, and low life expectancies. Richer, more highly developed countries have low birth rates and low death rates, with high life expectancies. Developed countries have fewer people, living longer and better. During the industrial revolution in Europe early in the 18th century, living conditions improved and death rates went down. The immediate effect was that population growth rates increased sharply. The remarkable thing was that as development progressed, birth rates came down as well, without any systematic population policies or family planning programs. This *demographic transition*, occurring over a number of decades, was experienced by all modern, developed countries.

During the industrial revolution, economies grew, living conditions improved, and mortality rates fell along with fertility rates, with the net result that real incomes rose continuously. But the process was really not so simple:

> In Europe, and later in Japan, the pattern of declining mortality and fertility was not so orderly – nor is it today in the developing countries. In a few places fertility decline preceded mortality decline; in others, fertility did not start falling soon after mortality did. And economic growth – if narrowly perceived as industrialization, urbanization, and the shift from family to factory production – was neither necessary nor sufficient for the demographic transition.
>
> In England fertility within marriage did not begin to fall until the 1870s, almost 100 years after the start of the Industrial Revolution and at least as long after a sustained decline in mortality had begun.[21]

One reason for the delay in England was that, while there was considerable economic growth, 'at least after 1820, it was the upper- and middle-income groups that captured most of the income gains.'

The demographic transition occurs at different rates in different ways at different times for different reasons. One major demographic change was the decline in death rates in countries undergoing industrialization, resulting in relatively rapid population growth rates in western countries. A second major change was the decline in birth rates following industrialization, which decreased these countries' growth rates below the world average.

> A third major demographic trend began around the time of World War II. A dramatic decline in death rates occurred in the underdeveloped countries ... This decline was caused primarily by the rapid export of modern drugs and public health measures from the developed countries to the underdeveloped countries. The consequent 'death control' produced the most rapid, widespread change known in the history of human population dynamics.[22]

Thus there has been a transition of the transition. During the industrial revolution rapid population growth was associated with increasing wealth, but after World War I rapid population growth has become associated with poverty.

Indeed, the economic-growth-driven demographic transition in the wake of the industrial revolution may have been a unique historical event. In many poor countries of the world today, death rates are declining not because of genuine development and improvement of overall living conditions, but because of the importation of specific health care techniques such as immunization programs. Some countries may now be stuck in their underdevelopment. And with the conditions of poverty and the institutional structures that prevail in many poor countries, technical innovations in health care can accomplish just so much.

The prevailing explanations for changes in population growth rates centered on economic growth and health care services miss the essentially political character of demographic change. As Frances Moore Lappé and Rachel Schurman suggest, 'high birth rates among the poor can best be understood ... as a defensive response against structures of power that fail to provide, or actively block, sources of security beyond the family.'[23] A well-off fisherman who has plenty of options, such as the possibility of moving to other fishing spots, will simply move on when the catches are not good. But a poor and desperate fisherman who has no good alternatives can do only one thing when the resource dwindles down: he puts out more lines. Economically, a poor family's producing more and more children is comparable to a desperate fisherman's putting out more and more lines. Both the fisherman's and the family's behaviors are shaped by the nature of the alternatives they face.

A rich fisherman puts out more lines because he can. A poor fisherman puts out more lines because he has no good alternatives. Similarly it appears that, up to a point, richer people have more children because they can, while poorer people have more children because they must. The pattern is suggested by a study in southern Egypt. The number of children was higher for whose who worked larger farms, but for any given farm size, the number of children was lower among those who owned their land than among tenants.[24]

Families continue to have babies even when the opportunities their children will face are meager. When people are desperate and have few alternatives the 'lottery mentality' takes hold, convincing people they have some possibility of doing well even if their concrete experience tells them their chances are slim. Fishermen keep fishing long after most of the fish are gone.[25] Of course they do give up when there is no longer any doubt that the resource has dried up. In extreme situations such as famines, when it becomes evident that there are no prospects at all, fertility rates decline sharply.

The metaphor here is that described by Garrett Hardin as the 'tragedy of the commons.'[26] Prior to the enclosure movement in England, when pastures were open, the incentives faced by each individual led him to place more and more cattle to feed on the common pastures. That ultimately led to destruction of the commons environment. The strategy of adding more and more cattle made sense for individuals, however, because while each individual benefited from feeding his own cattle, the negative effects were distributed through the community as a whole. As the economists say, there were 'negative externalities' that had little immediate and direct impact on the individuals.

When the threat of destruction became apparent, those who were more powerful and could make strong claims on the resources fenced in large sections of the area for their private use. The benefits drawn from the area still were large, but the distribution of those benefits was radically changed.

Large private landholdings, often tied closely to antidemocratic regimes, have quite direct effects on fertility:

> So, we must ask what are the consequences for fertility when at least 1 billion rural people in the Third World have been deprived of farmland? In many countries, including Brazil, Mexico, the Philippines, India, and most of the Central American countries, landholdings have become increasingly concentrated in the hands of a minority during a period of rapid population growth ... In this context, without adequate land or secure tenure, and with no old-age support from the government or any other source outside the family, many poor people understandably view children as perhaps the only source of power open to them. For those in extreme poverty, children can be critical to one's very survival.[27]

Thus, under anti-democratic institutional arrangements, where people have little say about how the resources around them are to be managed, most people have little effective access to resources and few opportunities. Under such conditions of scarcity, birth rates and children's mortality rates both remain high.

In the logic of the situation, a more equitable remedy to the tragedy of the commons would be for the participants to join together, analyze the problem, and realize that they would all be better off if they created some way to manage the commons together. If they agreed on fair rules by which they could jointly limit the access of individuals to the commons, in the long term they would all be better off.

Population growth and poverty are related to the nature of the physical environment, but not so directly as suggested by concepts such as carrying capacity. The connection is always mediated by a social structure that determines the ways in which resources are used and, more to the point, governs the ways in which the benefits of resource use are allocated. The critical issue is not the size of the population itself or the size of the population in relation to overall resource endowments. It is the nature of the social, political, and legal arrangements that mediate access to resources. Arrangements that are open to full and equal participation by all affected parties are likely to lead to more even distribution of the benefits from the resources, and thus to adequacy for all. Resources and general well-being are distributed more equitably in democracies than in non-democracies.

Many analysts see population growth alone as the source of poverty, hunger, destruction of the environment and many other major problems of our times. As one observer put it, 'policy makers tend to see high fertility as the intractable villain, creating acute population pressures and oppressive socioeconomic conditions in developing societies; consequently, programs to treat these onerous problems have been geared almost exclusively to birth control.'[28] A leading demographer acknowledges that '98 percent of the resources and effort should be devoted to social and economic development,' but he and his organization then focus their work narrowly on population control.[29] Demographers recognize that socioeconomic development is important in limiting population growth, but their recommendations usually propose only conventional family planning programs. These programs usually are not based on any explicit analysis of the roots of the social problems or of population growth in the concrete local circumstances; they are based on prevailing myths and metaphors. They do not go to the roots of the problem, and thus do not offer lasting remedies.

People from developed countries, through their governments and through many well-funded private agencies, are keen to promote family planning in Third World countries. Their work is generally well-intended, and based on the belief that it will help the Third World and the rest of the global community. But it is based on very shallow analyses of the problems. If the main concern is to protect the earth's resources and to control the rate of pollution and depletion, it is important to expose …

the myth that the impact of the population explosion stems primarily from poor people in poor countries who do not know enough to limit their reproduction. Numbers per se are not the measure of overpopulation; instead it is the impact of people on ecosystems and nonrenewable resources. While developing countries severely tax their environments, clearly the populations of rich countries leave a vastly disproportionate mark on the planet.

The birth of a baby in the United States imposes more than a hundred times the stress on the world's resources and environment as a birth in, say, Bangladesh. Babies from Bangladesh do not grow up to own automobiles and air conditioners or to eat grain-fed beef. Their lifestyles do not require huge quantities of minerals and energy, nor do their activities seriously undermine the life-support capability of the entire planet.[30]

In this light, since each baby born in rich countries will consume far more resources and generate far more polluting wastes than each baby born in poor countries, population control is more urgent in the North than in the South.

Conventional population control programs imply 'blaming the victim.' They press poor countries to make substantial adjustments and assume that people in richer countries need not make any adjustments. Indeed, the pressure on the South appears to be designed to protect the North from having to make any changes. Certainly none of the proposed strategies involve any significant costs to the North. If there is such a terrible imbalance between population and resources, why not promote programs of consumption control in the North?

Pressing people in the Third World to have fewer children can mean asking them to forgo one of the very few assets to which they have access. Even if their children's economic prospects are not promising, they are asked to take fewer lottery tickets, and cut back on the hope that comes with taking the chance that at least one of their children will do well.

Popular magazines headline the population story as one of 'Too Many Mouths.'[31] They view Third World babies simply as gaping mouths needing to be fed. But babies come with hands and heads too. Most people would become net producers if given a decent opportunity to do so. This was demonstrated when China's new policy of allowing families to earn private income 'unexpectedly created an incentive to have more children to help earn the income.'[32]

The major environmental problem worldwide is the fact that many people lack adequate opportunities to make good use of the physical resources around them. Landlessness, lack of capital, inadequate markets, and other constraints prevent their undertaking the productive work they would gladly do if they had decent opportunities. When people have decent opportunities they are producers, and not just consumers.

In some places this lack of opportunity may be due to an absolute insufficiency of resources. A small island may have so many people living on it that it must either import food or export people. But that sort of situation is rare. In most cases the problem is that the available resources are not well managed for the purpose of supporting the local population.

Bad management may be in the form of anarchy – the absence of management – but more frequently it is an inequitable, undemocratic form of management, one which concentrates the benefits from the use of the resources in the hands of a few. Plantation agriculture, for example, is often wrongly praised as being highly efficient. Its real appeal is the fact that plantations concentrate the benefits of the work of many laborers into the hands of a few owners.[33]

If farmers in the Third World were paid at the same rate as first world farmers for each bushel of grain they produced, they would become more productive and they would be more secure regarding their own futures. Birth rates and infant mortality rates in their communities would decline. Perhaps those concerned with reducing population growth rates should recommend a policy of equal pay for equal work or for equal products worldwide. The appropriate remedy for poverty, hunger, and children's mortality is to improve people's opportunities. People need to be secure in knowing that they will be able to live out their lives with dignity.

Reducing population growth rates may not reduce the extent of hunger and poverty at all. India, for example, has reduced its fertility levels sharply, but this in itself has not resulted in significant improvements for the poor. With any given gross national product, lowering population growth rates automatically means higher levels of GNP per capita. That is arithmetic, not social progress. Lowering population growth rates could result in the poorer section of the population's capturing even smaller shares of the GNP.

A White House Task Force on Combating Terrorism, chaired by the then Vice President George Bush, concluded that 'population pressures create a volatile mixture of youthful aspirations that when coupled with economic and political frustrations help form a large pool of potential terrorists.'[34] The typical response is not to analyze and correct the injustices faced by the poor, but simply to reduce their number. Many people view population control in the Third World as essential to First World security. Their perspective is narrowly self-interested. It amounts to using population control as a form of cultural genocide against the poor, the ultimate remedy of those who blame the victims.

Improved child survival rates and overall development help to limit the rate of population growth, but these alone will not reduce population growth rates fast enough. Similarly, family planning programs are important, but by themselves they are not enough. An overly narrow focus on population control can become dangerous if it is advocated in place of significant social change. Focusing too narrowly on population issues can mean blinding oneself to fundamentally important social, economic, and political factors underlying these problems. Treating population growth as if it alone was the source of social and environmental problems distracts attention away from the basic political and economic forces at work.

The quality of a family's lives depends heavily on it social power, which in turn depends on the quality of its alternatives; that is, its opportunities. The availability of opportunities depends not only on the natural environment (e.g., how much land there is) but also on the social structure through which resources are managed (who controls the land). Both the population and the poverty problems are at root problems of powerlessness. Their remedies must be based on strategies of empowerment.

INTERNATIONAL OBLIGATIONS

Many observers, including the World Bank, understand that poverty cannot be eliminated through economic growth alone.[35] Advanced industrial nations acknowledge this by the fact that none of them has a pure free market economy; instead, they see the need for having some sort of income transfer and social welfare programs. About 25% of national incomes are channeled through the public budget to social services, unemployment benefits and welfare payments.[36] All developed countries have seen that relying on charity alone is not enough.

The only major market economy in which there is no acknowledged responsibility of the rich with respect to the poor is the global economy. With official development assistance so meager and so misdirected in relation to the need, it is evident that globally there is no clear sense of duty toward the poor. There is no social safety net at the global level.

It has been estimated that for $20 billion a year it would be possible to meet the health, nutrition, education, and water and sanitation goals agreed at the World Summit for Children of 1990. An additional $5 billion would be needed to meet family planning goals. This total of $25 billion would be half the amount spent on cigarettes in Europe per year, and less than the amount spent on beer in the United States each year.[37] Yet UNICEF's annual budget at its highest ever was $938 million in 1992.[38] In some years the city of Stockholm has spent more for children's day care alone than UNICEF had to spend for all its programs worldwide. UNICEF's budget is not only meager, it is also voluntary, with three-quarters of it coming from governments and one-quarter coming from nongovernmental sources including greeting card sales. This does not show a strong sense of obligation toward children worldwide.

The explanation for this systematic neglect is fundamentally political:

> When so much could be done for so many and at so little cost, then one
> central, shameful fact becomes unavoidable: the reason that these
> problems are not being rapidly overcome is not because the task is too
> large, or too difficult, or too expensive. It is because the job is not being
> given sufficient priority. And it is not being given sufficient priority
> primarily because those most severely affected are almost exclusively
> the poorest and least politically influential people on earth.[39]

People seem inclined to dismiss the plight of the children of Haiti or
Malawi by saying it is unfortunate that they were born in poor nations. But
they were not born into a poor world. Preventing the extreme miseries of
poor children is not beyond the world's means. Perhaps it is time to get
beyond the hat-in-hand approach to official development assistance,
asking governments for more international charity, and instead begin to
take the view that the children of the world are *entitled* to better lives.[40]

Many observers have essayed on the widespread harm caused by the
international debt crisis. Bank loans are not the only unfulfilled
obligations, however. *The Declaration of the Rights of the Child* of 1959
says 'mankind owes to the child the best it has to give.' *Owes.* This too
can be viewed as a kind of unpaid debt, one that has resulted in immense
harm. Perhaps it is time to put the note in writing, to begin to acknowledge
what it is that all societies, and humankind as a whole, owes to each child.
Is there at least some minimum level of obligation to which we can
commit ourselves?

Part II
Children's Problems

3 Mortality

The number of children dying each year has been declining steadily, but the numbers are still enormous. Recent estimates of the number of under-five deaths in the developing world for selected years are as follows:[1]

1960	18 900 000
1970	17 400 000
1980	14 700 000
1990	12 700 000

The number of under-five deaths for the world as a whole in 1992 is estimated at 13 393 000.[2] This means there are about 36 700 dying each day, more than a million each month.

The children's mortality rate is the number of children who die before their fifth birthday for every thousand born alive. The rate fell sharply between 1950 and 1980 but declined more slowly in the 1980s.[3] The trend suggests the decline in under-five mortality worldwide may not be steady and decisive. Some observers now believe that the rapid global spread of the AIDS disease may eradicate all the gains in child survival rates of the last decade.

Children's deaths account for about one-third of all deaths worldwide. In northern Europe or the United States children account for only two to three percent of all deaths. In many less developed countries more than half the deaths are deaths of children, which means there are more deaths of young people than of old people.[4] The median age at death in 1990 was five or lower in Angola, Burkina Faso, Ethiopia, Guinea, Malawi, Mali, Mozambique, Niger, Rwanda, Sierra Leone, Somalia, Tanzania, and Uganda. This means that in these thirteen countries at least half the deaths were of children under five. In the United States the median age at death in 1990 was 76, and in the best cases, Japan, Norway, Sweden, and Switzerland, it was 78.[5]

About one-third of the children who die each year are African, although they account for little more than ten percent of the world's population of children.

In the United States in 1910 the infant mortality rate – the number of children dying before their first birthdays for every thousand born alive – was 124. The rate dropped steadily from 47 in 1940 to 10.9 in 1983, but then the speed of decline diminished rapidly. The infant mortality rate has been going down in the United States, but not as fast as in many other nations, with the result that the United States' standing in the rankings has deteriorated. In 1983 the United States ranked only seventeenth among the nations of the world. In 1991 the United States' infant mortality rate was 11, and 21 other countries had even lower rates. According to a report of the United States Congress, 'in contrast to the dramatic decline in the rate of infant mortality between 1950 and 1980, progress on reducing infant deaths has slowed to almost a halt in recent years'.[6]

The number of children who die each year can be made more meaningful by comparing it with other mortality figures.

There have been about 101 550 000 fatalities in wars between the years 1700 and 1987.[7] That yields an average of 353 833 fatalities per year. William Eckhardt estimated that the total number of civilian and military deaths due to warfare in 1991 was 443 500, and that the yearly average between 1986 and 1991 was 427 800.[8] These figures can be compared to the more than 12 million children's deaths in each of these years.

The most lethal war in all of human history was World War II. There were about 15 million battle deaths.[9] If in civilian deaths are added in, including genocide and other forms of mass murder, the number of deaths in and around World War II totaled around 51 358 000.[10] Annualized for the six year period, the rate comes to about 8.6 million deaths a year – when children's deaths were running at well over 25 million per year. This most intense war in history resulted in a lower death rate, over a very limited period, than results from children's mortality year in and year out.

Counting late additions, at the end of 1987 there were 58 156 names on the Vietnam war memorial in Washington, D.C. That is less than the number of children under five who die every two days throughout the world. A memorial for those children who die worldwide would be more than 250 times as long as the Vietnam memorial, and a new one would be needed every year.

Historically, governments have killed many of their own citizens outside of warfare. According to R. J. Rummel, in the twentieth century 'independent of war and other kinds of conflict – governments probably have murdered 119 400 000 people ... By comparison, the battle-killed in all foreign and domestic wars in this century total 35 700 000.'[11] His more recent estimates bring the total number of people killed by governments outside of war to about 170 million in this century. While this figure is far higher than the numbers killed in warfare, it is far lower than the number of children's deaths over the twentieth century. Early in the century the world's population was smaller but the children's mortality rate was higher. Estimating an average of, say, 20 million children's deaths per year would yield a figure of over 1.8 billion for the number of children's deaths in this century, more than ten times the number of people killed by governments.

Children die for many different reasons. The practice of infanticide has been widespread.[12] Even if children were not directly murdered, they were often abandoned or 'exposed' in ways that, but for the 'kindness of strangers' who might rescue them, could lead to their deaths.[13] In some cases children have been killed as a matter of government policy. King Herod, angered at the flight of Jesus, Mary and Joseph to Egypt, ordered the killing of all the male infants of Bethlehem.

Child abuse and neglect is still widespread in modern times, in both rich and poor countries, and many children die as a result. Millions of children live and die on the streets. In some countries street children are systematically killed. Children are being counted among the casualties of warfare at a steadily increasing rate. Often children are pressed to participate in armed combat as soldiers. State-sponsored torture of children has taken place in Argentina, El Salvador, Iraq, and South Africa.

The immediate cause of death for most children, however, is not murder or incurable diseases such as AIDS, but a combination of malnutrition and quite ordinary diseases. Table 3.1 shows the distribution of causes for 1986. Given adequate resources, diseases such as diarrhea, malaria, and measles are readily managed problems.

Even with the best of care the children's mortality rate can never be reduced to zero. In 1991 the lowest rate in the world was in Sweden where

Table 3.1   Estimated annual deaths of children under 5 by cause, 1986

Cause	Number (millions)	Proportion (percentage)
Diarrhea	5.0	35.4
Malaria	3.0	21.3
Measles	2.1	14.9
Neonatal Tetanus	0.8	5.7
Pertussis (Whooping Cough)	0.6	4.3
Other Acute Respiratory Infections	1.3	9.2
Other	1.3	9.2
Estimated Total	14.1	100.0

Source: James P. Grant, *The State of the World's Children 1987* (New York: Oxford University Press, 1987), p. 111.

there were only five deaths of children under five years of age for every thousand children born. If the world's resources were fully devoted to minimizing children's mortality, presumably the children's mortality rate could be reduced to about five everywhere. But that is a very demanding standard. It is quite reasonable, however, to suggest that if our worldwide priorities called for it, the worldwide average children's mortality rate could be reduced to, say, 10 per thousand live births. In 1991, twenty one countries had children's mortality rates of 10 or less.

If the children's mortality rate had been 10 for all countries in 1991, children's deaths would have numbered 1 410 000. This can be taken as a conservative estimate of the 'minimum possible' number of children's deaths. The actual estimated number of children's deaths for 1991 was 12 821 000.[14] The difference, 11 411 000, can be taken as a reasonable estimate of the number of 'unnecessary' or excessive children's deaths. Thus about 89 percent of the total number of deaths of children under five were 'unnecessary' or excessive.

The immediate causes of the massive deaths of children in clinical terms are well known, but we also need an understanding in social terms. Why are the world's children devastated by so much malnutrition and disease? Describing the condition of children around the world is not nearly as difficult as deciding how we should understand it.

PRIORITIES, NOT POVERTY

If we consider not only the clinical factors but also the social context we would see that almost all deaths of small children are due to some form of abuse or neglect, whether by the immediate family or by society at large. Even congenital birth defects are largely preventable with improved prenatal care; even accidents are to a large degree preventable.[15]

If enough resources and attention are given to small children, most would thrive. Many do not do well because their families are desperately poor. But focusing on the children and their families alone blinds us to the ways in which their conditions reflect the policies and actions of their societies. What is the role of government policy?

Many countries spend very little on children. Poverty is their explanation. But contrary to common assumptions, poor countries, like poor people, do have money. Poor countries are not uniformly poor; most have a middle class and a wealthy elite. They all manage to muster sufficient food and medical services for the wealthy. Soldiers don't go hungry. Even poor countries find money for monuments and armaments.

Poor countries are constrained in what they can do, but viewed globally, surely the limited allocation of resources to serving the interests of poor children is due more to the ways in which available funds are used than to the absolute shortage of funds.[16]

Specific deaths may be beyond the control of the immediate family or community, but *patterns* of mortality can be influenced by public policy. The failure to introduce effective policies and programs for reducing children's mortality (immunization, for example) should sensibly lead to charges of abuse or neglect by government.

The plight of children arises not so much out of the bad things that have been done directly to them as out of the many good things that have not been done for them. In the aggregate, much more harm results from child neglect than from direct child abuse. The failures of governments in relation to children are partly due to bad policies and programs, but more often to absent and inadequate programs resulting from the treatment of children's programs as low-priority items in national budgets. Children could be fed adequately in almost every country in the world, even the poorest among them, *if* that were regarded as high priority in government circles. Massive children's mortality is not necessary and inevitable.

That the problem is national priorities rather than national poverty is nowhere more clear than in the richest country in the world. The infant mortality rate in the United States is now about ten per thousand, which is quite good. But how do we come to terms with the fact that about twenty other developed countries have even lower rates, rates that are declining even faster than in the United States? Twenty percent of the children in the United States are under the official poverty line. That is not because the United States is a poor country.[17]

Government officials say that of course they don't want children to go hungry or die – and they don't. The problem is that they place so many other concerns at a higher priority. Where there are serious problems of hunger or homelessness or children's mortality, decision-makers claim that they *cannot* deal with the problem because they don't have the resources. Often the truth is that they *will not* respond to the problem. Children's well-being could be sharply improved if that objective was of high priority to governments. *Cannot* is an attempt to evade responsibility. The *cannot* defense should not be accepted as an excuse where low priority – *will not* – is the truthful explanation.

Children, especially poor children, are not attended to because they do not have the power to demand attention from public and private agencies. For some children the situation is worse than being ignored. The powerful often find ways to use children to serve their own interests, whether those interests are economic or sexual or military. Whether it is a matter of neglect or direct abuse, it is the interests of others that are served; the interests of children are ignored.

Small children cannot make their own claims for recognition of their rights; they require surrogates to speak on their behalf. A number of organizations, private and public, national and international, have emerged to take up the advocacy of children. International agencies such as the United Nations Children's Fund, Defence for Children International, and Save the Children do a great deal, and within countries there are organizations such as the Children's Defence Fund in the United States that are very effective. But much remains to be done. Millions upon millions of children still die unnecessarily each year.

DENIAL

The low priority accorded to children is closely linked to their invisibility. The numbers of children who die year after year are remarkable, but even more remarkable is the fact that so few people know them. Wars and terrorism and airplane crashes are in all the newspapers, but the massive mortality of children is not. Why is that? I think there are several major reasons:

Distance. The massive mortality of children is viewed as something that takes place far away, beyond where you and I can reach to do anything about it.

Racism. Powerful white people in developed countries do not show as much concern for the deaths of people of color as they do for other white people.

Nationalism. Closely related to racism, nationalism means that people feel that their nation's resources should be devoted to solving their own nation's problems, not those of other nations. Charity may be given overseas, but there is little sense of obligation or duty to those in other countries. There is no sense that children of, say, Malawi, are also children of the world, and thus are *entitled* to a share of the world's resources. Nationalism is just one of many levels of tribalism by which we distinguish *our* children from *their* children.

Events orientation. The news media are geared to reporting on events, not on steady-state conditions. Famine events such as that in Somalia are reported, especially when they yield dramatic photographs. Most children's deaths, however, are associated with chronic malnutrition, a steady condition that is dispersed throughout the world, especially in Asia,

Africa, and Latin America. In general, people are much more capable of seeing direct violence than they are of grasping indirect or structural violence in the social order.

Triage. There is a deep concern that 'solving' the problem of massive children's mortality will result in runaway population growth, resulting in deterioration in the quality of life everywhere. Thus there is a notion that, sad as it may be, some must be sacrificed for the benefit of others. The best known spokesman for this view is biologist Garrett Hardin, who argues that we mustn't let everyone climb into the lifeboat lest it be swamped and sink.

People tend to deny problems when they don't know what to do about them. Certainly the long-term denial of the threat of the AIDS disease by many governments has been partly because they didn't know what to do about it. But the techniques for saving children are simple and straightforward. Children need only simple things like food and shelter and attention.

The world has the technical capacity and the material resources to reduce children's mortality sharply, but does not. We know how to end hunger technically, but lack the political will. I think we are afraid that any workable solution would require those of us who are rich and powerful to forego some of our advantages.

The denial of children's mortality is due more to an unexamined fear that saving them will in some way require sacrifice in the quality of our own lives. We prefer massive costs to others who are small, vulnerable, and far away to modest and uncertain costs to ourselves.

INTENTIONALITY

In some killings, witnesses observe the accused caught with a 'smoking gun,' and the accused is known to have motives for taking the life of the victim. In other cases, the accused may acknowledge having caused the death but argue that the gun went off accidentally, or say that he was temporarily insane and thus not responsible for his action. In criminal trials, distinctions are made according to the nature of the intentions:

Homicide is divided into four different types: *Criminally negligent homicide* (sometimes called vehicular homicide) is an unintentional killing resulting from indifference or reckless disregard for human life, such as speeding through a school zone. *Manslaughter* is killing someone intentionally in the heat of passion; unintentionally while committing a violation or a misdemeanor; or unintentionally while performing a lawful act in a negligent manner, such as while cleaning a loaded gun. *Second-degree murder* involves malice, which means that the killer must have intended to cause death or to inflict severe bodily harm. *First-degree murder*, the most serious form of homicide, involves both malice and a premeditated decision to kill someone.[18]

Similar distinctions can be made in connection with other sorts of death scenarios. Are the widespread deaths of children worldwide intentional in some sense? There is also the question of where the locus of these intentions might be. Who exactly is the responsible agent?

Most children's deaths cannot be described as murders. But that does not mean that they are accidental or natural or inevitable. Many can be described as resulting from a form of negligent homicide. Negligent homicide is still homicide in that the deaths are avoidable and unnecessary.

Can governments commit negligent homicide? Certainly it should be possible to charge governments with crimes of omission, crimes of neglect. Consider the case of *Joshua DeShaney* v. *Winnebago County Department of Social Services*, brought before the United States Supreme Court. The child, Joshua, had been beaten by his father, causing him to be retarded and permanently institutionalized. A county social worker who knew of the abuse took no action. A majority of the court ruled that the state had not inflicted the violence, and thus was blameless. In his dissent Justice William J. Brennan argued 'inaction can be every bit as abusive of power as action. ... I cannot agree that our Constitution is indifferent to such indifference.'[19]

In another sort of illustration, it has been suggested that the government of Bangladesh should be held responsible for the more than 100 000 flood and cyclone deaths in the summer of 1991 because of its failure to provide appropriate defenses against these very predictable events.[20]

Most criminal law deals with those who take actions that should not have been taken; it does not deal so effectively with failures to take action that should have been taken. This is true whether the failure to act is attributed to individuals or to governments.

This skew means that child abuse gets much more attention than child neglect, despite the fact that far more children's deaths can be associated with neglect. Neglect may be difficult to observe in individual households, but at the societal level the systematic neglect of children shows up in high morbidity and mortality rates.

We tend to draw too sharp a line between *deliberate* and *neglectful*. *Deliberate neglect* describes the pattern of many governments' responses to the needs of children. The term is not an oxymoron; it is not self-contradictory. If the failure to attend to children's needs persists over time, even in the face of repeated complaints and appeals, that neglect can be described as intentional or deliberate. Neglect can be understood as the failure to do something that should be done – and that failure may or may not be intentional. If it persists and it is obvious, it must be regarded as intentional.[21]

There is a difference between not knowing what your actions will lead to and what is described in law as 'reckless disregard' for the predictable consequences of one's action. Manufacturers of cars and pharmaceuticals are expected to pull their products off the market if they learn they have serious harmful effects. When infant formula was first promoted in the Third World, it may not have been anticipated that it would kill babies. But when international governmental and nongovernmental organizations documented and warned and campaigned about the problem, and the World Health Assembly passed guidelines to control the behavior of sellers of infant formula, and *still* the sellers persist in selling the product in a way that is known to kill babies, that is unforgivable.[22] It is a form of killing.

Usually killings are concentrated in a particular time and space. The deaths of children, however, are dispersed all over the globe, and they are sustained over time. There certainly is no central command structure causing these deaths to happen. There is nothing like the Wannsee conference of January 1942 at which the Nazis systematically set out their plans for the extermination of the Jews of Europe.

There is that difference. The widespread deliberate and sustained neglect of children is not the calculated program of a few madmen assembled at a particular moment in history. The massive mortality of children is more frightening precisely because it occurs worldwide with no central coordination mechanism. The culpability is not individual but systemic.

HATRED?

The plight of children can be explained by the indifference of policymakers to the well-being of children. Children are ignored or they are used to serve other people's interests, and apparently the interests of the children themselves simply do not matter very much.

Is it just a matter of indifference, or do some societies harbor a desire to harm children? Marian Wright Edelman, president of the Children's Defense

Fund in Washington, D.C., is one of the most articulate advocates for change in United States policy toward children. Reporting on her views, on May 19, 1991 the *San Jose Mercury News* headlined 'There's a War on, Our Children Are the Target. In May/June 1991 *Mother Jones* magazine, also reporting Edelman's views, offered a cover highlighting 'America's Dirty Little Secret: We Hate Kids'. Could they really mean *hate*? Do we really *target* kids, or is that just hyperbole, designed to attract attention? Do our societies go beyond simply ignoring kids, and actually want to harm them?

In his 1974 anthology on the *History of Childhood*, Lloyd deMause argued that it is not simply a matter of neglect. There are darker forces at work, a real deep-rooted malice, an urge to sacrifice children. More recently he has suggested that 'Direct budget cuts in child aid and recessions that mainly affect children are modern equivalents of ancient child sacrifice – only our sacrificial priests are now presidents, budget committees and Federal Reserve chairmen'.[23]

On the whole, is public policy merely indifferent to the well-being of children, or does it actually show signs of hatefulness? Is there an active desire to hurt children?

In my view there is no widespread societal motivation to harm children for its own sake, out of intrinsic hatefulness. But there is a well-established pattern of accepting the sustained and undeniable harm that befalls children as societies pursue other interests. While there may be no widespread intention to harm children directly, there is widespread acceptance of their being harmed indirectly, as a kind of 'collateral damage' from other activities regarded as more important. In that sense there is instrumental hatefulness. The idea is frightening, but given the history of human capacity to do – or tolerate – violence to other human beings, it cannot be dismissed.

There are many programs to serve children, in the United States, in other countries, and in the world as a whole. But the persistent inadequacy of these programs, especially for poor children, does result in persistent harm, and often death.

The point is ultimately inescapable. Deliberate neglect of children, sustained over an extended period, leads to definite harm; thus it is hateful behavior. It is not forgivable in the way that momentary inattention might be forgivable. The conventional distinction between negligent homicide (manslaughter) and deliberate homicide (murder) is meaningful only as it refers to a singular, fleeting event. You may get away with the story that your gun went off accidentally the first time, but if the same thing happened repeatedly the story would not be accepted. No court would view repeated, sustained killings, with full knowledge, as accidental.

The widespread deliberate neglect of children by governments must be understood as being, in a way, intentional. But it is also important to distinguish it from deliberate targeting, with hateful desire to harm, as in the Holocaust, or the Armenian genocide, or King Herod's systematic killing of the children of Bethlehem.

GENOCIDE?

On June 24, 1981 a group of 52 Nobel Prize laureates issued a *Manifesto Against Hunger* which began:

We appeal to all men and women of goodwill . . . to bring back to life the millions who, as victims of the political and economic upheavals of the world today, are suffering from hunger and privation.

Their situation has no precedent. In a *single year, more people suffer than all those who died in the holocausts of the first half of this century.* Every day spreads the outrage further, an outrage that assaults both the world around us and our own spirit and conscience.

The Nobel laureates compared the massive deaths from hunger and privation with deaths resulting from genocide. Would it be reasonable to go further and say that the treatment of children worldwide, allowing the deaths of over 12 million children under five each year, itself amounts to a form of genocide?

The *Convention on the Prevention and Punishment of the Crime of Genocide* was adopted by the United Nations General Assembly on December 9, 1948 and entered into force on January 12, 1951. According to article II:

In the present Convention, genocide means any of the following acts committed with intent to destroy, in whole or in part, a national, ethnical, racial or religious group as such:
(a) Killing members of the group;
(b) Causing serious bodily or mental harm to members of the group;
(c) Deliberately inflicting on the group conditions of life calculated to bring about its physical destruction in whole or in part;
(d) Imposing measures intended to prevent births within the group;
(e) Forcibly transferring children of the group to another group.

Children do constitute a group, but they are not a national, ethnic, racial, or religious group, the only victims recognized in the genocide convention. Also, the massive mortality of children is not the deliberate action of readily identified actors in the pattern characteristic of other commonly recognized genocides.

Some argue that genocide should be defined narrowly to prevent the debasement and trivialization of the concept. The difficulty is that a narrow definition may suggest that other kinds of large-scale mortality that are permitted to take place are less important. The sensible alternative is to systematically acknowledge that there are different kinds of genocide associated with different categories of victims and different forms of intentionality. This is the approach advocated by Israel Charny in his taxonomic scheme. He defines genocide in the generic sense as the willful destruction of a large number of human beings, except as that might be necessary in self defense. He then suggests that in distinguishing different categories of genocide, the degree of willfulness or intentionality should be assessed, leading to rating of different degrees of the crime of genocide.[24]

Perhaps the definitions used in assessing homicides could be adapted. Just as there can be first, second, or third degree murder, so too there might be first, second, or third degree genocide. Further distinctions must be made, however, to take account of sustained deliberate neglect.

The deaths of children throughout the world differ in many ways from the Holocaust and other atrocities commonly described as genocides. The differences, however, are not sufficient to dismiss the issue. The conclusion is virtually inescapable: *children's mortality is so massive, so persistent, and so unnecessary it should be recognized as a kind of genocide.*

Anne Frank, the girl who wrote the famous diary while hiding from the Nazis in Amsterdam, died in the Bergen-Belsen concentration camp in Germany in March 1945. She was not shot or gassed, but died of typhus. Is her death any less of an atrocity because the immediate cause of death was a disease and not gas or a bullet? Does it matter that the Nazis did not specifically plan the typhus?

Why is it that we are deeply concerned with the abuse and neglect of children by their families but give so little attention to the abuse and neglect of children by their societies and their governments? No matter what the intentions of political leaders and no matter what name it is given, there are massive horrors that befall children around the world. We are asked to remember the genocide of World War II, but sometimes we forget why we are to remember.

Where children's mortality rates are much higher than they need to be, the government's policies may amount to a form of genocide. When not just one child but children as a class are not adequately nourished and cared for, that constitutes an ongoing crime by society. And as a crime there should be mechanisms in law for correcting that manifest injustice, including means for calling not only parents and local communities but also governments to account. The foundation of that mechanism would be the clear recognition in law and practice of children's rights.

4 Child Labor

Children work all over the world, in rich countries as well as in poor countries. They do chores for their families, and many go out to fields and factories to earn modest amounts of money. Children are more likely to work if their families are poor. Children's work can be an important part of their education, and it can make an important contribution to their own and their families' sustenance. There can be no quarrel with that. The concern here, however, is with child labor. Child *labor* can be defined as children's working in conditions that are excessively abusive and exploitative. It is not clear where exactly the boundary line between acceptable children's work and unacceptable child labor should be located, but there are many situations in which there can be no doubt that the line has been crossed. A study prepared for the United Nations provided numerous illustrations:

> Thousands of girls between the ages of 12 and 15 work in the small industrial enterprises at Kao-hsiung in southern Taiwan. ... Some children [in Colombia] are employed 280 metres underground in mines at the bottom of shafts and in tunnels excavated in the rock. ... Most carpet-makers [in Morocco] employ children between the ages of 8 and 12, who often work as many as 72 hours a week. ... [In Pakistan] slave traffickers buy children for 1600 rupees from abductors. They cripple or blind the weakest, whom they sell to beggar masters. ... one million Mexican children are employed as seasonal workers in the United States.[1]

In 1985 the police in Bangkok found a three-year old girl chained in the cellar of a factory in which she was forced to make heroin into pellets.[2] Thousands of children have been smuggled from South Asia to the Gulf states where they are forced to serve as jockeys in camel races.[3] The following chapter examines the international dimensions of one of the more outrageous forms of child labor, prostitution, the sexual exploitation of children for profit.

Children are exploited for their labor throughout the world. The horror stories regarding children in carpet mills, brick factories, and prostitution rings are well documented. Often the conditions under which children work is influenced by the nature of the international markets for particular products. Rugs made in Kashmir by small children, for example, are all destined for the international market. Children who help their mothers peel shrimp in sheds in Thailand also are responding to the demands of an international market. In some cases, however, the fact that quality standards are higher and rules generally are more stringent for exported products may mean that children are more likely to be relegated to work serving domestic markets. This appears to be the case in the manufacturing industries of Thailand, for example.

Many children are caught up in the bonded labor system, especially in South Asia and Latin America. In the succinct explanation of the International Labour Office (ILO):

> The employer typically entraps a 'bonded' labourer by offering an advance which she or he has to pay off from future earnings. But since the employer generally pays very low wages, may charge the worker for tools or accommodation, and will often levy fines for unsatisfactory work, the debt can never be repaid; indeed it commonly increases. Even the death of the original debtor offers no escape; the employer may insist that the debt be passed from parent to child, or grandchild. Cases have been found of people slaving to pay off debts eight generations old.[4]

In many cases the potential for exploitation is enhanced by the fact that there are no written contracts.

In Pakistan, an estimated 20 million people work as bonded laborers, 7.5 million of them children. The carpet industry alone has perhaps 500 000 bonded child workers. Afghan refugees in Pakistan, and their children, are now included in Pakistan's pool of bonded laborers.

Anti-Slavery International estimates that in India there are 5 million adults and 10 million children who are bonded. It has been reported that 'several million children between the ages of 5 and 14 are in chronic bondage in agriculture; around a million are to be found in the brick-kiln, stone-quarry and construction industries; hundreds of thousands in the carpet-weaving, match and firework industries, as well as in the production of glass bangles and in diamond-cutting and polishing.' A fact-finding committee sent by the Supreme Court of India to Uttar Pradesh and Bihar found

> ... large numbers of children between 6 and 9 working on carpet looms. Parents are given advances in exchange for their children's labour. But the children are paid very little and, with the fines levied for punishments or mistakes, there is no opportunity to pay off the debt. The children are forced to work long hours under close watch and are often not allowed to go outside. Those who try to escape are beaten or tortured.[5]

Children work in rich countries as well. In the United States, for example, in 1988 about 28% of all 15 year-olds were working. In striking contrast with poor countries, in the US children from low-income families are *less* likely to be employed than children from high-income families. In the United States, poor youth have high levels of unemployment.[6] Of the employed 15 year-olds, about 18% worked in violation of federal child labor regulations governing maximum hours or minimum ages for employment in certain occupations.[7] Many working teenagers are injured on the job.[8] Enforcement of child labor laws has been weak in many states, apparently due to the greater concern with protecting the interests of employers.

Paradoxically, the acceptance of child labor tends to be higher where there are higher surpluses of adult labor. The addition of children to the labor force helps to bring down wage rates, which in turn makes it more necessary to have all family members employed. The widespread employment of children keeps them out of school, and thus prevents the buildup of human capital that is required if poor nations are to develop.

Economic growth does not necessarily result in the reduction of child labor. Thailand's economy has been growing rapidly in the late 1980s and early 1990s. It is viewed as one of the great success stories not only of southeast Asia but of all of the Third World. Despite this rapid economic growth, however, widespread child labor persists. In January 1992 the government reported filing charges against the owner of a sweatshop in Bangkok

... where 31 workers between 9 and 20 were employed making paper cups. Some of the children rescued by the police had been so badly beaten they could hardly walk. All had been forced to work 18 hours a day sitting on a cement floor to fulfill their daily quota. None was ever allowed to leave the sweatshop.[9]

Millions of children work, many under grossly exploitative conditions. The ILO has estimated that in the year 2000 there will still be at least 37 million working children under 15.[10]

REMEDIES

Many excellent studies have documented the problem of child labor in many different countries. The oldest human rights organization in the world, Anti-Slavery International (formerly the Anti-Slavery Society), based in London, has sponsored a number of country case studies in its Child Labour Series. The ILO is now publishing a series called the ILO Child Labour Collection beginning with studies on the Philippines and Sri Lanka, and also a book on designing projects relating to child labor.[11] Certainly publicizing child labor is important, but too often critics bemoan the awful working conditions without offering any recommendations for what should be done about it.[12]

Where there is action, often it is in the form of passing child labor laws. Internationally, the ILO takes the lead. The abolition of child labor was one of the guiding principles articulated in its constitution of 1919.

The ILO works through its International Labour Conference which, over the years, has adopted numerous conventions and recommendations relating to child labor. The conventions are subject to ratification, and create legally binding obligations on the States Parties. Recommendations serve as guidelines for national policy. Much of its work was concerned with setting minimum ages for employment in different economic sectors. In 1973 the Conference established a general instrument on the subject, the Minimum Age Convention (No. 138) and Recommendation (No. 146). In essence, ILO Convention 138 establishes fifteen as the general minimum age for employment. The minimum is fourteen for nations 'whose economy and educational facilities are insufficiently developed,' and eighteen for any employment 'likely to jeopardize the health, safety, or morals of young persons.' Under some conditions that minimum can be reduced to sixteen. As of 1992, only thirty-nine nations had ratified that Convention.

Whether ratifying or not, many nations have adopted national laws to control child labor that conform to the ILO framework. United States law, for example, conforms to Convention 138, although the United States has not ratified it – or most other ILO conventions.

The *Declaration of the Rights of the Child* adopted in 1959 said 'the child shall not be admitted to employment before an appropriate minimum age; he shall in no case be caused or permitted to engage in any occupation or employment that would prejudice his health or education … ' Article 32 of the *Convention on the Rights of the Child* of 1989 says much the same thing, and calls upon States Parties to set minimum ages and regulate the conditions of employment of children. It in effect defers to ILO leadership with regard to child labor issues.

Many of the nations that have ratified ILO Convention 138 are not enforcing it. Whether or not they have ratified the convention, in many countries national laws to control child labor are not vigorously enforced. India, for example, has been ignoring its child labor laws for decades.[13]

Child labor is illegal in Pakistan. Thailand has a number of government agencies concerned with children such as the Women and Children's Division in the Labor Department, the Welfare Department, and the National Youth Council and the Division of Youth Development under the Community Development Department of the Ministry of the Interior. Thai law prohibits the employment of children under twelve, and the employment of children between twelve and fifteen is supposed to be regulated. But the regulations are consistently violated. Ambitious child and youth development plans are included in the national development plans. Still, Thai efforts to correct child labor abuses have been hampered 'by inadequate budget resources devoted to inspection and enforcement, and to low penalties and fines which did not sufficiently deter potential violators.'[14] In practice the agencies and the laws have not been sufficient to protect the interests of children in Thailand.[15] There is considerable evidence that 'the authorities are in collusion with the owners of unregistered establishments.'[16] Similar patterns prevail throughout the world.

Efforts to enforce child labor legislation can disadvantage children by driving enterprises into more furtive operating conditions, removing them from public view. When children are prohibited from working they may continue working illegally, but without benefit of minimum wages or health and safety regulations.

There have been many examples of political mobilization in behalf of working children, but these programs have limited impacts and are difficult to sustain.[17] In some cases local nongovernmental organizations are effective in addressing child labor problems:

In Pakistan, for example, the Bonded Labour Liberation Front has helped release thousands of bonded labourers . . . It has also embarked on an innovative education programme, including the establishment of 77 schools across the country, providing basic education for 3 300 children of bonded families.[18]

At the World Conference on Human Rights held in Vienna in June 1993 the Bonded Liberation Front of Pakistan joined with the Bonded Labour Liberation Front of India, INSEC-Nepal, and the Justice and Peace Commission of Bangladesh in the South Asian Coalition on Child Servitude to demand:

(i)   That the UN World Conference on Human Rights should ask the governments of all importing countries to enact suitable legislations banning import of goods made fully or partially by children. Only those goods bearing a label from the authorised agency vouching for 'Free from child labour' be allowed to enter the country. Similarly, the exporting countries also be asked to take similar steps for banning of goods made by children.

(ii)   Appointment of National Commissions on bonded labour including child servitude vested with statutory power to identify, release and rehabilitate bonded labour. Laws relating to abolition need to be enacted expeditiously in countries where they do not exist.

(iii)   To stop all loans, aid or support by any of the UN organizations or Development Banks to any project which is likely to involve or perpetuate bonded labour and/or child labour.

As these activists from South Asia recognize, there is some potential for using law and policy relating to international trade as a means for influencing child labor practices. To illustrate, the U.S. Trade and Tariff Act of 1984 calls upon nations exporting into the US under the Generalized System of Preferences (GSP) 'to have taken or be taking steps' to afford their workers internationally recognized workers rights.[19] One of the five workers' rights criteria in the GSP law is a minimum age for employment of children. Several reviews by the interagency Subcommittee on the Generalized System of Preferences have included investigations regarding child labor.

Thailand, for example, has been reviewed several times. In June 1987 the AFL-CIO petitioned the government to withdraw GSP privileges from Thailand because of violations of workers rights, 'most flagrantly the prohibition against child labor, which for many boys and girls in their early teens amounts to involuntary servitude.' In April 1988 the U.S. government decided to continue Thailand's GSP benefits on the grounds that Thailand was 'taking steps' including raising the minimum age for employment from 13 to 14.[20] The AFL-CIO petitioned again with regard to Thailand in June 1991. A review was conducted, and in June 1992 the review was extended to December 1992 in order to monitor developments with regard to child labor and the right to organize. The review was extended again in December 1992 'in order to give the newly-installed civilian elected government more time to address concerns about workers rights.' In June 1993 the review was extended again, to December 1993. The extension was based on the Thai government's statements that it was taking steps such as increasing child labor inspections, extending compulsory education, and reducing the legal work day for 13 to 15 year olds from eight to six hours.[21]

Whether for Thailand or other countries, instead of actually imposing trade restrictions on nations alleged to be violating child labor age restrictions, the U.S. Department of Labor's response has often been simply to extend the reviews. Moreover, United States law only 'calls upon nations exporting under the GSP *to have taken or be taking steps* to afford their workers internationally recognized workers rights, not to 'respect' those rights.'[22] It appears that in the U.S. as in much of the world, trade interests dominate over human rights interests.

BUSINESS-LIKE SCHOOLING

Those who do offer proposals for dealing with the exploitation of children fall into two major camps, the *abolitionists* who want to end child labor, and the *ameliorationists* who want to improve the conditions under which children work. Neither camp has been very effective, mainly because their arguments have been politically naive. Both national and international law regarding child labor is frequently ignored, in rich as well as in poor nations. Child labor laws are regularly ignored in practice because they do not take full account of the social, political, and economic forces that sustain child labor. Yes, one can say children shouldn't work, but how then are they and their families to eat? Yes, one can say they should have better lighting and better toilet facilities in their workplaces, but how exactly are these extra costs to be paid, and what will motivate that payment? One of the major impediments faced by the Bonded Labour Liberation Front in Pakistan is the fact that liberated workers have no good alternative opportunities. As a result, those in bondage are sometimes reluctant to be liberated.

Where children, parents, employers, and governments all feel they get some benefit from the existing practice and see no attractive alternatives, they will ignore and circumvent efforts to alter the situation. Attempts have been made to provide better alternatives for children in various forms, but they have consistently collapsed under the burden of their costs. Is it possible to break out of this dilemma?

Historically, compulsory schooling and the control of child labor in the West has been motivated by two major considerations: (1) organized labor found it advantageous to remove children from the labor pool so adult wage rates would be higher, and (2) the building of skill levels or 'human capital' through education increased earning capacities. Schooling was an investment. In Third World countries, too, greater effort should be made to organize labor and to assure that schooling is in fact a productive investment.

How can this investment notion be used in Third World situations? Presently, schools in many Third World countries are not likely to build up useful, money-earning skills. The schools' performance levels are abysmally low, partly because they are funded by government regardless of how they perform. They are not attractive to children or their parents because they see little value in attending school. Parents are certain only of the fact that children who attend school forgo the opportunity to do immediately useful work in the fields or on the streets.

Many vocational schools have been created, often with support from private charities. Their success record has been mixed, and their scale remains small in relation to the size of the child labor problem. The difficulty is that usually such schools depend on external subsidies that are not large enough and are not sustained through time.

Perhaps such schools have not flourished because they have not been organized in a business-like manner. Vocational schools could be organized as private businesses, businesses that would succeed as economically viable operations if they were effective in instilling money-earning skills in their students.

The challenge, of course, is to find ways to pay for such schools. At least part of the school's costs can be covered with the school's earnings. The schools can be organized as combination work-study operations in which students gain practical experience by providing a variety of products and services for the local market.

In addition, to cover long-term financing, investments can be made in the students themselves. Techniques might be adapted from highly successful micro-loan programs such as the Grameen Bank in Bangladesh. That program has a number of special features:

> ... first, its clientele is essentially class-homogeneous – it caters exclusively to the landless and those owning 0.5 acres or less of land. Second, it follows a group approach to loan disbursement: borrowers must form groups of five persons each, each group selecting its own chairperson and secretary and holding weekly meetings. While loans are given to individuals there is an implicit group pressure and responsibility for repayment. Third, the loans are given without collateral, for any viable income-earning activity of an individual's choice ... Fourth, it recognizes the especially vulnerable position of women within the family ... Fifth, the concept of empowerment by collective activity and solidarity is emphasized in meetings and in special training programmes. Sixth, repayment is made easy by

enabling loans to be repaid in weekly instalments at a meeting in the village itself to which the bank worker comes for this purpose. Seventh, built into the system are various social-security schemes such as a group savings fund set up primarily to advance consumption loans; an emergency insurance fund against default, accident, and deaths; and various other schemes such as for house-loans, and so on. Eighth, to ensure that bank ownership stays with the members, each member has compulsorily to buy shares in the bank.[23]

By 1990 the Grameen Bank had made loans to more than 700 000 of the poorest women in Bangladesh, with an average loan size of $67, 'and the repayment rate is an incredible 98 percent.'[24] Similar programs now exist in at least thirty different countries. The Grameen Bank and many similar micro-loan programs throughout the world have good records of success in their enterprises and good records of loan repayment. They vary in structure, but all have some sort of social support system integrated with the lending program. Instead of focusing on support for starting new enterprises, a comparable lending program could be devised to help individuals pay school tuition to learn marketable skills.

Putting these ideas together, the recommendation here is simply this: *Private vocational schools could be created with curricula designed to build skills that would enhance long-term earning capacity in the local setting. Tuition could be paid through loans against future earnings.*

Requiring children to work for years to pay off a debt may seem uncomfortably similar to the situation some children face as bonded laborers. There are important differences here, however. No child should be asked to do this without the consent of both child and parents. There must be very clear and explicit contracts and repayment schedules. The consequences of default on the loan should be plain and limited.

Past studies of loan programs for education have concluded that their prospects are questionable, but they have focused on higher education, conventional approaches to schooling, and conventional approaches to lending.[56] The focus on higher education is unfortunate because there would likely be greater individual and social benefit from improvements in primary and secondary school than from improvements in higher education.

Studies that estimate economic benefits of schooling based on results obtained historically with government-funded schools do not take account of the much higher level of benefit that could result from high quality, sharply focused, specially designed, business-like private schools of the sort envisioned here.

Studies of the effectiveness of tuition loan programs tend to assume ordinary lending arrangements. In both poor countries and rich countries, loans for education have had high default rates. The proposal here, however, is that the lending facility should be designed in a way that draws on the experience of micro-loan programs such as the Grameen Bank in Bangladesh.

Social support mechanisms can play an important role in facilitating repayment of tuition loans. For example, parents, relatives, and perhaps community members could share in the liability so that they are contractually obligated to pay if the child does not. This would strengthen the parents' and relatives' incentives to provide encouragement and support for the child in studying and, upon graduation, in seeking gainful and stable employment. Properly designed, vocational schools of the sort described here could help to strengthen families and communities.

Apart from conveying technical skills, the school also would serve as a social support system during and after the student's attendance at the school. Faculty and staff members would be expected to develop long-term deep relationships with the students and their families. Graduates would be expected to return frequently to talk with current students and to help maintain the school with money, with their skills, and with whatever other resources they can muster. The feeling of the school would not be that of a factory churning out standardized products but of a large extended family. No student would have the right or the requirement to attend the school. Instead, acceptance into the school should come to be viewed as a privilege.

The school would have to be of first-rate quality in teaching skills that would be of value locally, whether these are skills of carpentry, plumbing, truck-driving, or anything else that may be in demand. Market research would be needed to discover which skills are in demand locally. Particular attention should be given to the kinds of skilled jobs that outsiders take in the local area. The school also could offer training in entrepreneurship so that graduates would be better prepared to find and develop their own opportunities.

A school of the sort proposed here would be a self-sufficient institution, surviving on its own success. It would not depend on a permanent external subsidy from government or private sources. If the school is not effective, the earning power of its students would not be increased. They would find it difficult to repay their tuition loans. If enough students default on their loans, the school's cash flow would suffer, and eventually it would dry up and disappear. This self-testing characteristic is missing from government supported school systems. Government-funded schools ordinarily have no strong feedback cycle, no reinforcement schedule to keep their performance level up. Many are doomed to being funded inadequately, assuring their mediocrity. And they are doomed to being funded perpetually, assuring their perpetual mediocrity.

This proposal for business-like vocational schools can be appealing to both the political left and the political right. It is designed to help the poor, but it is based on using the free market directly to liberate the poor from their plight. These schools would not be unending drains on public resources. They would require capital from the outside only for startup; after that, they could be self-sustaining. Of course continuing contributions would always be welcome to allow such schools to reach more children.

Such schools could be started as small experiments. Small boards of interested individuals could take the responsibility for drawing up concrete plans and budgets suited to local circumstances. Startup funding might be obtained from local industrialists who have themselves moved from rags to riches and are willing to create that possibility for others. Clarity of vision together with a good measure of optimism could be put together to start small seed programs with vast possibilities.

Such schools and tuition loan programs might be established on the basis of resources and resourcefulness already available within poor countries. But the possibilities would be greater with backing from governmental and nongovernmental international organizations. The World Bank, in particular, should see that schools of this kind would have beneficial effects for national economies while at the same time benefiting children, in sharp contrast to the usual structural adjustment policies of the international lending agencies. Such schools would constitute investments in human capital in a very literal sense.

5 Child Prostitution

Child prostitution refers to situations in which children engage in regularized sexual activity for material benefits for themselves or others. These are institutionalized arrangements – sustained, patterned social structures – in which children are used sexually for profit. Child prostitution is an extreme form of sexual abuse of children and an especially intense form of exploitative child labor.

The core concern here is the highly exploitative character of child prostitution. Most prostitution is exploitative, but for mature men and women there may be some element of volition, some consent. The assumption here is that young children do not have even the capacity to give valid, informed consent on such matters.

Child prostitution is widespread, but it is not possible to assess its magnitude with any precision. Except in some centers of pedophilia, children account for only a small segment of the prostitution trade overall. Even so, the numbers are large. It has been estimated that about 5000 boys and 3000 girls below the age of 18 are involved in prostitution in Paris. The Ministry of Social Services and Development in the Philippines has acknowledged that child prostitution rivals begging as the major occupation of the 50 000 to 75 000 street children who roam metropolitan Manila. The number of underage prostitutes in Bangkok numbers at least in the tens of thousands.[1] In India the number is surely over 100 000. It has been estimated that there are about 600 000 child prostitutes in Brazil.[2] The number of child prostitutes worldwide is probably well over one million.[3]

Reports say that in Bangkok, 'girls scarcely weaned are handed over to pimps for the equivalent of a small sum of dollars and very soon find themselves shut up in some brothel for life.' Girls can be bought for $100 or $200 in Macao, or for about $500 at auctions in India. Children play an important role in sex tourism.

This chapter is not a general survey of child prostitution around the world, but rather it is an examination of the ways in which child prostitution activities in different countries are *linked* with one another. These linkages are regularized and institutionalized.

Child prostitution activities cross national borders in several ways. There is *trafficking*, the movement of prostitutes, and those who will become prostitutes, from one region to another. And there are *traveling customers.* These include not only tourists but also business and military travelers. In response to all this, there are efforts at *international control*, by governmental and nongovernmental organizations working internationally to limit child prostitution. The focus here is on international linkages as they relate to child prostitutes, defined here as those under 16 years of age.

In some places, such as India and Thailand, child prostitution was deeply ingrained as part of the culture well before foreign soldiers or tourists appeared in large numbers. There are many local customers. Some Japanese and other tourists may use the child prostitutes in the 'tea houses' in the Yaowarat district of Bangkok, but traditionally most of their customers have been locals, especially local Chinese.[4] Similarly, in the sex trade near the American military bases in the Philippines before they closed down, more than half the customers were local people.[5] There is big money associated with the foreign trade, but there are bigger numbers in the local trade. This chapter focuses on international liaisons, but this does not mean that most customers of child prostitutes are foreigners.

TRAFFICKING

International trafficking for purposes of prostitution has a long history that is well documented and widely ignored. In the middle of the 19th century there was trafficking of young children from England to the continent, especially to Belgium, France, and Holland for purposes of prostitution. At the turn of the century many young girls were purchased in China, taken to the United States, and sold in open markets or directly to individuals.[6] There was large-scale trafficking of Chinese women into Malaya: 'In 1884, at least 2000 out of 6600 Chinese women in Singapore were prostitutes. Most of these girls were between the ages of 13 and 16.'[7] By the 1930s, under the *Mui Tsai* system, there was extensive traffic in women and girls between southern China and Malaya:

> Although the young girls entered Malaya supposedly for the domestic labour market, many mui tsai were sold to brothels. Often they came under the strict control of the secret societies which were involved in their importation into Malaya and Singapore. In 1863 alone, 500 young girls were coerced from China by secret societies. ... These girls were between the ages of 13 and 16. These young girls were meant not only for the brothels in Singapore but were also distributed to the mining and other commercial towns in Malaya, and other parts of South-East Asia.[8]

During the 19th century there was extensive traffic in Jewish girls from Eastern Europe. In 1903 Arthur Moro of London's Jewish Association for the Protection of Girls and Women reported:

> We have positive evidence that to almost all parts of North and South Africa, to India, China, Japan, Philippine Islands, North and South America and also to many of the countries in Europe, Yiddish speaking Jews are maintaining a regular flow of Jewesses, trafficked solely for the purpose of prostitution. We know that they were taken to brothels owned by Yiddish speaking Jews.[9]

Many others were involved in international trafficking early in this century:

> Overseas at Buenos Aires, The Rand, Manchuria, and other stops on the international vice circuit, the French were equally well-represented in all aspects of commercial vice. Italians and Greek traffickers sent their tribute to the voracious brothels of the Middle East and North Africa. Furthermore, in terms of participants, the Chinese and Japanese played the biggest role of all ... [10]

With Stroessner's rise to power in 1955, Paraguay became a major source:

> The large demand for prostitutes in the cities, combined with the easy availability of girls from the countryside, has stimulated the traffic in women to other countries. There is evidence that young peasant girls from Paraguay are taken to the United States and Europe for prostitution. In the past several years over 700 girls from the rural area of Caraguatay are reported to have come into the United States in groups of ten to twenty, passed through Miami and Chicago, and then by bus to New York City.[11]

Eleven-year-old girls have been taken from the hill tribes of Burma and smuggled into Bangkok.[12] In 1981 a representative of a Hong Kong nightclub, working with collaborators in Guangdong Province, took 41 girls from China to be forced into prostitution in Hong Kong.[13] Undoubtedly most international trafficking is in women over the age of 16, but some children do get swept up in the tide. Specific ages are rarely reported, but it seems reasonable to guess that at least some under-sixteens are included.

Some migration that is nominally for other purposes has the effect of supplying prostitutes. Sometimes children who are supposedly being adopted are in fact used for sexual purposes. In one case a 14-year-old Filipina girl was 'ostensibly adopted by a Dutch woman of Filipino origin who brought the girl into the Netherlands where she forced her to engage in prostitution.'[14] An NBC report shows 'the ease with which children can be adopted abroad and then brought to the United States to be sexually abused.'[15]

'Catalog' or 'mail order' brides often end up as prostitutes. After the young woman arrives in the new country, the marriage may not take place, or if it does it might come apart after a very short period. In some cases the abandoned woman, stranded in a strange country, turns to prostitution. In some case she is turned over to a specific pimp or brothel, in accordance with the broker's original intent.

In the 19th century, ritual marriages, undertaken without the required civil registration, were used as the means of procuring young Jewish girls from Eastern Europe:

> Procurers were known to go through the traditional ritual and then take their legally unmarried and largely unprotected partners off to a domestic or foreign brothel. ... In 1892 twenty-two men were convicted in Lemberg for procuring girls from small Galician towns with promises of jobs as servants, and selling them to brothels in Constantinople, Alexandria and points east of Suez. The Austrian consul in Constantinople had rescued sixty of them from virtual imprisonment the year before.[16]

Similar means are still being used. The German ambassador to Thailand has said that 'a terrifyingly high number of marriages of German men in Thailand – who appear there as tourists – aim only at bringing young Thai women to the Federal Republic in order to force them into prostitution there.'[17]

In India, fake marriages are a common means for drawing young women into the trade. In some cases the woman may sustain both an arranged marriage and prostitution simultaneously:

> Says Beena, a Delhi prostitute originally from Tibet: 'Most of us came as child brides and were sold off to brothels. Once we got in there was no way of getting out.' Today Beena lives a double life. In the morning she helps her husband sell readymade garments on the streets of New Delhi and at night, she paints her face and solicits customers in the notorious G.B. Road area. 'My husband wants me to do this,' she says in a tone of pain mixed with anger. 'Men only want our money. No one wants to love us.'[18]

Women who travel to foreign countries for arranged marriages are particularly vulnerable because they do not have any local family support system to provide an alternative. The age distribution of those drawn into fake marriages and then forced into prostitution is not known, but it is likely that at least some of them are younger than sixteen.

In many societies girls are sold into prostitution directly by their parents. Undoubtedly most of these girls are under 16. Most girls that are sold work locally, but some are taken by their procurers to distant countries, to replenish the stock in their brothels.

Migrating women are likely to become prostitutes. Young women travel abroad with the expectation that they will work in factories or as entertainers, waitresses, or servants. Some, deceived from the outset, are channeled directly into brothels where they are held by force. Some drift into prostitution after the original work arrangements deteriorate or disappear.

Many go to work abroad in a form of international indenturing in which children from poor families serve as house servants for rich families.

Unfortunately, indenturing often leads to exploitation and abuse of children. The seduction or rape of the parlor maid by the master of the house was the subject of many a nineteenth century novel. The woman was frequently blamed and cast out either pregnant or with a young child. A long way from home, unable to return to her family because of shame or the financial burden resulting from the penalty clause in her indenture contract, she turned to prostitution as her only means of survival.

The realities of contemporary indenturing are just as harsh. Children as young as 8 in Thailand, the Philippines, and other countries are sold by impoverished parents to agents from Bangkok and Manila. Instead of being placed with rich families, the minors are diverted to brothels in distant cities. A 15-year old prostitute who we interviewed had traveled from Santo Domingo to St. Maarten and told a story almost identical to the Victorian melodrama just mentioned. She went to work as a maid in the house of a radio personality at the age of 12. He seduced or raped her, and she was pregnant by the age of 13. After the infant was born, the baby was taken from her, and the offender applied to the courts for custody on the grounds that the mother was immoral. She was expelled from the house and resorted to prostitution.[19]

The pattern of domestic service functioning as a path to prostitution was well established in central Europe by the turn of the century: 'At Lemberg in 1909 for example the police reported that two-thirds of the registered prostitutes had been in service beforehand.'[20] It remains an important path to prostitution. Reports from Haiti say that young girls are employed as domestic help specifically to provide sex for the family's sons. There is a pattern followed by young girls hired as household help in Haiti:

> Exploited, ridiculed, lost in the big city, girls who are totally cut off from their parents are the most victimized ... Without any options, they are led to prostitution. After being abused by the sons of the house and then its master, the family throws them out. To survive, they become prostitutes and later they become abandoned single mothers.[21]

Most international travel occurs in the procurement stage, but there is also some travel of prostitutes after they are already in the trade. Many move to more lucrative markets, especially Japan.[22] Sometimes the move is only temporary. For example, major events such as world fairs or major sports events that draw large numbers of people attract prostitutes as well. Some may travel of their own volition, and some may be brought or sent by their pimps. However, there is no indication of extensive international travel by child prostitutes after they are recruited. They do travel within countries under the control of their pimps.

TRAVELING CUSTOMERS

While international trafficking refers to the delivery of prostitutes to the countries of customers, there are also systematic means for delivering customers to the countries of the prostitutes. Tourists and business travelers play important roles. Military 'rest and recreation' programs, and the location of military bases in less developed countries also bring customers from richer countries to prostitutes in poorer countries. And there is a steady international traffic of pedophiles (those who prefer sexual relationships with children) to areas catering to that trade.

Tourism

Many tourist destinations have flourishing prostitution industries, and many of them make special efforts to accommodate tastes for very young girls. A visitor to Hong Kong in the 1960s describes a 'special massage establishment on Cameron Road.'

The special massage establishments use very young girls from twelve to fifteen or sixteen as masseuses. There are hundreds in the Kowloon area, tucked away in the rear rooms of apartments, and the young girls there are slaves in every sense of the word. Since the Communist take over of the mainland there has been a steady flow of refugees, many landed illegally from 'snake-boats', to Hong Kong. They are only too willing to sell their young daughters to the traffickers. The usual price the traffickers pay for a ten-year-old virgin girl is H.K. $1600. As I discovered that night in the special massage establishment, they get their investment back on the first night she works for them, as they charge H.K. $1600 for the services of a virgin.[23]

Some prostitution evolves to accommodate ordinary tourists on ordinary excursions. The availability of child prostitutes may be just one of the many amenities that make their vacations interesting. In some cases, however, tours are established specifically for tourists for whom sex is the primary objective. In the Philippines, for example, it seems child prostitution has been promoted as a direct result of government policy:

In the early 1970s the country deliberately went in for tourism as an important source of income. Every effort was to be made to attract tourists to the Philippines and schemes were deliberately laid to use sexual services in the marketing of tourism and as a tourist attraction. Red light districts sprang up with brothels, 'massage-parlors' and so on, both in the capital, Manila and in tourist areas such as Puerto Galera and Boracay. The hotels started up so-called 'hostess services.' Child prostitution developed to add to the variety in the 'market.' Certain people understood that this was a niche for making a lot of money. More and more paedophiles in many places in the world became aware of the fact that the Philippines had developed almost into a sanctuary for them.[24]

There is sex-oriented tourism to some richer countries, particularly Holland and some of the Scandinavian countries, but tourism focused on child prostitutes is based in poorer countries. The customers are relatively rich, whether they come from rich or poor countries. Most are from the United States, Europe, and Japan, and some come from the Middle East.

Comfortably off men from the Middle East constitute a considerable proportion of those creating a demand for prostitution in Asian countries, India included. It is claimed, for instance, that approximately

1 in 10 of the customers in Bombay's red light district is a man from the Middle East. It is also claimed that Arabian businessmen have pseudo-marriages arranged for them by middle men for a price. The 'marriage' lasts just for the length of the man's holiday or business stay in India. As soon as he returns home, the relationship, as far as he is concerned, is as though it had never existed. The girl is left behind, defiled, cast out and often pregnant.[25]

Apparently they have a special interest in child prostitutes. 'Tourists from the Middle East are particularly enthusiastic about "deflowering" virgin girls. They are thus easy prey to enterprising pimps who know how to sell their experienced child prostitutes as "virgins."'[26] In the Philippines:

> The biggest number of customers are white males from the industrialized countries and prefer girls who are less than 12 years old and boys a little older. They pay them in cash. The Japanese come second and they are fond of older teenage girls and give clothes, jewelry, cameras and other amenities as payment. A small but significant group are Filipinos. These are older men locally referred to as dirty old men, DOMs. But generally child prostitutes still prefer to have sex with foreign men.[27]

The demands of wealthy tourists lead to increasing supplies of child prostitutes. The Centre for the Protection of Children's Rights in Thailand found that 'during 1985–88 when tourism was heavily promoted by the government, the sale of children into prostitution boomed. Of all the families they spoke to who had sold their daughters into prostitution, 35% had sold one daughter in the 12 – 16 age group and 25% had sold two daughters.'[28] The demand is explained by one visitor to Bangkok who said he was there for just one reason, girls: 'Fourteen-, fifteen-year old girls. I've already been to Sri Lanka and Korea, but this is the best place to find them: the girls are real fresh here, straight from the hills.'[29]

In 1984 fire destroyed a brothel in Phuket, Thailand, a major resort area. Five girls, ranging in age from 9 to 12, were found dead in the ruins of the locked basement. A film, *Tomorrow Will There Be a Rainbow*, tells the story of how their poor families in northern Thailand had sent them out to earn money.

The children are exploited economically not only by being paid very little but also by being cheated. A 14-year-old from Cebu in Manila's red light district 'was sold to a brothel where she was devirginized by a

Japanese. She stayed with the Japanese for a week, returned to the casa to get her pay but was told she still owed them money.'[30]

The children pimp for each other:

> At the casas we visited, the recruitment process was simple: you brought in your friends who needed cash. As one ages, you start pimping for the younger ones. Glenda is 14 ... semi-retired after two years as a child prostitute and now manages younger girls who she beats up when they don't follow her orders.[31]

The child prostitutes work long hours:

> Robinson's Plaza, Harrison Plaza, Ali Mall, Luneta – you see them especially on week-ends, hanging around, sending out signals to prospective customers. *Spartacus*, an international guide for pederasts, once described Harrison Plaza as a 'fish market,' open from ten in the morning to ten at night with 'several hundred boys available at one time in that area.'[32]

Few children operate wholly independently, but some are much freer than others. Street children come and go more or less as they wish, and undertake a variety of different activities, while other children may be permanently confined to a brothel. One study found that with regard to child prostitution ...

> Street children have, on average, only a few customers. As a rule they only use this way of making money when absolutely necessary. In the sample of 1000 children in the Philippines only 17% had customers every day. Conditions are in general completely different for children controlled by the syndicates. These children may be forced to have sexual intercourse up to 20 times a day.[33]

Some organized sex tours specialize in sex with children. Investigative reporters for the National Broadcasting Company found travel agencies in West Germany and England offering child sex tours to Thailand. One of the reporters 'purchased a child sex tour from a London travel agent. When he arrived in Thailand at his destination, a pimp whom he met through the Bangkok branch of the multinational travel agency delivered a 13-year-old girl to his hotel room.'[34]

Apart from the sex tours, tourism promotes prostitution indirectly. There is the symbolic effect of rich tourists demonstrating lavish lifestyles, and tempting young people to go after easy money. In addition, there are strong economic pressures. The tourist trade brings in wealthy people who can afford to pay high prices for all kinds of things. Accordingly, local merchants increase their prices, which leads to rapid inflation. The many local people whose incomes do not increase as a result of tourism find they can no longer afford the inflated prices. Desperate for new sources of income, some may turn to prostitution.

In many parts of the world there are patterns of circular migration in which poor people go off to richer countries to work, but with the intention of returning home after a time. Often these are men or women who travel without their families, to work in various forms of unskilled labor. These migrations of 'guest workers' are encouraged by the sending countries because they have severe underemployment problems, and the repatriation of earnings may account for a large share of the poor countries' income.

Migrating men often become the customers of prostitutes. In Peru:

> The history of the exploitation of Peruvian Amazonian resources of wood, rubber, and oil has been paralleled by a history of prostitution in the same area. Short-term migrant workers live in camps or enclaves, and companies supply prostitutes for their sexual needs. It has been reported that the demand for very young girls (12 to 16 years) is very high in Inquitos, and that virgins are offered as gambling prizes.[35]

Business people sometimes use their opportunities to travel, or to relocate for extended periods, to take advantage of young children. Consider this account of a Britisher working in the Philippines for a multinational oil company:

> Steve has an apartment in the Malate area and both invites young kids (mostly boys – but also a few girls) not only to his apartment but to eat in restaurants etc. He also gives a small amount to kids who bring in other kids. Usually the age range of the kids would be 8 – 14 with a few a little older. Sometimes, he has them take a shower or play with each other naked on the bed while he makes video documentaries. Sometime early this year, the police raided his apartment and found him and five other boys playing naked.

Testimony regarding his behavior was taken from children by Bahay Tuluyan, a church-based program responding to the needs of women and children in Malate-Ermita, the major red-light district of Manila. The organization staged a march to the immigration authorities asking that he be deported. They were not successful.

As Russia and the countries of Eastern Europe turn toward capitalism and become increasingly open to foreign investment, the sex trade flourishes, and many youngsters are caught up in that trade. According to the director of a pediatric hospital in Ho Chi Minh City, 'since the massive arrival of businessmen from Japan, Hong Kong, Taiwan, the sex business is rising,' and many businessmen coming to Viet Nam seek children 10- to 12- years old.[36]

The internationalization of business relates to prostitution in other ways as well. Many multinational corporations establish manufacturing plants in Third World countries and hire young, single girls to work on the assembly lines. Their role is similar to, and sometimes linked to, that of girls working in the sex industry:

> In neither manufacturing or sex industry can women workers expect economic security nor sufficient earnings over the long run. ... The similarities and overlap between light manufacturing and sex industries are further brought home by the fact that women displaced from assembly plants may seek work in hotels and brothels. Some factory women supplement their meagre wages by moonlighting as prostitutes. ... Young women unable to find or keep a job, a strategy which often involves submitting to the sexual advances of factory supervisors, may cross over the gates to the beer houses which have sprung up around the industrial estate.[37]

In 1993 *Time* magazine ran a cover story on 'Sex for Sale' and also did a companion piece on 'Defiling the Children'. It told of child prostitution within countries, and also described the attractiveness of Thailand, the Philippines, and Sri Lanka for pedophiles.[38]

Military Travelers

Prostitution, including child prostitution, occurs on a large scale near military bases and military 'rest and recreation' areas. This occurs at both domestic and overseas bases. Since there has been so much projection of U.S. military power abroad since World War II, frequently it has been U.S. servicemen and civilians attached to bases in foreign countries who were the customers.

Up until the closing of the bases in 1992, the pattern was particularly visible in the Philippines. In the 1970s and 1980s, thousands of Americans were stationed at 25 bases and other military facilities in the Philippines. The largest were Clark Air Base (55 000 hectares) and Subic Naval Base (26 000 hectares). Thousands of American military personnel were stationed at Subic Bay, but the numbers went up sharply when the Seventh Fleet visited. There also were many American civilians working at the base. Thus businesses in the nearby town of Olongapo were geared toward accommodating the Americans at the base. There were thousands of 'hospitality girls.' Olongapo was described as Asia's biggest brothel.

In 1982 a serious outbreak of venereal disease led to the hospitalization of 12 girls between the ages of 9 and 14. It was this incident that triggered Father Shay Cullen, who had been running a drug rehabilitation center, to launch a campaign to end the prostitution in Olongapo. In 1989 he reported that naval intelligence agents at Subic had found that children from 11 to 14 were being offered by an organized group to pedophile servicemen. In addition, he says 'hundreds of people from Europe, the United States, and Australia come to Olongapo City to buy and sell sex with children between 6 and 16.'[39] The local mayor, prosecutor, and other officials refused to act on the information. Cullen was asked to leave the country, and pressured by the base commander. His life was threatened many times.

In Thailand, the American presence during the Indochina war accelerated the development of prostitution. During 1962–76 there were tens of thousands of U.S. military personnel stationed at seven air bases in different parts of Thailand supporting operations in the Indochina war. Hundreds of thousands flew into Thailand for 'rest and recreation' visits. Bars and brothels mushroomed near the bases and the R&R centers, especially in the Northeast. In 1964 the police department estimated there were 400 000 prostitutes in Thailand. After the departure of the United States forces the women in the trade shifted to resort areas such as Pattaya, or went overseas to work in Japan, Singapore, Hong Kong, Germany, Switzerland, Holland and elsewhere.

Many establishments are operated by local people and appear to be local operations but in fact are owned and controlled by foreigners. For example, it has been estimated that Americans own a majority of the bars in Barrio Barreto and Subic City, two smaller prostitution areas outside Olongapo in the Philippines: 'They are able to own bars through marriage to a Filipina or using a Filipino front. Bar owners are the 'upstanding' members of the city – the Lions Club, the Rotary Club, etc. and have their own Bar Owners Association.'[40]

The rapid growth of United Nations peacekeeping missions in the early 1990s raised a new cause for concern. Following the Paris Agreements of

October 1991, the United Nations created UNTAC, the United Nations Transitional Authority in Cambodia. It fielded 15 900 peace-keeping troops and 6100 administrators, and with a budget of $2.8 billion, was the largest field operation in the history of the United Nations. With many young men away from home, and with money in their pockets, finding themselves among people who had little cash income, prostitution in Cambodia flourished. Child prostitution became an important part of the trade, with children kidnapped, and raped, bought, and sold.[41]

Too little attention has been given to the children of prostitutes and the problems they encounter. They are prime candidates for entry into the trade. In Honduras, children born to women who have been forced to work in brothels 'are taken over by the owners and become part of the establishment.'[42] The prospects of prostitutes' children may depend on whether they are the products of international liaisons. In the Philippines, for example, it has been found that relatives of the prostitute were more willing to look after the child if he or she were a pure Filipino than if the child resulted from a relationship with a Caucasian. 'Amerasian' children were more likely to remain in the prostitution environment.[43]

Pedophiles

Most of the traveling customers of child prostitutes are men. In some cases they are women, such as the middle-aged white European women who travel as tourists along the coast of Kenya. The customers may be heterosexuals, homosexuals, or pedophiles. They may or may not be homosexual. Pedophiles – mostly men, but occasionally women – constitute a very distinctive group of customers.

Certain areas have become known as centers of pedophilia. In the Philippines, international pedophilia was recognized as a problem as far back as 1599, when the Spanish Royal Audiencia issued an ordinance prohibiting Chinese settlers from practicing 'sodomia' with the 'Moro and Indian boys of these islands.'[44]

In modern times, Pangsanjan, about 40 miles southeast of Manila, has been an international center of pedophilia. Its sordid reputation became even more well known when American filmmakers came to town to shoot scenes for *Apocalypse Now*. The word spread and foreign men took up residence, including an American who ran a prostitution business. That American was arrested in 1988, 'along with six other Americans, five West Germans, three Australians, two Belgians, a Japanese and a Spaniard. Most have since left the country.' But one Swiss national 'married the sister of his 15-year-old male lover and has applied to return home not with his wife but with his new brother-in-law.' It has been estimated that in the town of 22 000, 65 percent are under 18, and one-third of these – almost 5000 – are child prostitutes.[45]

The situation in Pangsanjan changed radically after 1988 when the government cracked down. In the first raid, 23 pedophiles from around the world were caught and deported, and more raids followed after that. It has been reported that the pedophile trade has now been virtually eliminated in Pangsanjan.[46]

Manila has its share of the pedophile trade:

> In Manila, as in other similar centers, the growth of child prostitution is alarming. In this case, the pimps visit the poor rural areas and negotiate to buy children or lease them for about $50.00 per year. Young children, both girls and boys from the age of about eight, are taught to perform sexual acts for voyeurs and later placed in brothels which cater to pedophiliacs.[47]

Pedophilia has become a major concern in Sri Lanka as a result of the vigorous promotion of tourism that began in the 1970s. By 1980 child prostitution was well established, especially in the resort areas. 'Men from all parts of the world come each year to Sri Lanka to satisfy their sexual and emotional needs, and, having visited once, they come back again and again. ... Boys as young as ten years old ... are easily attracted into prostitution.'[48]

The 'beach boys' that cruise the resort areas are numerous and well organized:

> It has been found that though a rough estimate of about 10 000 boys are 'moved' from resort area to resort area by their 'agents' with whom the 'deals' are made, there are other boys from the ages 8–16 who have now emerged acting independently, and making their contacts individually or in small groups. They ape the older boys who are 'professionals' in these practices. What is disturbing is that paedophiles are coming in search of still younger and younger boys for the purposes of sexual pleasure. In a season or two these sexually exploited children are abandoned.[49]

Many of the pedophiles take rooms in small hotels on a monthly basis, and re-enter the country annually to make contact with 'their boys.' Tourism in general has fallen sharply because of the ethnic and political violence in the country since 1983, but the hotels catering to pedophiles have maintained high occupancy rates.

Jack Anderson, a famous newspaper columnist, described Bangkok as 'the hub for international child prostitution. ... Europeans and Americans make up a big share of the clientele and have even cashed in on the business side.'[50] Andersen also mentioned the case of a Utah man arrested by Thai police because he was suspected of running a house of prostitution for pedophiles under the guise of an orphanage. Two other Americans were arrested in 1989 for running a child sex ring. American men have been arrested in Manila for similar reasons.

Pedophiles around the world have established vigorous communication networks through publications such as the *Spartacus Gay Guide* and *PAN* magazine from the Netherlands, and the *Paedo Alert News*, and through organizations such as the Lewis Carroll Collector's Guild and the North American Man-Boy Love Association (NAMBLA).[51]

ECONOMIC PRESSURES

Large differences in the income levels of the peoples of different countries have little effect when everyone stays home. But when poor people travel to rich countries, or rich people travel to poor countries, whether as tourists, business people, or soldiers, the inducements promoting prostitution are enormous. With large differences in wealth levels and increasing ease of transportation, beginning in the 19th century 'prostitution became a multinational enterprise.'

In the late-nineteenth century commercial prostitution changed in one crucial respect. Routes of supply lengthened and the traffic became international. ... the popularity of brothels diminished among clientele and inmates, both of whom began to find them confining ... This change of taste squeezed the profits of commercial vice, based as they were on the economies of scale of the large brothel. Fortunately for the entrepreneurs, the sex imbalances created by the disproportionate emigration of European men meant that there was a foreign requirement for prostitutes. The steamship and the telegraph made it possible to respond to the new market situation. There is an uncanny parallel between the real crisis of commercial prostitution and the alleged crisis of capitalism in the same period, each resolved by expansion overseas.[52]

International prostitution accelerated rapidly in the 20th century, largely as a result of the expansion of international relationships of every kind. The process is economic:

The demand for sexual service is most significant where men congregate in large groups separated from home and family. The sexual demands of military men, traveling, businessmen or sailors, and immigrant laborers create a major market for women's bodies. That market is kept supplied through procurers and gangs that run the traffic in women and children.

Procurers work the poverty-stricken countryside of Third World nations as well as bus and train stations of major cities, acquiring girls and young women. They maintain a constant supply to serve the market.[53]

Trafficking for purposes of prostitution follows general patterns of international trade: there is a net flow from poorer to richer countries, and the more highly valued commodities go to the richer countries, or at least to richer people. For example, there is a regular flow of Nepalese and Bangladeshi girls into India, apparently because Nepal and Bangladesh are poorer than India, and thus their girls can be obtained more cheaply than Indian girls.

In some places the market in women is institutionalized enough to sustain regular auctions. There have been reports of women being sold through auction in Buenos Aires in the 1920s.[54] An unconfirmed report speaks of auctions in Zanzibar, the island part of Tanzania, as recently as the 1970s.[55] In India 'the slave bazaar is so well organized a woman can be kidnapped in Bangladesh and moved across India for sale in Pakistan. Some women are auctioned like cattle at transit centers located just outside big cities.'[56] One reporter tells of a row of business hotels along Showa Avenue in Ueno, Tokyo that 'has become an auction block for human bodies':

Young Thai girls were being auctioned off left and right at knock-down prices before my eyes. I couldn't stand to watch it. . . . Dealers came from all around – Nara, Osaka, the Kansai area. The highest bid was 750 000 yen (about US$3 000) for six months service, but one little black girl went for only 200 000 yen (US$800).[57]

In China, according to one report:

The women are transported hundreds of miles from their home and sold at auctions in many of the provinces in the north-west and the coastal regions. Some are only 13 or 14. They are displayed at markets or, in one notorious case in 1988, paraded semi-naked down the main street of a town in Central China.[58]

The idea that the receiving country earns substantial amounts of money from sex tourism may be an illusion because of the foreign control. Yayori Matsui, describing Japanese sex tours to the Philippines, says 'very little foreign money stays in the Philippines; most of it ultimately goes back to Japan:'

> Japanese tourists are buying package tours from Japanese travel agencies, traveling on Japan Air Lines, staying at hotels owned by Japanese capital, enjoying sight-seeing tours arranged by Japanese travel agency branches, picking up women at Japanese-managed clubs, dining at Japanese restaurants, buying souvenirs at department stores backed by Japanese investments, and returning to Japan the same way they came – Japan Air Lines.[59]

Child prostitution activities are economic, but there is a fundamentally political dimension as well. Power relationships are of central importance. One writer observes:

> The powerful, the haves, the better armed, those more equipped with modern technology and communication systems, and those who produce more, no matter how, have their way in this world. The powerless and have-nots are perennially victimised. And the children are the poorest and most helpless in terms of those power-oriented values.[60]

Another observer elaborates:

> The main issue that must be confronted in pedophilia and child prostitution is the element of exploitation. Exploitation exists where the relationship is unequal in terms of power. We speak of exploitation in several senses:
>
> There is the *exploitation of the child*, who is often too young to be aware of the implications of the relationships they enter. ...
>
> Second, we deal with *class exploitation*. The child prostitutes are often recruited from economically depressed families, who also lack the political power to fight excesses of the pedophiles. ... In the context of capitalism, there is massive commodification of sex. The child is reduced to a commodity to be exchanged mainly for money. ...
>
> Finally, we deal with *national exploitation*. We [in the Philippines] have become so desperate about earning dollars that we now prostitute our children to fuel our dying economy. ...[61]

Sex tourism can be compared with the use of foreign labor by multinational corporations in overseas plantations or factories. In many countries, laborers on plantations owned by foreigners are better off than laborers on locally-owned plantations. Similarly, prostitutes serving tourists are likely to be better off than those serving local clients:

> Indeed, whatever the contribution of tourism to the growth of prostitution in Thailand, it should be emphasized that the women working with *farangs* are in many respects the 'elite' among the prostitutes: they earn significantly more than those working with Thais, enjoy greater independence, and are rarely controlled by pimps or pushed into prostitution against their will – which is otherwise quite a common phenomenon.[62]

The objection to foreign clients of prostitutes, like the objection to multinational corporations, is not that they are more exploitative than locals, but precisely that they are *foreign* exploiters.

DOMESTIC LAW

Many countries have laws explicitly prohibiting child prostitution or other more general laws which could be used to control the practice, but they are rarely implemented. For example, in India, article 23 of the constitution prohibits trafficking, and the Suppression of Immoral Traffic Act of 1956, amended in 1986, addresses the issue of child prostitution in particular. However, the law has had little useful effect.[63]

Several different kinds of legal and institutional responses have been developed in the United States. In 1977 about 600 000 juvenile females and 300 000 juvenile males in the United States were involved in prostitution.[64] In 1992 another source estimated that there are 2.4 million children involved in juvenile prostitution each year.[65] These are very uncertain figures.

Four major pieces of national legislation relate to child or juvenile prostitution: (1) the Protection of Children Against Sexual Exploitation Act, (2) the Child Abuse Prevention and Treatment and Adoption Reform Act, (3) the Runaway and Homeless Youth Act, and (4) the Missing Children Act, all passed in the late 1970s and early 1980s. About half the states have legislation explicitly directed at juvenile prostitution.[66] Increasingly, legislation in the United States reflects the view that 'the juvenile prostitute should be treated as a victim of adult sexual misconduct, rather than as a youthful perpetrator of criminal acts.'[67] Much of the legislation appears to be generally ineffective, at least as measured by numbers of convictions under the respective acts. There is very little case law regarding child prostitution, and very little legal analysis.[68]

One lawyer feels that 'only when we enact and enforce tough criminal laws against the customers as well as the pimps who exploit these children will we significantly reduce the tragic problem.'[69] But this is a very limited repertoire of action. D. Kelly Weisberg recognizes that a narrowly legalistic approach to the problem is not likely to work:

Alternative goals of prevention, punishment, and rehabilitation should be carefully explored to determine which goals best conform to the problem. In addressing a problem such as juvenile prostitution, it is simplistic to believe that punishment will eliminate the problem, since such an approach has failed with adult prostitution.

Too often, the legislative response to a social problem – especially one involving child victims – is enactment of harsher penalties for adult perpetrators; yet this approach ignores the plight of the victims. When addressing a social problem such as juvenile prostitution, an emphasis on prevention and treatment appears to be more effective if the goal is to assist the youth involved.[70]

Police can act in a non-punitive manner toward juveniles. In Lexington, Kentucky, for example, the police department has an Exploited and Missing Child Unit which uses teams composed of one police officer and one social worker. It views the youth as victims, and concentrates on providing support services to them, while developing investigations leading to the arrest and conviction of customers and pimps.[71]

One part of the federal legislation on juvenile prostitution 'appears to be very effective':

The Runaway and Homeless Youth Act, which provides funding for runaway shelters nationwide, helps both male and female adolescent prostitutes who are runaways. Several federally funded runaway shelters have exemplary programs that address the specific needs of adolescent prostitutes. Three such centers are Bridge Over Troubled Waters in Boston, The Shelter in Seattle, and Huckleberry House in San Francisco.[72]

Apparently interventions are likely to be more effective when they provide not punishment but support for troubled children.

INTERNATIONAL CONTROL

International Governmental Organizations

Many organizations work within individual countries to combat child prostitution, but our concern here is limited to those that work internationally. Several international governmental organizations (international organizations whose members are national governments) play a role.

The **International Criminal Police Organization**, INTERPOL, acts as an information exchange and as a liaison body between police forces of different countries; it does not have the power to investigate specific crimes. The international effort to control 'white slavery' was one of the major factors leading to INTERPOL's creation.[73] In 1974 INTERPOL's General Secretariat prepared a document on *Traffic in Women: Recent Trends*, but its sketchy information did not include any data on the ages of the women.[74] In 1988 INTERPOL conducted an International Symposium on Traffic in Human Beings.

The **International Labour Organization**, ILO, has sponsored some studies and conferences on child labor, and child prostitution has been mentioned in those contexts, but the organization does not address the issue systematically.

The **United Nations Children's Fund** (UNICEF) has a program on Children in Especially Difficult Circumstances that includes the issues of labor exploitation and child abuse. Its work on child prostitution is done quietly.

Within the United Nations system, in addition to UNICEF and ILO, the **Working Group of Experts on Contemporary Forms of Slavery** also is concerned with the exploitation of children. Human rights in general is the responsibility of the Economic and Social Council of the United Nations. ECOSOC has a subsidiary Commission on Human Rights, which in turn has a Sub-Commission on Prevention of Discrimination and Protection of Minorities. That Sub-Commission receives reports from a number of Working Groups, one of which is the Working Group of Experts on Contemporary Forms of Slavery. Since 1975 it has held sessions each summer at United Nations headquarters in Geneva.[75]

In 1982 ECOSOC commissioned 'a synthesis of the surveys and studies on the traffic in persons and the exploitation of the prostitution of others.' The report spoke of the traffic of north African women to Europe, South Americans to Melbourne, women from Hawaii and California to Japan, and Thai women to Switzerland, giving special attention to the traffic based on fake marriages. It also attacked sex tours. The report said that 'confined in the bondage of prostitution, women and children await their liberation. This fight is as necessary as the fight against the drug traffic and the fight against racism.'[76] Apparently the report did not lead to any significant action.

In 1990 Vitit Muntarbhorn of Thailand was appointed by the Commission on Human Rights to serve as Special Rapporteur on the sale of children. His first report, submitted at the end of 1990, and his second report submitted at the end of 1991 (with an addendum on Brazil in early 1992), provided a good deal of useful information on child prostitution and also on child pornography and child labor.[77]

International Nongovernmental Organizations

For the purposes of this discussion, international nongovernmental organizations (INGOs) are nongovernmental organizations that work in several different countries, not necessarily those with membership from several different countries. Several INGOs give child prostitution a prominent place on their agendas.

Anti-Slavery International (formerly the *Anti-Slavery Society*) in London, founded in 1839, is the world's oldest human rights organization. It gives a great deal of attention to child labor, and in that context it frequently addresses the problem of child prostitution.

Defence for Children International, headquartered in Geneva, advocates children's interests worldwide. It has national offices in many countries, and publishes the quarterly *International Children's Rights Monitor*. DCI-USA and DCI-Netherlands have given particular attention to child prostitution.[78]

The **International Abolitionist Federation** was founded by Josephine Butler, a woman from Liverpool who worked to abolish prostitution in England in the 19th century. She was joined in her efforts by Alfred Dyer, whose special concern was the rise of child prostitution in England. He campaigned to raise the age of consent from 12 to 18, to curtail procuring of young girls for prostitution. He focused on the traffic of young English girls to the continent, where they were forced into prostitution.[79] The Federation, founded in 1875, is headquartered in Lausanne, Switzerland. The IAF's major objective is controlling traffic in persons and the exploitation of the prostitution of others. It opposes the regulation of prostitution itself. The IAF has organized numerous conferences to further its cause. The main theme of its September 1990 conference in Geneva

was 'The Exploitation of Prostitution: Violation of Human Rights;
Children, The First Victims.'

The **International Catholic Child Bureau**, headquartered in Geneva,
has been working actively on children's rights issues, and on child
prostitution in particular. It publishes a periodical on *Children Worldwide*.

The **International Feminist Network Against Female Sexual Slavery**
grew out of the Global Feminist Workshop to Organize Against Traffic in
Women held in Copenhagen in 1980. The IFN's first meeting in
Rotterdam in 1983 led to the creation of a network of local groups to
address the problems of prostitution in every region of the world.[80] In
1984, with the assistance of the United Nations Non-Governmental
Liaison Service, the group conducted a consultation to examine
prostitution and other forms of exploitation of women.[81]

The **International Save the Children Alliance** has supported a variety
of projects relating to child prostitution, including a study by its
Norwegian arm, Redd Barna, on the sexual exploitation of children in
several developing countries.

International Federation Terre des Hommes is a private social
services organization headquartered in Lausanne, Switzerland. It has
supported work in Sri Lanka and Thailand on the problem of child
prostitution.

End Child Prostitution in Asian Tourism, ECPAT, is an organization
and international campaign intended to carry out the objective spelled out
in its name. It grew out of an Ecumenical Consultation on Tourism and
Child Prostitution organized by the Ecumenical Coalition on Third World
Tourism in Chiang Mai, Thailand in May 1990. ECPAT has established its
headquarters office in Bangkok, and has 14 offices, in the region and in
some of the nations that send sex tourists. It has been effective in
mobilizing nongovernmental organizations to work together to control
child prostitution in Asia, and has drawn the support of government
officials throughout the world.[82] ECPAT is the only international
organization for which child prostitution is the major issue of concern.

International Law

In many countries the law regarding prostitution is applicable to children,
and in some cases there are laws relating specifically to child prostitution.
The concern here, however, is primarily with international law.

Many international human rights declarations and agreements over the
past century are related to child prostitution. One important stream of

international law is that related to children, and another is that centered on prostitution, slavery, and the exploitation of women.

In 1871, at the International Medical Congress in Vienna it was proposed that uniform international law should be established to regulate prostitution. However, this effort, like the Contagious Diseases Acts implemented in Great Britain between 1864 and 1869, was primarily to protect men from disease, not to protect women.

An international conference in Paris in 1902 led to an *International Agreement for the Suppression of the White Slave Traffic*, signed in Paris 1904. Its purpose was to commit governments to take action against 'procuring of women and girls for immoral purposes abroad.'[83] This led to the 1910 Mann Act in the United States which forbids transporting persons across state or national boundaries for prostitution or other immoral purposes. *An International Convention for the Suppression of White Slave Traffic* was signed in Paris in May 1910. Protocols amending both the 1904 and 1910 agreements were signed at Lake Success, New York in May 1949.

In September 1921 a *Convention for the Suppression of the Traffic in Women and Children* was signed in Geneva, and in October 1933 a *Convention for the Suppression of the Traffic in Women of Full Age* was signed in Geneva. Protocols amending both were signed at Lake Success, New York in November 1947.

In 1949 a United Nations *Convention for the Suppression of the Traffic in Persons and of the Exploitation of the Prostitution of Others* was adopted in 1949 and came into force in 1951. The United States has not signed the convention.

In December 1956 the United Nations *Supplementary Convention on the Abolition of Slavery, the Slave Trade and Institutions and Practices Similar to Slavery* came into force.

In 1981 a *Convention on the Elimination of Discrimination Against Women* came into force.

An overview of the evolution of children's rights is provided later, in Chapter 9. The two streams of international law, relating to children and to prostitution and related issues, come together in Article 34 of the new *Convention on the Rights of the Child*, which addresses the issue of child prostitution directly:

States Parties undertake to protect the child from all forms of sexual exploitation and sexual abuse. For these purposes States Parties shall in particular take all appropriate national, bilateral and multilateral measures to prevent:

(a) the inducement or coercion of a child to engage in any unlawful sexual activity;

(b) the exploitative use of children in prostitution or other unlawful sexual practices;

(c) the exploitative use of children in pornographic performances and materials.

As indicated above, there are organizations working to control child prostitution, but the level of effort by the international community is nowhere close to what is needed.

Cultural Relativism

In Pangsanjan in the Philippines, some parents who depend on their children's incomes have resisted attempts to end child prostitution. In many places agencies of government, including police forces, are actively involved in prostitution, including child prostitution. In the late 1970s, when a film was made on child prostitution in the Philippines, the government was furious – at the film.[84] In Thailand, the large-scale development of prostitution for the promotion of tourism was critically reviewed in a British documentary film, *Foreign Bodies*. Many government officials in Thailand were more upset with the negative publicity created by the film than by the facts that it portrayed. The same thing happened in 1989 when ABC-TV in the United States produced a documentary on child prostitution in Thailand. If local people and local governments have no objection to child prostitution, should outsiders leave them alone?

In dealing with child prostitution or with human rights generally, should rights be recognized as different in different cultural settings? If in Samoa fathers traditionally twist their children's ears to discipline them, should you intervene, or should you say 'that's all right, he's Samoan'? What does the answer depend on? Do you intervene if you witness the incident in California but not if you see it happen in Samoa?

Intervention in other people's lives always raises serious ethical questions. Interventions across borders, across cultures, and across political worlds raise even more questions. Should powerful white men from rich countries ever involve themselves with disadvantaged people in poor countries? Intervention that is not only across borders, across cultures, and between worlds but also involves the most intimate issues of sexuality raises enormous ethical problems. Confronting all these difficult issues, one might leap to the conclusion that no one should ever mess with anyone else's life. But being unresponsive to problems can be unethical too.

The problem of cultural relativism is especially important in international work, but the problem comes up within individual countries as well. In most Asian countries it is Christian women's groups that are most outspoken in their concern about child prostitution. There are considerable differences between them and their Buddhist and Muslim counterparts, even if there is never any direct confrontation over those differences.

At a children's advocacy conference in the summer of 1989 a young woman from a Muslim country was upset about the draft *Convention on the Rights of the Child*. She was outraged that its negotiators made special accommodations for Muslim countries because their laws and customs with respect to adoption and other practices were different from those in western countries. She asked why Muslim children should not be entitled to the same rights and the same protection as other children throughout the world. The charge was not that the Westerners who dominated the negotiations were being culturally insensitive, but that they were being too sensitive!

Certainly there are great variations in cultural attitudes toward child prostitution. What is regularly accepted as simple fondling in some cultures may be viewed with horror as child sexual abuse in other cultures. One way to make the issue less problematic is to be careful about definitions. What exactly is it that should be controlled? Article 34 speaks specifically of 'the exploitative use of children' in prostitution. This language is comparable to that in Article 6 of the *Convention on the Elimination of All Forms of Discrimination Against Women* which calls for the suppression of the 'exploitation of prostitution of women.' The International Abolitionist Federation works to implement this objective. Following the convention and the federation, the issue is not prostitution as such but the *exploitation of the prostitution of others* that is important. The core problem is exploitation.

Of course there are cultural variations in tolerance for exploitation, too. How should that be handled? My personal answer is that I want to show respect for others' views of what is right and wrong, but I also want to act with integrity, with respect for my own views of what is right and wrong. I want to take account of others' ways, but ultimately my action must be based on my own values and my own understanding of the situation. I would not accept, say, the killing of children, in any society just because those who did it thought it was right. I would try to be culturally sensitive in how I approached the problem, but that would be more a matter of strategic considerations (how could I be most effective?) than a concern about the propriety of intervention.

One way to deal with the problem of cultural relativism is to say that the international law of human rights is about *universal minimum human rights*. International conventions on human rights should be based on universally recognized rights. Of course this means that international law can codify only the 'lowest common denominator' of rights that are widely accepted. Individual countries should be free to make more stringent specifications of human rights, and to vary among themselves, provided that they recognize and work within that baseline universal minimum. This understanding implies that international human rights law would cover only a narrow base of issues. But the fact that the law focuses on only a few major issues, and is codified without exceptions, could make it much more powerful.

Historically the sexual abuse of young children occurred on a limited, localized scale, but modernization has changed that. Persistent poverty, the temptations of high-income life styles, and easy travel have created enormous pressure toward prostitution either of oneself or one's children. Females are recruited into lives of prostitution while still under 16. With elaboration of the pedophile trade, there is more interest in the prostitution of children as children. There is also widespread interest and a thriving international trade in pornography involving children.

Despite the formulation of new laws and the heroic efforts of some individuals and organizations, child prostitution worldwide appears to be growing rather than declining. There are new forces promoting child prostitution, for it is now clear that 'children and adolescents around the world are increasingly sought out as prostitutes, in part because customers consider them more likely to be free of the virus that causes AIDS.'[85] The prospects are grim. Much more vigorous action is needed.

Widespread child prostitution marks some nations as distinctly uncivil societies. To the extent that child prostitution is sustained by international linkages of travel and commerce, global society also falls short of acknowledging and implementing its responsibilities toward children. Some actions have been taken to control child prostitution, both nationally and internationally, but it is going to take much more to end the outrage. The international community could take more decisive action to implement Article 34 of the *Convention on the Rights of the Child*. As a beginning, it would be useful to survey existing national laws and implementation mechanisms regarding child prostitution and, on that basis, design model laws and agencies for effectively controlling child prostitution within countries and internationally.

6 Armed Conflict

Armed conflicts hurt children in several ways.

Wars kill and maim children through their direct violence.

Warfare is not limited to combat among professionals. Children are killed in attacks on civilian populations, as in Hiroshima and Nagasaki. In Nicaragua, many children were maimed or killed by mines.[1] The wars in Afghanistan in the 1980s and in Bosnia in 1993 have been especially lethal to children. Many children have been killed and injured in the *intifada* in the territories occupied by Israel.[2] As the news media show us, the horror stories are endless.

Wars now kill more civilians than soldiers, and many of these civilians are children. Children are being counted among the casualties of warfare at a steadily increasing rate over the past century:

> In the last decade alone, an estimated 1.5 million children have been killed in armed conflicts. A further 4 million have been disabled, maimed, blinded, brain-damaged. At least 5 million have become refugees, and 12 million more have been uprooted from their communities.[3]

Why have children become so much more vulnerable? Historically, conflicts involving set-piece battles in war zones away from major population centers killed very few children. However, wars are changing form, moving out of the classic theaters of combat and into residential areas where civilians are more exposed.

But it is not only a matter of exposure. Civilians are killed not only accidentally (so-called 'collateral damage') but also deliberately – even if the intention is denied. Children are being targeted. In the massacre of Lidice, Czechoslovakia, the Nazis systematically killed or dispersed all the children. Children were systematically killed in the massacre at El Mozote in El Salvador in 1981.[4] Terrorists often make a point of going after children. Neil Boothby explains:

> As paradoxical as it may be, this is occurring precisely because children are so precious to many of us. To destroy what is of highest value to someone is clearly among the most effective forms of terrorism

imaginable; to kill and injure children is to rob a family or an entire group of its future. What better way to undermine whatever popular support may exist for any given cause than to attack the very beings we love and value most in life?[5]

Although our focus here is on armed conflict, it should be recognized that there is a great deal of violence against children in repressive conditions short of active warfare. Thousands of street children have been killed with impunity by death squads in Latin American countries. According to Amnesty International:

> In the 1980s there is widespread imprisonment, torture, and killing of children by governments. In South Africa alone, according to official statistics, the government detained approximately 2000 children under 18 between July 1985 and January, 1986. ... Immediately after arrest, children may be beaten for several hours while under interrogation. Children have been hit with fists, sjamboks (whips), rifle butts, and kicked.... In Iraq, the authorities arrested approximately 300 children and teenagers in the northern town of Sulaimaniya in late 1985. At least 29 of the detainees were reported to have later been secretly executed. ... At about 3 p.m., August 1, 1986, government soldiers entered the small village of Morakondre in Suriname in search of armed opposition troops. When they left, Cakwa Kastiel, a three-year-old child, was dead. He had been shot in his mother's arms.[6]

The many cases of violence against children in South Africa clearly were not 'isolated incidents where one policeman oversteps the mark but rather a consistent pattern that is occurring countrywide.'[7]

A striking aspect of modern warfare is the apparent willingness to sacrifice the young, both one's enemies and one's own. In some cases children have been held as hostages by their own national leaders. When the Serbs laid siege to Srebrenica in April 1993, the Moslem leaders in Bosnia did not want their women and children and injured to be evacuated; in effect they wanted to hold their own people hostage in order to strengthen their claim on the territory.

The violence to children can continue long after the warfare is concluded. Children are frequently hurt in the aftermath of warfare by leftover mines.[8] It has been estimated that 'using current mine-clearing techniques, it would take 4300 years to render only twenty percent of Afghan territory safe.'[9]

The casualty rate for children is increasing not only because they are more exposed and have become deliberate targets, but also because children are used as soldiers.

Often children are pressed to participate in armed combat as child soldiers, harming them both physically and psychologically.

Children can be the agents as well as the victims of violence. Increasingly, older children (10 to 18 years old) are engaged not simply as innocent bystanders but as active participants in warfare:

> ... thousands of children are currently bearing arms in at least 20 ongoing conflicts. Even children as young as nine years old are used as frontline combatants in unwinnable battles, as decoys to lure opposing forces into ambush and as human mine detectors to explode bombs in front of advancing adult troops.[10]

In some cases children 'have been expected to commit violent murders against unarmed civilians as a kind of rite of passage into combat forces' and 'boys were sometimes forced to kill other children of similar ages in order to save their own lives ... [11] In Peru:

> According to deputies of the Peruvian Parliament, the 'Sendoro Luminoso' ('Shining Path') guerrilla movement uses more and more frequently *minors to perform assassinations* because under Peruvian law they cannot be charged for crimes committed before the age of 18.[12]

The Minister of Education of Iran said that in 1987, 150 000 school children volunteered to fight in the Iranian army; school children represented 60 percent of all volunteers in the army.[13]

There are many reports of forced recruitment of school children as combatants by the Mozambique National Resistance (MNR, or Renamo). They have been used as scouts and spies, and as part of their training as guerrillas, they have been forced to kill prisoners.[14]

The child soldiers of Uganda

> ... will carry with them the scars of violence and war. They are mature beyond their years, but the respect shown them is frequently because of the weapon they proudly carry. ... Child soldiers are increasingly deployed in guerrilla and conventional wars in developing countries, yet we have little or no information on how this affects them.[15]

Neil Boothby says that 'in my clinical experience, psychological disturbance has been greater among children who perpetuated violence than among those who were victims of it.'

There are perhaps 200 000 child soldiers under fifteen in the world.[16] In June 1993 children were reported to be fighting in at least twenty-four wars.[17]

Wars sometimes harm children indirectly, through their interference with normal patterns of food supply and health care.

Many children died of starvation during the wars under the Lon Nol and Pol Pot regimes in Kampuchea in the 1970s. In February 1975, 40 percent of the children admitted to the Catholic Relief Services Children's Centre died, most within 24 hours of admission.[18] In 1980–86 in Angola and Mozambique about half a million more children under five died than would have died in the absence of warfare. In 1986 alone 84 000 child deaths in Mozambique were attributed to the war and destabilization.[19] The high mortality rates in Angola and Mozambique were due not only to South Africa's destabilization efforts but also to their civil wars. The famines in Ethiopia in the mid-1980s and again in the late 1980s would not have been so devastating if it were not for the civil wars involving Tigre, Eritrea, and other provinces of Ethiopia. Civil war has also helped to create and sustain famine in the Sudan.[20] In 1992 it was estimated that 'at least a quarter of all Somali children under the age of 5 are believed to have died as a result of famine and civil strife ...'[21]

The interference with food supplies and health services is often an unintended by-product of warfare, but in many cases it has been very deliberate. According to the late Jean Mayer:

Starvation has been used as an instrument of policy many times: against the South during the American Civil War, against France by the Prussians in 1870, against the Central Powers by the Allies during the First World War, against the city of Leningrad by the Germans during World War II, and against the Viet Cong by the United States during the Vietnamese conflict. In the situation in Nigeria, where I was present as an observer, starvation was being used as a weapon of terror by the Nigerians and as a weapon of propaganda by the Biafrans. At no time did I see any shortage of food in the Biafran army, which was nonetheless defeated. The persons who are most vulnerable in a fight like that, as the present situation in Ethiopia illustrates, are not combatants but children, pregnant and nursing women, and the elderly – those who die first in a famine. The weaponry of starvation is worse than indiscriminate, like bacteriological warfare; it discriminates against those who, by any standard, least deserve it.[22]

In the genocidal killing of the kulaks in the Ukraine and surrounding areas in the early 1930s, about four million children died as a result of the deliberately imposed famine and other 'de-kulakization' programs.[23] According to one account, in the late 1960s in the Nigerian civil war, 'a number of great and small nations, including Britain and the United States, worked to prevent supplies of food and medicine from reaching the starving children of rebel Biafra.'[24] In the 1990s, similar patterns have been seen in Bosnia, Somalia, and Sudan.

In some cases the disruption of the infrastructure can have deadly effects well beyond the conclusion of the war. It has been estimated that more deaths resulting from the Gulf War occurred *after* the conclusion of the war than during the war itself. Of the total deaths of Iraqis attributable to the war, approximately 109 000 were to men, 23 000 to women, and 74 000 to children. Of these, an estimated 56 000 military personnel and 3500 civilians died from direct war effects.[25] By this analysis, taking account of the war's effects on health both during and after the war, there were more children's deaths than combat deaths resulting from the Gulf War.

Chapter 3 described the massive mortality of children, and the following chapter describes the widespread malnutrition. Why do these problems persist in such vast numbers? UNICEF's Director of Public Affairs says:

> The answer is that malnutrition and disease have been powerfully reinforced in the second half of this century, especially over the past two decades, by a multiplier agent of terrible effectiveness. That agent is armed conflict, and it is the principal reason many of these children have had no vaccines and oral rehydration – or sufficient food.[26]

Wars cause great psychological damage to children.

The psychological trauma that war causes for children received a great deal of attention during World War II.[27] As Alison Acker observes:

> The war in Central America has an emotional effect, too. Children who have watched their parents murdered, who have been raped or tortured themselves, children who have been orphaned, abandoned, imprisoned, and beaten, may well have been damaged for life. There is no one

officially measuring the trauma, much less attempting to heal the traumatized, only a dedicated few who battle official indifference.

It is remarkable how few studies there have been of children from other wars. There is scant information on the children of the concentration camps in Germany and Poland, on the Vietnam boat people's kids, on the children of the disappeared people of Chile and Argentina.[28]

The book *Fire from the Sky: Salvadoran Children's Drawings* conveys a sense of the effect these wars can have on children.[29] The impact on children of the Hiroshima bombing has been studied, and there have been several efforts to explore children's perceptions of the prospect of nuclear war.[30] The effects of the long-lasting civil violence in Northern Ireland on children has been documented,[31] as has the impact of the long war in Lebanon.[32] An analysis of the effect of continuing violence on the children of Uganda found that 'The Ugandan youth are not indoctrinated with hatred or desire for revenge. They have no real enemies, but they are tired of war, violence, coups, and army men. They do not hate. They do not love. They hope.'[33] The psychological impact of war on Croatian children has been assessed.[34]

Several studies were made of United States' children's reactions to the Vietnam war. Some have been concerned with themes such as 'accepting the necessity for war.'[35]

The psychological impacts of warfare on children have been investigated frequently, and have produced a great deal of information that is useful in designing therapeutic treatments for them.[36] Curiously, there have not been nearly as many studies of the direct physical impacts of warfare on children.

Even short of active warfare, the establishment of armed forces can be harmful to children in several ways.

High expenditures on armed forces can result in inadequate provision of resources for the care of children.

Many have observed the contrast between the small budget allocations for health and the enormous allocations for defense in many countries of the world. President Dwight Eisenhower made the much-quoted observation that 'Every gun that is made, every warship launched, every rocket fired, signifies, in the final sense, a theft from those who hunger and are not fed, those who are cold and not clothed.' World Bank figures show that the 43 countries with the highest infant mortality rates (over 100 deaths per 1000 live births) spend three times as much on defense as on health.[37]

In 1986 Pakistan's Finance Minister, Mahbub-ul-Haq, asked:

... must we starve our children to raise our defence expenditures? For the sad fact is that from 1972 to 1982, the health and education expenditures of the low-income developing countries went down ... while, at the same time, the defence spending of the developing world rose from $7 billion to over $100 billion. When our children cry in the middle of the night, shall we give them weapons instead of milk?[38]

UNICEF asks if it can really be said that it is too expensive to save children 'when 3.5 million children a year are dying of diseases which can be prevented by immunization at an additional yearly cost which is less than the price of five advanced fighter planes?'[39]

Soldiers often father mixed-raced children who are likely to be abandoned.

Active warfare, occupations, or the establishment or overseas bases often lead to the births of large numbers of children of foreign soldiers by local women. Many of these children must be raised without fathers, and some are abandoned altogether. The lucky ones are adopted or live in homes such as the Elizabeth Saunders Home for Mixed-blood Children established outside Tokyo after World War II,[40] but many end up scavenging in the streets.

Many children of U.S. servicemen were abandoned around the U.S. military bases in the Philippines:

The *Philippine Daily Inquirer* reported that there are about 3000 abandoned and neglected children of American and Filipino parentage 'who have mostly ended up on the streets as beggars, vendors, scavengers, baggage boys, shoe shine boys, and car and bus cleaners.'[41]

There are 'nearly 85 000 Amerasian children in varying states of need in nine Asian nations and many more elsewhere throughout the world,' most fathered by U.S. servicemen, businessmen, and civilian government workers.[42] These children generally are treated as social outcasts.

Largely as a result of the efforts of the Pearl S. Buck Foundation, Asian-American children born as a result of the Vietnam War and some of their relatives have been allowed to emigrate to the U.S. A new Amerasian Act was signed into law in December 1987, with about $5 million budgeted to fly the children and their accompanying relatives to the U.S. by 1990. There are somewhere between 8000 and 15 000 Amerasian children eligible for resettlement. Under the U.S. Orderly Departure Program the children and their relatives can emigrate at the rate of 1900 a month.[43]

When the bases in the Philippines themselves were abandoned, a group of Filipino Amerasians filed suit in U.S. District Court in San Francisco asking the U.S. Navy for support and damages for the children left behind in the Philippines.[44]

In Bosnia, as in other wars, many babies born to rape victims have been abandoned.[45] Remarkably, studies of the horror of rape in warfare pay little attention to the consequences for children who are born as a result.[46]

Warfare can result in large numbers of unaccompanied children.

UNICEF was created out of the need to attend to the many thousands of children cast adrift in Europe after World War II.[47] Wars, natural disasters, and other kinds of problems have led to the repetition of similar situations all over the world.[48] Children who are orphaned or who are separated from their parents are fortunate to be survivors, but they are specially vulnerable to direct physical violence, disease, malnutrition, and impaired social development. In some cases children are separated from their parents haphazardly, in the chaos of war, and in some cases children may be systematically evacuated for their own protection.[49]

TRADE GUNS FOR BUTTER?

It is often suggested that too much money is spent for defense in both the rich and poor countries of the world, and that some of that money might instead be used to relieve hunger and to promote children's survival and development. One of the most renowned proponents of this view is Ruth Leger Sivard, whose regular tabulations of *World Military and Social Expenditures* provide the basic data. The idea is prominent in the work of the Children's Defense Fund, especially in its publication, *A Children's Defense Budget*.[50]

The reasoning is sometimes questionable. It is sometimes charged that beyond signifying a gross misallocation of funds, large defense budgets actually cause widespread hunger and child mortality. While money not spent on arms might conceivably be used to alleviate the symptoms of hunger, that does not mean that large defense budgets in themselves cause hunger. Enormous amounts of money are spent on other things such as, say, cars or space exploration, but no one says that those expenditures cause hunger. Also, in the U.S. national defense is the exclusive responsibility of the federal government while other human concerns are addressed primarily at the state and local levels. The appropriate comparisons are not about federal allocations alone, but about the allocations to the human services and defense sectors overall, from all sources.

Offering no explanation for the skewed priorities, the arguments imply that the misallocations are simple mistakes. The critics almost seem to expect that once they show how many children could be saved if one less battleship were purchased, the political leaders will thank them for pointing out the error and correct it in the next budget cycle.

Nevertheless, many countries' budgets stay sharply skewed in favor of defense year after year. If security means the protection of our most precious assets, child survival should be high on the agenda of all defense departments. Why isn't it? Why does this enormous misallocation persist? What are the forces that keep it in place? Whose interests are served by military establishments and warfare?

Many observers suggest that national security should be redefined to take fuller account of human welfare, but they don't have much effect.[51] Perhaps they all make the same mistake – believing that the purpose of defense systems is what it is claimed to be by defense establishments. Perhaps the real, operational function of defense establishments is not so much to maintain the security of the people as a whole as it is to assure that the powerful will remain in power. This proposition seems to explain their behavior much better than their conventional rhetoric, and it certainly helps to explain why proposals for alternative understandings of security are not welcomed.

Why would leaders in developed or in developing countries agree to spend less on maintaining their armed forces if it is those armed forces that keeps them in power? The director of the Institute for the Study of Rural Resources in Bangladesh asked:

> Whose security is being defended, that of an economic or political class, or that of the entire population of the country? Wages are kept down and cheap labour enclaves maintained, strikes are prevented and supplies of raw material are obtained from the Third World at low prices, all in the name of national security. ...
>
> Militarization of the police and of paramilitary organizations is going ahead at a tremendous pace in the Third World today. And this militarization is required to support the internal power structure and to maintain the *status quo* within various developing countries.[52]

The linkage between hunger and military expenditures is not simply in the budgetary allocations; it is also in the ways in which those armed forces are used to sustain repressive regimes. More hunger and more children's deaths result from the structural violence of repression than from the direct violence of warfare.

Defense budgets protect the interests of the powerful through the ways in which the arms are used, and also by the ways in which the money spent rewards political allies of the powerful. To some extent defense budgets constitute a form of welfare for the rich.

Governments suggest that defense establishments serve all of their people's interests, but defense serves mainly the rich, not the poor. Poor people are still trying to get, while the rich want to protect what they have already got. Poor people don't buy burglar alarms or hire guards to stand outside their doors. They don't have a stake in the *status quo* in the way the rich and powerful do. It is no wonder that poor people are far more concerned with development than with defense. If the poor were the ones who allocated the world's resources, far less would be spent on defense and far more on child survival.

Governments like to suggest that military threats, whether internal or external, affect virtually all the people's interests, and large 'defense' establishments serve all the nation's citizenry more or less equally. But it should be recognized that the interests of a nation's governing elites generally are different from those of its people, and especially from the interests of the poor among them. Analysis on the basis of class makes the issue clear. Security is a rich people's issue, while child survival is a poor people's issue. The decisions are made by the rich because the rich are also the powerful. As a result there is an enormous bias in the system in favor of defense and against child survival.

Weapons are symptoms of the insecurity of the powerful. While government leaders may be preoccupied with hardware and its role in ensuring their power, for most people in the world the security issue is about having enough to eat, and something to wear, and a place to live, and some way to keep their children alive and well. Conventional governmental security policy diverts resources away from these fundamentals of real human security.

INTERNATIONAL HUMANITARIAN LAW

International lawyers distinguish between international *human rights* law and international *humanitarian* law. Humanitarian law focuses on situations of armed conflict. Both are reviewed here as they relate to children in armed conflict situations. An overview of human rights law in relation to children is provided later, in Chapter 9.

The four Geneva Conventions of 1949 are the major sources of the law of armed conflict. The *Convention Relative to the Protection of Civilian Persons in Time of War* is of particular importance for the protection of children. The others are the *Convention for the Amelioration of the Condition of the Wounded and Sick in Armed Forces in the Field*; the *Convention for the Amelioration of the Condition of Wounded, Sick and Shipwrecked Members of Armed Forces at Sea* and the *Convention Relative to the Treatment of Prisoners of War.*

After negotiations at the Geneva Conference on the Reaffirmation and Development of International Humanitarian Law beginning in 1974, two supplements, *Protocols Additional to the Geneva Conventions* of 12 August 1949 were adopted in June 1977. *Protocol I* applies to international armed conflicts, while *Protocol II* applies to non-international armed conflicts. The four Geneva Conventions of 1949 together with these two protocols comprise the core of *international humanitarian law*, the human rights law that applies in situations of armed conflict. By May 1993 181 states had become parties to the Geneva conventions, making them the most widely ratified conventions in history. 124 states had become parties to Protocol I, and 115 had become parties to Protocol II.[53] Although the United States has ratified the 1949 Geneva conventions, it has not ratified the two protocols.[54]

In 1974 the United Nations General Assembly adopted a *Declaration on the Protection of Women and Children in Emergencies and Armed Conflicts*, Resolution 3318 (XXIX) of 14 December 1974. The declaration made six points, such as the proclamation that 'attacks and bombings on the civilian population, inflicting incalculable suffering, especially on women and children ... shall be prohibited,' but as a non-binding resolution, no means for enforcement were included.

In the *Convention on the Rights of the Child*, Article 38 is the only one focused on situations of armed conflict. It says:

1.   States Parties undertake to respect and to ensure respect for rules of international humanitarian law applicable to them in armed conflicts which are relevant to the child.

2.   States Parties shall take all feasible measures to ensure that persons who have not attained the age of 15 years do not take a direct part in hostilities.

3.   States Parties shall refrain from recruiting any person who has not attained the age of 15 years into their armed forces. In recruiting among those persons who have attained the age of 15 years but who have not attained the age of 18 years, States Parties shall endeavour to give priority to those who are oldest.

4.   In accordance with their obligations under international humanitarian law to protect the civilian population in armed conflicts, States Parties shall take all feasible measures to ensure protection and care of children who are affected by an armed conflict.

Article 39 is also relevant. It says:

States Parties shall take all appropriate measures to promote physical and psychological recovery and social re-integration of a child victim of: any form of neglect, exploitation, or abuse; torture or any other form of cruel, inhuman or degrading treatment or punishment; or armed conflicts. Such recovery and re-integration shall take place in an environment which fosters the health, self-respect and dignity of the child.

Other articles call upon governments to provide special assistance to children deprived of their families or to children who become refugees.

Article 38 reiterates established international humanitarian law, including the seventeen articles in the fourth Geneva Convention of 1949 specifically concerned with the protection of children. Paragraphs 2 and 3 echo paragraph 2 of Article 77 of *Protocol I* to the 1949 Geneva Conventions.

Article 38 is known as *the* armed conflict article, but with regard to protection from recruitment, it has little to offer. While the rest of the convention is generally applicable to 'every human being below the age of 18 years,' Article 38 makes a point of allowing children under 18 to take direct part in hostilities and to be recruited into a nation's armed forces.[55] It is all the more extraordinary because these provisions are already embodied in the international humanitarian law to which the article refers. If the article calls upon nations to respect international humanitarian law as a whole, why restate its provisions only with respect to age limits for exposure, especially when the article offers no improvement?

The answer is more historical than legal. In the ten years it took to negotiate the convention many participating nations pressed to have the age limits increased. But there was strong pressure in opposition, primarily from the United States. A December 1988 news report on the negotiations regarding the minimum age for combat said:

> In recent years, many countries have dropped their objection to raising it to 18 years old. But some countries, including the United States, say it would be too difficult for their armed forces to separate out those younger than 18 in time of war. The United States allows enlistment at 17 with parental consent.
>
> This week the United States, backed only by the Soviet Union, prevented the acceptance of a compromise solution that would have required countries to 'endeavour to prevent' children from 15 to 18 from going to war.
>
> An American text requiring countries to 'take all feasible measures' to keep children younger than 15 off the battlefield was accepted instead.[56]

According to some reports the United States was isolated on this issue, but by another account

> ... both the Arab States and the USA used pressure against raising the minimum age of recruitment to 18. The UK government, which has volunteer soldiers at 16, was also in opposition but was content to let the USA be the spokesman. A few 16 year olds were in the Falklands War and 200 were at the front in the Gulf War of 1991, so the UK was even less ready than the USA to make a compromise by raising the minimum to 18. The USA seemed to be opposed, less on principle than on procedure. The government's military advisers insisted that the proper place for raising the minimum age was not the UN Human Rights Commission but the diplomatic conferences on international humanitarian law (as from 1973–1977) at which the military was present.[57]

By the conclusion of the negotiations the U.S. position prevailed, with Article 38 saying that governments 'shall take all feasible measures to ensure that persons who have not attained the age of fifteen years do not take a direct part in hostilities.'

The irony is that despite its winning many concessions from others in the negotiations, the United States still has not signed the convention. This is strongly reminiscent of the United States performance at the Third United Nations Conference on the Law of the Sea. The United States won many concessions from others during the long hard negotiations from

1974 to 1982, but refused to sign the new United Nations Convention on the Law of the Sea for more than a decade, and then only after obtaining more concessions.

Although it does not have the force of law, in the *Declaration and Plan of Action* approved at the World Summit for Children in September 1990 national governments made major commitments to take action in behalf of children. With regard to armed conflict, the world leaders promised:

> We will work carefully to protect children from the scourge of war and to take measures to prevent further armed conflicts, in order to give children everywhere a peaceful and secure future. We will promote the values of peace, understanding and dialogue in the education of children. The essential needs of children and families must be protected even in times of war and in violence-ridden areas. We ask that periods of tranquillity and special relief corridors be observed for the benefit of children, where war and violence are still taking place.[58]

Rädda Barnen (Swedish Save the Children) asked to have specific language included regarding the use of children in armed forces but was unsuccessful. The statement on goals voiced the intention to 'provide improved protection of children in especially difficult circumstances and tackle the root causes leading to such situations,' but did not get any more specific than that.

IMPLEMENTATION

International humanitarian law setting out human rights for children in warfare focuses on two dimensions: one, as civilians, they will not be targets in any given war; and two, as children, they will not be recruited or used as soldiers. Neil Boothby feels that neither of these basic rights has been implemented.[59] However, Dorothea Woods (who prepares the monthly bulletin, *Children Bearing Arms* for the Quaker Office at the UN in Geneva) feels that the 1977 protocols' provisions concerning the recruitment of children under fifteen 'has been implemented to a considerable extent':

> ... the known violations are often made by movements in opposition to the government, e.g., in Afghanistan, Burma, Colombia, El Salvador, Guatemala, Kurds, Mozambique, Palestine, Peru, Philippines, Sudan, Timor East, and Uganda. Few of these movements have been accorded international recognition and so they do not feel bound by international

protocols. Even with these bodies, however, the international law protecting children has some impact. For example, in El Salvador, some of the guerrilla movements have refrained from kidnapping youngsters for military action and have said that the decision was made with respect for the international protocols on humanitarian law, and to demonstrate their own fitness to govern. ... They did not implement the protocols fully, but the international standards influenced their practices.

Sometimes the government is the transgressor, e.g., in Afghanistan, Cambodia, Chad, El Salvador, Guatemala, Somalia, Uganda, Vietnam. The fact that the children under fifteen are included in the armed forces of only three of the ninety plus ratifying powers points to the fact that few governments ratify these protocols unless they are ready to carry out the provisions.

Thus it appears the law does have some effectiveness, but much more needs to be done to implement it.

IMPLEMENTING ARTICLE 38

What can be done to assure that states parties comply with the modest standards of Article 38? Let us focus particularly on paragraphs 2 and 3, on the age at which children may be exposed to armed conflict. Primary responsibility for implementation of these rules rests with the national governments that accept the *Convention on the Rights of the Child*. The challenge to the international community is to find ways to *assure* that implementation. What can be done?

Any program of action should be based on careful research to determine the situations in different nations with regard to these rules. Neil Boothby has listed '25 countries since 1985 in which children under the age of 15 have made up significant portions of guerrillas, standing armies, or both.'[60] Information on law and practice with respect to children's involvement in warfare should be updated regularly by an agency with a mandate from the international community. What is needed is not a one-time research effort, but continuous monitoring. A solid monitoring program would produce information in a timely manner for human rights organizations and other agencies that could take appropriate action. It also would let nations know that they are being watched, and that people care a great deal about whether they expose children to armed conflict. Studies should be made of national laws with respect to the exposure of children to armed conflict, and of efforts to conform those laws to Article 38.

Organizations within each country concerned with the problems of children in armed conflict should be identified and supported in appropriate ways. In many cases these indigenous organizations will be best able to assess the current state of national law and practice.

The ICRC could review national laws with regard to children in armed conflict. National Red Cross societies may have more latitude than the ICRC. Some have already taken important initiatives with regard to ending the involvement of children in warfare:

> The American Red Cross and the Soviet Red Cross have had preliminary discussions on a joint venture to this end. It is our hope to be able to bring before an International Red Cross Conference before this century's end a resolution that calls on the world's governments and peoples to vow and enforce the exclusion of children from the world's killing fields. We hope to develop for that resolution the support of the world's now 149 National Red Cross and Red Crescent societies and the some 160 nations that are signatory to the Geneva Conventions.[61]

The National Red Cross societies also could play an important role in continuous monitoring of national laws and practices.

Information that is obtained could be used to strengthen programs of action to limit the role of children in armed conflict. Examples of appropriate legal language could be circulated to assist nations in strengthening their relevant laws. To assure more effective implementation of those laws, there should be clear accounts of the violations. Analyses should identify specific individuals in a position to correct violations, and political and legal action should be focused on influencing those individuals. Violators might be called to account through a systematic series of escalating steps, beginning with moderate inquiries addressed to appropriate government officials, and then building up to embarrassing publicity and threats of international sanctions. Responses appropriate to the concrete circumstances would need to be designed.

THE QUESTION OF AGENCY

Many things could be done for children involved in armed conflict, but there always looms the question of agency: who will do those things?

Which individuals, which organizations will take the action that is required, under what motivations, with what resources? Those who want to do something may not have good physical access and legitimacy, while those with access and legitimacy may lack the resources or the desire.

Controlling local violence is normally the responsibility of local governments. If the local government can't handle it the next higher level of government is obliged to step in, and if that does not work the national government is expected to intervene. In some cases it is not so clear who ought to act. There may be a breakdown of civil order, where the rule of law is no longer effective. However, in many cases there is no such breakdown, and local law remains important. As in all other arenas of human rights, it is national laws and national governments that ought to be the principal instruments for implementation of the legal rights of the child.

The overwhelming problem is that in regard to children in conflict situations the national government may be more the source of the problem than the solution. In that case there is a special responsibility for the international community to find ways to intervene in behalf of children.

Primary responsibility for implementation of international humanitarian law rests with the International Committee for the Red Cross. The ICRC is one of the three components of the International Red Cross, together with the League of the Red Cross and Red Crescent Societies and the recognized National Red Cross and Red Crescent Societies. Although it is financed by voluntary contributions from governments, the ICRC is a private Swiss organization, not an international organization. The committee itself is limited to 25 members, all Swiss. It is supported by a large number of delegates, all of whom must be Swiss citizens. The ICRC's major concern is the implementation of the four Geneva Conventions of 1949 and the two protocols of 1977, but as a private organization it is not constrained by the language of those agreements, and often goes beyond their specific mandates.[62]

In its work on behalf of the victims of armed conflict, the ICRC

> ... has always been particularly sensitive to the plight of children during wartime. Since the Second World War especially, it has endeavoured to alleviate their sufferings by helping in the drafting of laws for their protection, and by undertaking operations in countries affected by conflicts.[63]

Because of its belief that the problems of children are always closely intertwined with those of adults, however,

... the ICRC does not have specific programmes for children; or, to put it more precisely, the ICRC's programmes for children are always situated within a broader general context of assistance to the victims of conflict.[64]

Usually the ICRC works as quietly as it can, understanding that 'its low-profile diplomacy enables it to operate on both sides of a conflict.'[65] However the ICRC does at times publicly denounce serious and repeated violations of international humanitarian law. The International Red Cross and Red Crescent Museum in Geneva prepared a photograph exhibition on children in war shown at the exhibition gallery of the United Nations in New York during April and May 1991.

In the ICRC's perspective, implementation of international humanitarian law within nations means 'the State must first incorporate the treaties into its national legal order ... the States party are obliged to take the necessary measures in peacetime to ensure effective application of IHL in the event of armed conflict.'[66] The ICRC works through the national Red Cross and Red Crescent Societies to facilitate adaptation of national laws to implement international humanitarian law.

UNICEF also plays a role at the international level. In the context of its broader efforts in behalf of Children in Especially Difficult Circumstances, UNICEF has undertaken major initiatives for dealing with Children in Situations of Armed Conflict.[67] (Children in Especially Difficult Circumstances also includes Working Children and Street Children, Children Endangered by Abuse and Neglect, and Children Affected by Natural Disasters.) A discussion paper on *What More Can be Done for Children in Wars?* was prepared and circulated within UNICEF in April 1984.

A policy paper sent from headquarters to UNICEF field offices on October 31, 1986 on *Children in Especially Difficult Circumstances* provided guidelines and possible courses of action for dealing with children in situations of armed conflict. It also included a brief appendix on children as a zone of peace. Emphasis was placed on coordination with other international organizations, and with local non-governmental organizations provided they had the endorsement of their governments.

UNICEF sponsored The International Conference on Children in Situations of Armed Conflict in Africa: An Agenda for Action held in Nairobi in July 1987. The conference passed a resolution saying that the safety and protection of children and women during armed clashes should be an overriding concern of both combatants and non-combatants. African governments and the Organization of African Unity were urged to promote the concept of children as a zone of peace.[68] The zone of peace idea was elaborated by the late Tarzie Vittachi, former Deputy Director of UNICEF, in a slim volume called *Between the Guns*.[69]

In 1990, UNICEF's Guatemala office organized a conference on the impact of violence on children in Central America.[70] The April 1990 issue of the newsletter, UNICEF *Intercom*, focused on children of war.

UNICEF commissioned a major study on *Children in War: A Guide to the Provision of Services*.[71] It identifies ten major ways in which children can be affected by warfare and then addresses six major questions regarding what can be done about them. The major effects are (1) conflict; (2) loss of life; (3) injury, illness, malnutrition, and disability; (4) torture, abuse, detainment, and conscription; (5) unaccompanied children; (6) psychosocial distress; (7) displacement; (8) family impoverishment; (9) education disruption; and (10) social disruption. The questions posed are how can the relevant facts be ascertained; how can the risk group be identified and reached; what can be done to prevent and mitigate the effect; what emergency responses are appropriate; what can be done to prepare for the emergency response; and what can be done to facilitate rehabilitation and recovery?

This study provides useful guidance for concrete action 'on the ground.' There remains the question of what can be done at the global level. UNICEF, ICRC and other organizations play major international roles in looking after the interests of children in conflict situations, but they are constrained. UNICEF focuses on children but does not focus on situations of armed conflict. ICRC focuses on conflict but not particularly on children. As Neil Boothby points out, with regard to conflict situations

> ... there is still no viable structure for safeguarding and reporting on children's rights. In war and refugee situations, the International Committee for the Red Cross (ICRC) and the United Nations High Commissioner for Refugees (UNHCR) have mandates to do so. But normally both agencies undertake their tasks through quiet diplomacy with national governments ... Critics suggest that this tactic sometimes leads to situations in which protection issues can neither be aggressively pursued nor publicly disclosed.[72]

The *Convention on the Rights of the Child* also is limited. The Committee on the Rights of the Child is confined by the language of the convention itself and is not free to initiate new programs. Also, the committee's responsibilities cover all of the many different concerns addressed in the convention, so situations of armed conflict occupy only a part of its agenda.

There is now no international agency focusing on national policies and practices with respect to children in situations of armed conflict. There is no central agency systematically supporting and defending the many non-governmental agencies around the world that work for children in conflict situations on a local, national, or regional basis. There is no agency identifying the gaps in coverage. There is no body to coordinate the established agencies' work in this area. ICRC, UNICEF, and several other organizations include the issue of children in armed conflict on their agendas, but there is no international organization whose *primary* concern is children in armed conflict.

There should be one global agency that takes lead responsibility for coordinating work on behalf of children in armed conflict. In the absence of any single dominant agency dedicated to the issue, perhaps a *Liaison Group on Children in Armed Conflict* could be organized by concerned international organizations such as UNICEF, ICRC, UNHCR, the Committee on the Rights of the Child, Defence for Children International, the International Save the Children Alliance, OXFAM, Amnesty International, Rädda Barnen, Redd Barna, and the International Federation of Terre des Hommes.

The Liaison Group could meet perhaps once a year to review the existing situation and coordinate future action. It would not intervene directly into situations of armed conflict, but it could provide advice and support for appropriate organizations prepared to do that. It could help to devise strategies and programs for local organizations, and it could help to develop useful information. It would be the locus for cumulative learning and strategic planning. Its power would come not from its capacity to act directly but from its role in coordinating and focusing the work of many different agencies, each of which has different capacities, interests, resources, and skills.[73]

If such an agency were to succeed in aligning the efforts of the many concerned organizations, the possibilities for implementing the rights of children in armed conflict situations would be greatly enhanced.

7 Malnutrition

The World Health Organization defines nutrition as 'a process whereby living organisms utilize food for maintenance of life, growth and normal function of organs and tissues and the production of energy.' Malnutrition results when this process goes wrong, whether because of problems on the intake side or because of problems in processing the intake. There are various types of malnutrition including protein-energy malnutrition and specific micro-nutrient deficiencies. According to the World Health Organization the most important nutrition deficiency diseases are *protein-energy malnutrition*, which is important because of its high mortality rate, its wide prevalence, and the irreversible physical and sometimes mental damage it may cause; *xerophthalmia*, which is important because of its contribution to the mortality of malnourished children, its wide prevalence, and the permanent blindness it causes; *nutritional anemias*, which are important because of their wide distribution, their contribution to mortality from many other conditions, and their effects on working capacity; and *endemic goiter*, because of its wide distribution.[1] Xerophthalmia results primarily from vitamin A deficiency, anemia from iron deficiency, and goiter from iodine deficiency.

The most widespread form of malnutrition is protein-energy malnutrition (PEM), sometimes described as protein-calorie malnutrition (PCM). It is so prevalent that in the absence of other specifications, references to malnutrition are understood to indicate PEM. Kwashiorkor and marasmus are intense forms of PEM.

PEM is usually due to a lack of energy foods rather than to a lack of protein intake. The symptoms of protein deficit often observed in cases of severe malnutrition result from the fact that the protein that is obtained is diverted to fulfilling immediate energy needs, and thus is not available for the body building and maintenance functions normally fulfilled by protein. If energy supplies are adequate, the protein remains available for its body building and maintenance functions, a phenomenon described as *protein sparing*.[2]

CAUSES OF MALNUTRITION

It is useful to distinguish among the immediate, underlying, and basic causes of malnutrition.[3]

Immediate Causes

Malnutrition is caused by inadequate or improper dietary intake and disease. The two are closely linked because bad diets can increase vulnerability to disease, and many diseases result in loss of appetite and reduced absorption. Even with appropriate food intake, malnutrition can result from disease, particularly diarrhea or parasitic diseases. There may be enough good food coming in, but it may in effect run right out, or it might be diverted to the nutrition of parasites. Infection often leads to malnutrition. Disease often increases the body's food requirements. When children die at an early age, usually it is not malnutrition alone but the combination of malnutrition and disease that leads to death. The immediate causes can be understood as the *clinical* causes of malnutrition.

Underlying Causes

The underlying causes of malnutrition are inadequate access to food, inadequate care of children and women, and inadequate access to basic health services, sometimes combined with an unhealthy environment.

Inadequate food supply in the household can be a major factor in causing malnutrition. Often, however, the types of food and the methods of feeding are also important. The choice of weaning foods and feeding patterns are critical. At times children are given inappropriate foods such as tea. Some beliefs regarding appropriate foods and feeding patterns can result in deficient diets for pregnant or lactating women, or children.[4]

Some foods such as rice or maize have inadequate nutrient density, which means that small children cannot take in large quantities at one sitting. Children who depend on bulky carbohydrates must be fed frequently during the day or they will not get enough.

Malnutrition does not necessarily mean that household food supplies are inadequate. Sometimes it is more a matter of food *behavior* than of food *supply*. For example, the supply of food in the household may be adequate but its distribution within the family may be skewed against small children and in favor of the male head-of-household.[5] Of course this is not a significant problem where household food supplies are abundant.

Feeding with breastmilk substitutes clearly illustrates how malnutrition can arise from provision of the wrong kind of food. The promotion of infant formula is especially pernicious in Third World countries where sanitation is poor, literacy levels are low, and people are extremely poor. The result has been that infants fed with formula have had much higher infant mortality rates than breastfed infants. The health effects of formula feeding have been less severe in developed countries, but it is clear that morbidity levels are higher among formula-fed infants even in developed countries. Recent studies have shown that formula-fed infants are more likely to get cancer.

Thus, nutrition status is not determined simply by food supply, but rather 'nutrition is an outcome of three groups of factors: household food security, health environment and health services, and care. In other words, people should be well-fed, healthy, and well-cared for.'[6] Food, health, and care are viewed as the three pillars of good nutrition.[7] The underlying causes of malnutrition can be understood as relating to *household* level causes.

Basic Causes

The basic causes of malnutrition can be divided into three broad categories. First, there may be problems relating to *human resources*, having to do with inadequate knowledge, inadequate skills, or inadequate time. Second, there may be problems relating to *economic resources*, referring to inadequate assets in terms of money income, land, or other assets. Third, there may be inadequate *organizational resources*, such as inadequate schools, health care programs, or water supply systems. The basic causes can be understood as relating to societal causes of malnutrition.

Explanations of malnutrition commonly focus on the clinical and household levels, but an understanding is needed at the societal level as well. The endless marginalization of the poor in free market systems, described in Chapter 2, certainly is one of the basic causes of malnutrition in the world.

Amartya Sen and Jean Drèze argue that hunger is due primarily to a failure of entitlements rather than, say, to inadequate agricultural productivity or population growth.[8] Briefly:

> What we can eat depends on what food we are able to acquire. . . . The set of alternative bundles of commodities over which a person can establish such command will be referred to as this person's 'entitlement'. If a group of people fail to establish their entitlement over an adequate amount of food, they have to go hungry.[9]

It follows that the remedy lies in strengthening entitlements. In some analyses, the understanding is that this can be done only through increasing the household's capacity to produce or purchase food. I argue, however, that under some conditions people also should have a claim on the resources (not only food but also care and health services) of their societies based on their needs. In the following chapter I suggest that one way to do this is through the law. Children should have a fully implemented legal right to adequate nutrition.[10] Many problems of children derive from their powerlessness. Promoting recognition of their rights enhances their relative power in society.

MALNUTRITION AND MORTALITY

There is a strong association between protein-energy malnutrition and children's mortality, at least where the malnutrition is severe. Studies in Latin America suggest that in almost half of children's deaths, malnutrition is a significant underlying cause. In Indonesia, 'nutritional deficiency has been identified as an associated cause in 16 percent of the deaths of children aged 1–4.'[11] In rural Punjab, India it was found that 'on average, child mortality doubled with each 10 percent decline below 80 percent of the Harvard weight median. Children above the 80 percent level had mortality rates as good as those for children in four southern European countries.'[12]

A study of children in a rural area of Bangladesh showed that several different anthropometric measures (weight-for-age, weight-for-height, height-for-age, arm circumference-for-age, and arm circumference-for-height) all were effective in predicting mortality over the two years following the measurements. According to all of the indicators, severely malnourished children were at much higher risk of dying.[13]

The linkage between malnutrition and mortality is not always evident. In the late 1970s and early 1980s the infant mortality rate in Sri Lanka declined while the nutritional status of the bottom fifth of the population also declined.[14] Kerala has the lowest infant mortality rate of all the states of India, but it is also among the lowest in per capita intake of nutrients.[15] The average intake is low, but with nutrition programs providing a solid nutritional floor for the poor, apparently the distribution of food is much less skewed than it is elsewhere.

Children who are *severely* malnourished in terms of anthropometric measures certainly are more likely to die. For children who are mildly or moderately malnourished, however, the prospects are not so grim.[16] In the United States, for example, there is little linkage between malnutrition and children's mortality because the malnutrition is rarely severe.

There is no generally accepted procedure for determining the extent to which deaths are due specifically to malnutrition. Thus the major international data-gathering agencies – WHO, FAO, and UNICEF – do not provide estimates of the numbers of people who die from malnutrition each year.[17]

GROWTH MEASUREMENT

Different kinds of malnutrition have different kinds of manifestations. Because of its worldwide importance, the remainder of this chapter focuses on protein-energy malnutrition.

Assessments of PEM nutrition status are commonly based on anthropometric (body) measures. Measurements may be made of height, weight, or arm circumference, for example, and the results compared with appropriate norms. For a time the Gomez scale of expected weight (or height) for age was used. The extent of malnutrition was assessed in terms of the ratio of a child's weight to the expected weight for healthy children of the same age and gender, expressed as a percentage. Thus a child between 60% and 75% of the standard weight for his or her age would be said to be moderately malnourished. The preference now is to make the assessment in terms of the number of statistical 'standard deviations' below the expected weight (or height).

Regardless of whether percentages or standard deviations are used, questions were raised about the early tendency to treat anthropometric measures as direct measures of nutrition status. As W. Henry Mosley and Lincoln Chen observed:

> Customarily, growth faltering in a cohort of children is called 'malnutrition,' and this, in turn, leads to the inference that it is simply the consequence of dietary deficiency. There is now abundant evidence that growth faltering is due to many factors and that it may be more appropriately considered a nonspecific indicator of health status. … There is a growing body of evidence that 'malnutrition' among young children is as much dependent on maternal health factors and infections as it is on the nutrient deficiency. It is thus more appropriate to consider the levels of physical stunting and wasting in cohorts of children as nonspecific indicators of health status (as is the case with the level of mortality) rather than as a specific indicator of dietary deficiency.[18]

There is evidence that children grow better when their caregivers are warm and loving than when they are cold disciplinarians,[19] which certainly supports the view that nutrition status is affected by the quality of care, and is not solely the result of inadequate food supplies.

UNICEF points out that 'most malnutrition is not caused by shortages of food in the house' and that 'most feeding programmes fail to have any significant effect on children's nutritional status.'[20] One review of the effects of feeding programs on the growth of children showed that overall 'anthropometric improvement was surprisingly small.'[21] As the authors speculate, part of the reason may have been that there is often considerable leakage of food away from the targeted individuals, with the result that their dietary intake actually did not improve very much. However, a more fundamental reason may have been that food supply was not really a major problem to begin with, and the observed growth retardation could have been addressed more effectively with other kinds of programs, perhaps emphasizing immunizations or sanitation. The feeding programs may have not only reached the wrong individuals, but may have been altogether the wrong choice of remedy.

Thus the Mosley-Chen perspective has important policy implications. Where low-weight children have been found, the response typically has been to introduce some sort of feeding program. The reinterpretation of the weight or height data as being shaped by more than food supply leads to consideration of a much broader variety of remedies.

Anthropometric measures do not assess nutrition status directly; they assess developmental impairment or growth failure, the most extensive public health problem among children in developing countries. It results from the complex interaction of nutritional, biological, and social factors. Rates of physical growth and achieved body size have been accepted as markers of this syndrome. Growth failure may be partly due to dietary adequacy, but there can be other causes as well.

Different forms of growth failure can be described in these terms:

- *underweight or overweight*, for deviations of body weight from expected weight-for-age;
- *wasted or obese*, for deviations of body weight from expected weight-for-height; or
- *stunted*, for deviations of height below expected height for age.[22]

Growth retardation in the forms of wasting, stunting, and underweight are usually signs of malnutrition, but there are exceptional cases in which they result from other causes. Thus children who show growth retardation should be clinically examined to characterize their conditions more precisely. For our purposes, however, the degree of growth retardation can be taken as a reasonable indicator of the extent of malnutrition.

If the objective is to identify individual children in need of attention, it is most useful to assess the extent to which children are *wasted*, that is, the extent to which they have low weight for their height. Many children who are *underweight*, who have low weight for their age may have 'scars' of past malnutrition, and not signs of current problems ('wounds'). *Stunting*, in which children are short for their age, is due more to past than to current problems.[23]

It has now become clear that growth failure is most active between six and 24 months of age, which is thus the main 'window of opportunity' for prevention.[24] Actions targeted to children beyond two years of age will not be very useful in reversing their growth retardation because their low weight or height is likely to have originated in their first two years of life.

This has important implications for public policy. Many nutrition programs concerned with protein-energy malnutrition as indicated by low weight or low height are misdirected in terms of their intended coverage. School lunch programs, for example, are not likely to be of much use for reversing growth retardation. Rather than selectively targeting underweight or underheight individuals among older children, it would probably be more efficient and effective to focus the resources on all children up to two years of age.[25]

NUMBERS OF PEOPLE MALNOURISHED

Where field measurements cannot be made, rough estimates of the extent of PEM in a population can be formed on the basis of information on the overall food supplies, population size, and the distribution of food within the population. The Food and Agriculture Organization of the United Nations (FAO) and World Bank form estimates in this way. FAO estimated that in 1979–81, depending on the criterion used, there were between 335 and 494 million people in developing countries who were undernourished.[26] The World Bank estimated that in 1980 about 340 million people did not get enough energy to prevent stunted growth and serious health risks. About 730 million did not get enough energy to sustain an active working life.[27]

It has been estimated that about 20 million people in the United States are chronically malnourished.[28] Caution is required, however, because this figure is based on methods of estimation that are very different from those used by the international organizations.

Children's Problems

Table 7.1   Malnutrition in developing countries, 1975–90

	Percent affected		Number (millions)	
	1974–6	*1988–90*	*1974–6*	*1988–90*
GENERAL MALNUTRITION				
1. Population (all ages) with energy intake (kcals/caput/day) on average below 1.54 BMR over one year	33%	20%	976	786
	1975	*1990*	*1975*	*1990*
2. Children (under five years) with weight below–2 S.D. of reference	42%	34%	168	184
	1980s		*1980s*	
3. Women (15–49 years old) with weight below 45 kg.	45%		400	
MICRONUTRIENT MALNUTRITION				
4. Anaemia: women (15–49 years old) haemoglobin < 12 g/dl (pregnant) or < 11 g/dl (pregnant)	42%		370	
5. Iodine deficiency disorders (IDD) Goiter (all ages)	5.6%		211	
6. Vitamin A deficiency: children (under five years) with xerophthalmia	2.8%		13.8	

Source: United Nations, Administrative Committee on Coordination/ Subcommittee on Nutrition, *Second Report on the World Nutrition Situation* (Geneva: ACC/SCN, 1992), p. 2.

Recent data on malnutrition in developing countries, based on the work of several agencies of the United Nations, are reported in Table 7.1. In summary:

An estimated 20% of the population has inadequate food consumption. Growth failure affects one-third of children, and over 40% of women are underweight and/or anaemic. At least one billion people worldwide are probably affected by one or more nutritional deficiency.[29]

Table 7.2   Prevalence of underweight children under 60 months (5 years) of age in developing countries, 1975–90

Region	Percent underweight				Numbers underweight			
	1975	1980	1985	1990	1975	1980	1985	1990
	percent				in millions			
Sub-Saharan Africa	31.4	28.9	29.9	29.9	18.5	19.9	24.1	28.2
Near East/North Africa	19.8	17.2	15.1	13.4	5.2	5.0	5.0	4.8
South Asia	67.7	63.7	61.1	58.5	90.6	89.9	100.1	101.2
South East Asia	43.6	39.1	34.7	31.3	24.3	22.8	21.7	19.9
China	26.1	23.8	21.3	21.8	20.8	20.5	21.1	23.6
Middle America/ Caribbean	19.3	17.7	15.2	15.4	3.4	3.1	2.8	3.0
South America	15.7	9.3	8.2	7.7	4.8	3.1	2.9	2.8
Global Total	41.6	37.8	36.1	34.3	168	164	178	184
Total Under 5 Population in Developing Countries					402	434	493	536

Source: United Nations, Administrative Committee on Coordination/ Subcommittee on Nutrition, *Second Report on the World Nutrition Situation* (Geneva: ACC/SCN, 1992), p. 10.

It is widely accepted that if a child's weight is more than two standard deviations below the reference for his or her age, that child should be described as malnourished. The prevalence of underweight children is indicated in Table 7.2 and and Figure 7.1. As these data show, in developing countries at least 184 million children under five years of age are seriously underweight. Contrary to the common belief that the problem is most widespread in Africa, there are far more malnourished children in Asia than in Africa. More than half the developing world's underweight children are in South Asia.[30]

The relationship between the prevalence of underweight children and the gross national product per capita of the nations of the world is shown in Figure 7.2. The influence of income is strongest at the lower end of the range. The fact that several nations lie below the fitted regression line means that these nations have fewer underweight children than would be expected on the basis of their income levels alone. This deviation may be due in part to differences in the level of their public expenditures for health, education, and welfare. For example, in Chile, Jamaica, Costa

Figure 7.1   Prevalence of underweight children in developing countries, 1975–1990

Percent underweight children

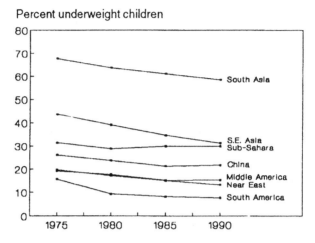

Source: United Nations, Administrative Committee on Coordination/ Subcommittee on Nutrition, *Second Report on the World Nutrition Situation* (Geneva: ACC/SCN, 1992), p. 10

Rica, Zimbabwe, and Egypt social support expenditures as a proportion of GNP ranged from 13% to 19%. In contrast, Mexico's social support expenditures were 4% of GNP and Indonesia's were 3% of GNP.[31]

Table 7.1 shows a decline in the proportion of children in developing countries who are malnourished, from 42% to 34%, but because of population growth there has been an increase in the numbers of malnourished children, from 168 to 184 million. The proportion of children in developing countries who are malnourished has declined, but the absolute number has gone up. Thus there are now more children on earth suffering from malnutrition than ever before in history.

Figure 7.2 Percentage underweight preschool children vs. GNP per capita

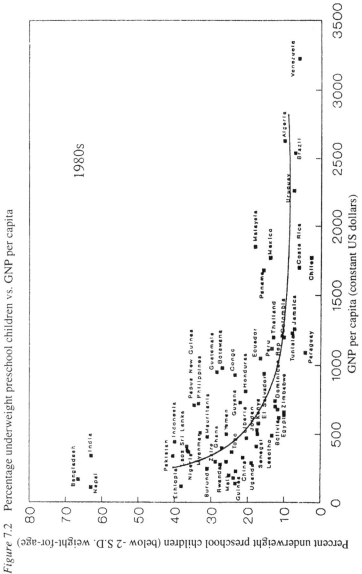

Notes: Data on prevalence of underweight children are based on actual surveys (latest available). GNP per capita is given for the same year that each country's anthropometric survey was undertaken.
Source: United Nations, Administrative Committee on Coordination/Subcommittee on Nutrition, *Second Report on the World Nutrition Situation* (Geneva: ACC/SCN, 1992), p. 9.

Part III
The Human Rights Response

8 Nutrition Rights

Increasing food production, nutrition education, feeding programs and all the other conventional approaches have important roles to play in ending hunger in the world, but so far they have not been adequate. Perhaps it would be useful to work more directly with the social/legal/political tools of entitlements, rights, responsibility, and accountability to get the job done.

HISTORY OF NUTRITION RIGHTS

When he was Director-General of the Food and Agriculture Organization of the United Nations (FAO), Addeke Boerma said that 'if human beings have a right to life at all, they have a right to food.'[1] More recently, Richard Jolly, Deputy Executive Director of UNICEF, said 'Freedom from hunger is a basic human right. It is unacceptable that 150 million children under five should be suffering from serious malnutrition in a world that has the capacity to prevent it.'[2] Certainly widespread malnutrition and the massive mortality of children associated with it is unacceptable. But what about the idea that freedom from hunger is a basic human right? Is it true? Can it be implemented?

The right to adequate nutrition (or right to food) concept has a long history.[3] In 1948 the *Universal Declaration of Human Rights* asserted in article 25(1) that.'everyone has the right to a standard of living adequate for the health and well-being of himself and his family, including food....'

On March 14, 1963 a Special Assembly on Man's Right to Freedom from Hunger met in Rome and 'issued an historic *Manifesto* calling on the governments and people of the world to unite in the struggle against man's common enemy – hunger.' The manifesto described the character and scope of hunger in the world, and asserted that 'freedom from hunger is man's first fundamental right.'[4] A variety of action programs such as increasing agricultural productivity and improving trade relations were suggested and moral concerns were expressed, but the idea that 'freedom from hunger is man's first fundamental right' was not elaborated.

The *International Covenant on Economic, Social, and Cultural Rights* was adopted by the United Nations General Assembly in 1966 and came into force in 1976. Article 11 says that 'The States Parties to the present Covenant recognize the right of everyone to an adequate standard of living for himself and his family, including adequate food, clothing, and housing ...' and also recognizes 'the fundamental right of everyone to be free from hunger ...'

In 1974 the World Food Conference issued a *Universal Declaration on the Eradication of Hunger and Malnutrition.* It asserted that 'Every man, woman and child has the inalienable right to be free from hunger and malnutrition in order to develop fully and maintain their physical and mental faculties.' That declaration was endorsed by the United Nations General Assembly in Resolution 3348 (XXIX) of December 17, 1974.

In September 1976 both the United States Senate and House passed right to food resolutions. It was the sense of the Congress that every person throughout the world has a right to a nutritionally adequate diet, and the United States should increase its development assistance until it reached one percent of the U.S. gross national product.[5]

In November 1984 the World Food Assembly, comprised primarily of representatives of nongovernmental organizations, met in Rome. Its purpose was to call attention to the fact that the promise made at the 1974 World Food Congress that 'within a decade no child will go to bed hungry' had not been fulfilled. Its final statement asserted that 'the hungry millions are being denied the most basic human right – the right to food.'

In 1991 the House Select Committee on Hunger chaired by Congressman Tony Hall, through House Resolution (H.R. 2258) advocating the Freedom from Want Act, urged the United States to propose a United Nations Convention on the Right to Food.[6]

In the *Convention on the Rights of the Child*, which came into force in 1990, two articles address the issue of nutrition. Article 24 says that 'States Parties recognize the right of the child to the enjoyment of the highest attainable standard of health ...' and shall take appropriate measures 'to combat disease and malnutrition' through the provision of adequate nutritious foods, clean drinking water, and health care. Article 27 says that States Parties 'shall in case of need provide material assistance and support programmes, particularly with regard to nutrition, clothing, and housing.'

The rights idea was voiced frequently at the International Conference on Nutrition organized by the Food and Agriculture Organization of the United Nations and the World Health Organization and held in Rome in December 1992. In his address opening the conference His Holiness Pope John Paul II said:

It is up to you to reaffirm in a new way each individual's fundamental and inalienable right to nutrition. The Universal Declaration of Human

Rights had already asserted the right to sufficient food. What we must now do is ensure that this right is applied and that everyone has access to food, food security, a healthy diet and nutrition education.

In the conference's concluding *World Declaration on Nutrition* the nations of the world agreed that 'access to nutritionally adequate and safe food is a right of each individual.' Yet there was nothing in the accompanying *Plan of Action for Nutrition* to elaborate that right, nothing providing for clear entitlements with effective accountability.

While the idea of the right to food appears in many different contexts in international law, most are not binding. In some cases, as in the *International Covenant on Economic, Social, and Cultural Rights*, the obligations are technically binding on the States Parties. However, because the obligations lack specificity and because there are no effective mechanisms for implementation and accountability, they are not binding in practice. With regard to food or other issues, 'the main problem in regard to social and economic rights has been to define the obligations corresponding to the rights. ... The obligations remain vague until the present. In the absence of effective international supervision, they have not been made clearer through case law.'[7]

Several nations have articulated nutrition rights in some form in their laws. Cuba's constitution assures that 'no child be left without schooling, food and clothing.' The Italian, Spanish, and Greek constitutions assure a right to health. In many countries there is language referring to other sorts of assurances, such as the right to social security (as in the Netherlands and Spain) that can be interpreted as implying nutrition rights. In most cases, however, the assurances are vague and have not been enforced through the courts. There is practically no elaboration in detailed statutes of distinct nutrition rights, and no legal enforcement.

Although there have been many expressions of concern, and many laudable anti-hunger programs at local, national, and global levels, the idea of the *right* has not yet been implemented. As Ved Nanda put it, 'no framework presently exists for the realization of the right to food, nationally or internationally.'[8]

On reviewing the hunger data, Philip Alston and Katarina Tomaševski observe that 'these statistics make hunger by far the most flagrant and widespread of all serious human rights abuses.' Alston adds that 'the right to food has been endorsed more often and with greater unanimity and urgency than most other human rights, while at the same time being violated more comprehensively and systematically than probably any other right.'[9] The idea that people should have a right to adequate nutrition is an old one, one whose vision has not been fulfilled.

WHY CHILDREN?

Many groups vulnerable to malnutrition should be protected – mothers, the elderly, the handicapped, unborn children, refugees, people in armed conflict situations, and so on. I suggest that the idea of the right to nutrition, in some form, will be far more acceptable if it focuses on children. There are several reasons for this.

First, no one can doubt the powerlessness of small children. Not even the most callous politician could tell a three-year old that if she wants to eat she should go out and work.

Second, it can be argued that saving a child's life is more valuable than saving an older person's life simply because there are more life-years saved. Similarly, the benefits from an improvement in the quality of life accrue over many more life years for a child than they would for an older person.

Third, there are well-developed means for assessing the nutrition status of children on an inexpensive and objective basis, using anthropometric techniques. There is a strong consensus among nutrition professionals on the interpretation of these data. Techniques for measuring malnutrition in other groups are not as well developed.

Fourth, anthropometric data collected around the world shows unambiguously that children's malnutrition is a massive problem.

Fifth, graphic news coverage of the suffering in places like Ethiopia and Somalia and constant calls for donations keep the issue in the public's consciousness.

Sixth, political work for children can be based on creating alliances among the many organizations concerned with children and the many organizations concerned with nutrition. Hungry children already have a well established constituency.

Seventh, the *Convention on the Rights of the Child* and the World Summit for Children of September 1990 have created a new appreciation of the rights of children.

Eighth, both the World Summit for Children and the Declaration and Plan of Action on Nutrition agreed upon in Rome in December 1992 call upon participating states to prepare National Plans of Action, on children in one case and on nutrition in the other case. The obligation to prepare these two plans gives states new opportunities for examining the nutrition needs of children.

All these reasons together lead to the judgment that obtaining recognition of effective nutrition rights may be more politically feasible for children than for others. One can begin with children, and later go on to address the needs of other vulnerable groups as well.

THE PRINCIPLE

Some free market advocates feel that governments should take no direct responsibility for dealing with hunger. They see government involvement with hunger as an unwarranted intrusion, distorting the play of market forces and creating economic inefficiency. As Jean-Phillippe Platteau observes:

> In Europe, it was precisely with the advent of capitalism that the old values and institutions (like the Poor Laws in England) guaranteeing food security for everybody came under the strong attacks of the heralders of the new 'laissez faire' order. Interestingly, incentive considerations were the main arguments which the latter put forward: only poverty can incite (force) the lower classes to work and, according to [Townsend's Dissertation on the Poor Laws of 1786] hunger is actually the most effective pressure, because it is 'peaceful, silent and continuous.'[10]

There was similar reasoning behind China's reforms designed to 'smash the iron rice bowl.'[11] Fortunately, however, many modern economists recognize that economic efficiency is not the same as social efficiency, and there are good reasons to intervene in the marketplace. In particular, there are good reasons to assert and defend human rights.

Many agree that, regardless of the type of economy, it is the duty of governments to assure that all their citizens can at least subsist:

> In this concept of subsistence rights and duties, the emphasis lies, not on 'feeding' or 'maintaining' people but on creating a social and economic environment which fosters development and hence need not depend upon charity. To take seriously the notion of subsistence rights and to value them as universally applicable 'minimal reasonable demands' on the rest of society means that the satisfaction of basic human needs must be a primary and explicit focus of development.[12]

Or, more simply, 'A government's basic job is to provide a system in which people can meet their own and their children's basic needs.'[13] The point is reaffirmed in Principle 25 of the *Limburg Principles on the Implementation of the International Covenant on Economic, Social and Cultural Rights* which says that 'States Parties are obligated, regardless of the level of economic development, to ensure respect for minimum subsistence rights for all.'[14]

It is the duty of governments to structure their societies in a way that prevents malnutrition. Under ideal governance there would be no need to even raise the question of a right to nutrition. The idea of nutrition rights comes up only because communities and governments are imperfect.

National governments have three kinds of obligations: to *respect*, to *protect*, and to *fulfill* nutrition rights. As articulated by the United Nations' Special Rapporteur on the issue, the obligation to respect the right to food 'calls for non-interference by the state in all cases where the individuals or groups can take care of their own needs without weakening the possibility for others to do the same.' The obligation to protect the right to food 'implies the responsibility of states to counteract or prevent activities and processes which negatively affect food security, particularly for the most vulnerable in society.' The obligation to fulfill requires the state to give 'assistance or direct provision' under some circumstances.'[15] In a similar more recent formulation, 'States must *respect* the freedom of individuals to take the necessary actions and use the necessary resources, either alone or in association with others, to facilitate the fulfillment of their needs ... the State must also *protect* individual freedom of action and use of resources as against other more assertive or aggressive subjects .... the State has the obligation to *fulfill* the expectations of all to enjoy the right to food ...:'[16]

If government ought to be providing certain kinds of services, especially with regard to the fulfillment of nutritional needs, then there is the vexing question: does the private sector's offering these services get the government off the hook, allowing government to evade responsibilities it really should fulfill? Should churches close their soup kitchens?

The solution lies in making distinctions, recognizing that there are some social services best left to the private sector while others ought to be provided by government. It is reasonable to call upon the local community to help out neighbors in temporary distress, from floods, temporary unemployment, or accidents, for example. People should gladly carry over some soup and blankets, directly or through their churches and clubs, to respond quickly to such transitory problems. But *chronic* hunger is a responsibility of government. Chronic problems reflect systemic failures, and thus are a fundamental responsibility of government.

Perhaps capable adults should not be fed by the state, but few would argue that small children in crisis should be ignored. Childhood malnutrition is one of those issues for which there should be a recognized obligation of government to provide some sort of services. As a matter of principle, *there should be a recognized legal obligation of government to provide services to assure that every child is adequately nourished.*

The family and the community also have responsibility for assuring that children are adequately nourished. The point is that there should be a clear duty of government, enshrined in law, to do what needs to be done if the family's and the community's response is inadequate. If the principle is accepted, there will still be a need for discussion of the exact nature of the services and the conditions under which they must be provided. The services provided by government could take several different forms, including not only direct feeding programs but a variety of health and care services as well.

This obligation would then help to assure that government is motivated to support the community in fulfilling its responsibility. Community groups working on the local malnutrition problem should be able to rely on their local and state governments for help, whether for money, contacts, transportation, or moral support and encouragement. It is the responsibility of government to help such community groups. Moreover, the government should be grateful for the opportunity to help the community use its resources to deal with local malnutrition, for otherwise the burden would fall on the government itself.

National legislatures should be persuaded to affirm the principle that children have a right to adequate nutrition. However, that is the beginning, not the end, of the action that is needed. Programs fitting local circumstances need to be designed to implement the idea. Indeed, in many cases legislators will be reluctant to affirm the principle unless they first get a clear picture of its implications for action.

There have been many efforts to gain recognition of a right to nutrition within individual countries and internationally. Unfortunately, this has often been equated with the general effort to alleviate malnutrition, and advocates of the right to nutrition have simply recommended ways of improving the production and distribution of food. Concerned people have created many different kinds of food supply programs ranging from programs designed to deliver food directly into the mouths of children, as in the Indian *anganwadis*, to the massive international transfer of food through the World Food Programme.

It is important to distinguish between the achievement of adequate nutrition and achievement of a *right* to adequate nutrition. Nutrition rights are based on the quality of protection one has against the occurrence of malnutrition. You can't tell how much protection people have against, say, fire, by asking people if their houses are on fire at the moment. To assess the quality of the protection one has to look into the institutional arrangements that are in place, ready to act if and when disaster threatens. The fact that most people in any given country are well fed tells us nothing about the situation of marginalized people, and it says nothing about what might happen in the future if wealth declines or government priorities change.

Past efforts to ameliorate malnutrition have all been valuable, but they have been matters of charity and chance, and not the implementation of real rights. True implementation of a right to something means not just providing some amount of that thing to some people; it means *assuring* that every individual who is entitled to it gets his or her full share of it.

We cannot tell a small child that we are sorry, but your family and perhaps your local government have failed you, and there is nothing that can be done about it. We cannot tell a small child that there is a war that simply must be fought on the other side of the world, so you will not have enough food. Children's nutrition should not be understood as a matter of priorities because when it is, children lose. Adequate nutrition for children should be recognized as an assured, unqualified right. The demand should be not merely for increased funding but for recognition that *children have a right to adequate nutrition*. The principle must be recognized. It then becomes sensible to discuss details of how it is to be fulfilled in different circumstances.

The motivating idea underlying the nutrition rights vision is that malnutrition can be reduced by establishing clear rights to adequate nutrition *in the law*, and assuring the implementation of that law. With such rights, individuals (or possibly groups) who are eligible because they are malnourished or at risk of malnutrition are entitled to specific services designed to prevent or alleviate that malnutrition. If those who are eligible do not get that service, they have effective means for complaining and getting that to which they are entitled. This remedy, this recourse, also is established by law.

The establishment and effective implementation of such law will not be *the* solution to the malnutrition problem. The nutrition rights approach does not replace existing programs for alleviating malnutrition, but rather it builds on and uses them. It can make feeding, health, and education-based nutrition programs more efficient and effective by making them more decisively goal-directed. Under such an approach, government no longer feeds people just to feed people. The obligation is not to deliver a specific quantum of food or services to all who are eligible, but to bring about a particular result: the end of their malnutrition. Many nations have a variety of nutrition-related activities, but they are not organized as a coherent program. A nutrition rights framework can provide a basis for aligning these activities so they work together systematically to achieve the goal of minimizing malnutrition.

This rights approach to dealing with the malnutrition problem might be criticized for being statist and top-down in its orientation. I agree that much of the work of combating malnutrition should be carried out with those who are poor and weak directly, through programs of empowerment.[17] I am concerned, however, that working exclusively on the empowerment of the weak may tend to absolve government of its responsibilities. In a curious way, working only to change the weak themselves implies a kind of blame-the-victim posture. Governments should be called upon to do their parts as well.

This rights-based approach to the problem of malnutrition is based on the understanding that malnutrition arises largely out of powerlessness. As Amartya Sen and Jean Drèze put it, marginalized people suffer from a failure of entitlements, which means that they cannot make adequate claims to food supplies and services in the marketplace or to the means for providing adequately for themselves. The appropriate response, then, is strategies of empowerment of the weak. The law can be used as one means for helping to empower the weak.

The nutrition rights approach is responsive to the failure-of-entitlements analysis, but it does not correct the root causes of the problem. It does not suggest a method for preventing disempowerment, but only a means of compensating for it. In that sense, nutrition rights are conservative, not transformative; they provide only symptomatic relief. Nutrition rights do not eliminate the underlying problem, but my view is that malnourished children should not have to wait for that.

MULTI-LAYERING

If they are to be effective, nutrition rights must be articulated in national law. National governments are the major agents of their implementation. However, comparable laws, rules, statutes, or guidelines also could be established and implemented at the sub-national level, in states, provinces, counties, and municipalities, for example. Such rules also can be established at the regional and global levels.

As indicated in the rings of responsibility image in Chapter 1, local agencies trying to deal with malnutrition should be backed by higher-level agencies to the extent necessary to assure that the problem is solved. This can be done in an orderly way. Nations can establish their own rights systems, with specific criteria and rules that apply to all their citizens. These criteria and rules may vary across nations, depending on their different circumstances. As proposed in Chapter 10, the international community can develop a rights system so that nutrition-related services to its member nations are based on clear criteria and rules favoring the weakest among them.

In much the same way, many nations are divided into smaller juris-dictions, perhaps provinces or states. These smaller units might be able to establish their own nutrition rights systems. In that case the national government could create a nutrition rights system in which the provinces (rather than individual citizens) were the primary units. Provinces could then be assessed in terms of their nutritional status (e.g., the proportions of children in each province who are malnourished according to standard measures), and the most needy provinces entitled to specific services. In some cases provinces in turn might manage their nutrition rights systems by focusing on still another administrative layer, districts within the province.

The same sort of approach could be used in the management of refugee camps. Individual camps could have clear guidelines for the allocation of food supplies among residents within them which at least approximates a rights system. The global authorities responsible for providing food and other services to the camps collectively also could have explicit rules to identify the most needy of the camps and assure that they receive special services.

Laws, rules, guidelines and principles can be introduced or adapted to conform to a nutrition rights system at the global, regional, national, state, or district levels. Even the rules of access to individual service programs can be modified to assure that clients are treated as if they had rights to the service.

Just as different levels have different responsibilities, they also can have different rights. For example, some services might be assured to individual children while others are assured for household, villages, or districts. The eligibles may include all children, households, villages, etc., or only those that meet specified health, economic, demographic, or other criteria. Thus multi-layering means there are distinct nutrition rights and responsibilities, both within units and across units, in a hierarchical structure.

CARROTS, NOT STICKS

The nutrition rights idea is based on the use of the law, but this does not mean that it should be based on punitive sanctions against wrongdoers. There may be some cases in which children go hungry because they have 'bad' parents. In such cases, the law should be more concerned with assuring that the children do not have to pay for the sins of their parents than with assuring that their parents do have to pay for them. In much the same way, it would be foolish for the international community to think about punishing bad governments when it should emphasize the positive things it can do for children victimized by such governments. Although it is obviously not always true, the law should be based on the presumption that people and governments want to do the right thing, but sometimes need added incentives or some sort of help. The law can be used not only in punitive ways but also in positive ways to support and reinforce doing the right thing. It can be used to mandate positive life-affirming actions, quite literally.

There may be concern that the use of positive reinforcements could be more expensive or less effective than the use of negative sanctions. The question is a reasonable one to raise. There is, however, a great deal of evidence in the history of child-rearing and also in the history of diplomacy to suggest that positive actions can be very effective and efficient. They should at least be tried and systematically assessed.

Malnutrition among children should be viewed as illegal, a condition that is not allowed, but this does not mean that anyone should be punished. The presence of a malnourished child should trigger a series of legally mandated positive actions by families, communities, and governments that are designed to end that condition.

Some people object to the rights approach on the grounds that other approaches (education, more caring communities, promotion of local self-sufficiency, etc.) are preferable. I agree that they are preferable. My view is that (1) by emphasizing carrots rather than sticks, the rights approach can be positive rather than negative, (2) the rights approach does not displace other approaches, but complements them, and (3) the rights approach is useful where other more conventional means prove inadequate, and they have proven inadequate. Moreover, (4) there does not seem to be any better means for reaching those who are most seriously marginalized.

FUNDING

Strengthening children's right to adequate nutrition means *assuring* that children get what they should have. It makes sense to press for fuller funding for programs so that all who meet the eligibility criteria can in fact get the service. But full funding this year does not assure full funding next year. Increased funding for nutrition programs certainly is worth pursuing, but it leaves children vulnerable to the see-saw of the budgeting process. Funding may be increased for a time, but with the next war or drought or bank crisis, the budgeters are likely to say there is not enough money, and funding for the programs will be ratcheted down again. Even when funding is adequate there may be nothing to assure that *all* who are eligible actually receive the services to which they are – or should be – entitled.

Those who meet the eligibility qualifications should not have to do without the services because someone says there is not enough money. Those denied services for which they are qualified should have clear and readily accessible legal recourse, just as retirees who do not get their social security checks have a legal basis for demanding what is theirs.

Hard rights provide assured entitlements; services are not provided only 'if possible' or 'if budgets allow.' A right to service implies *first call* on public resources, so that these are paid for first, before anything else. Those most in need are served first. Increasing funding for service programs does not in itself alter the balance of power. It is important to assure that those who are eligible for such programs receive the services as *a matter of right*. Effectively implemented rights strengthen the weak in the face of the strong and thus benefit them over the long run.

CAPPING ENTITLEMENTS

The idea of the right to nutrition has not advanced partly because there is resistance to any suggestion that individuals ought to have the right to demand that they be fed. No one wants the neighborhood vagrant to have a right of access to his or her personal cupboard. No one is proposing that. The proposal is that carefully designed governmental programs should be established to assure that no child should have to suffer from sustained malnutrition.

There is resistance to the idea of economic rights of any kind because there is a fear that opening that door would obligate the society to unlimited demands for costly services.[18] But first call does not mean an unlimited call. Unquestionably, entitlements must be capped, and they must be well targeted. Well-framed rights are based on clear, detailed criteria regarding who is eligible for services. The law regarding children's right to adequate nutrition should spell out the nature of the service to be provided, and establish clear limits regarding age and other considerations. The criteria can be set to keep the pool of eligible people to a manageable size. The idea of a right to adequate nutrition will not be politically feasible unless the obligations imposed on others by that right is capped, and a good way to cap it is by limiting it to very young children.

The law with regard to children's nutrition rights could be formulated quite simply. It might say, for example, that all pregnant women are entitled to at least a specified minimum of prenatal care; that all pregnant women and mothers of children under three years of age are entitled to a specific program of nutrition education; and that children under three years of age are to be weighed at least every three months. It could say that the government is obligated to provide services to any child who failed to gain weight (or at least a specific amount of weight) in a three month period in accordance with the best professional advice of nutritionists. Details regarding the exact nature of the services would not have to be spelled out in the main body of the law, but statutes and regulations could be formulated to provide guidance.

Some of the services rendered could be at the community level. For example, the government might find that establishing a good immunization program and effective sanitation systems help to prevent children's growth retardation, and that doing so reduces the amount of services that must be delivered at the individual level.

Treatment protocols could vary according to particular national circumstances. While the specific services could vary, laws of this form could be used to implement the principle that vulnerable children are entitled to adequate nutrition as a matter of right.

On the average, developing countries have been devoting only about ten percent of their annual budgets to human priority issues: nutrition, water supply, primary health care, primary education, and family planning.[19] Thus even poor countries could do more with their existing resources. The main argument of the rights approach, however, is not that nations should spend more but that they should spend better. The resources that are available should be targeted and managed to be more effective in ending malnutrition. The implementation of nutrition rights can help to accomplish that objective.

In extremely poor countries, systematic identification of children who are malnourished or at risk of malnutrition may be enough to stimulate increased attention. If children do get more attention from their parents and from their communities simply because they are identified as malnourished, the cost to government for remedial services could be kept very low. No matter how meager resources may be, malnourished children have the right to be identified and given special attention.

USING EXISTING PROGRAMS

The work of ending childhood malnutrition worldwide should be focused where the problem is most intense, but it may be more feasible to develop the methods where the problem is moderate and capacities to respond to the problem are large. In this sense, developed countries such as those in western Europe, Japan, and the United States are well placed to provide leadership in showing how children's right to adequate nutrition could be made into a hard right.

In the United States there will be some ideological resistance to the establishment of any sort of economic right. In the law, however, the distance to be traveled is not great:

> The U.S. Supreme Court has ruled that there is no fundamental federal constitutional right to such goods as food, shelter, or education, but the rights to the basics of life are frequently set out in federal or state statutes or state constitutions. For example ... the AFDC statute gives federal matching funds to states 'to furnish financial assistance ... to help maintain and strengthen family life' And state welfare statutes frequently require that payments be adequate to meet basic needs. While such requirements are often ignored in practice, their existence in federal and state law demonstrates that many of the principles and rights embedded in article 27(3) [of the *Convention on the Rights of the Child*], already are to be found in a significant part in U.S. law.[20]

No new service programs need to be developed; if all who were eligible for programs such as the Special Supplemental Food Program for Women, Infants and Children (WIC) and Aid to Families with Dependent Children (AFDC) did in fact participate, hunger could for all practical purposes be ended. The *Medford Declaration to End Hunger in the U.S.* asserts that 'If we fully utilize existing public programs – in conjunction with the heroic efforts of voluntary food providers in local communities – we can end hunger very soon.'

The United States has designed an elaborate nutrition monitoring system,[21] and it has many different kinds of nutrition programs. However, the monitoring system looks in many different directions and serves many different objectives. It looks more at the consumption habits of middle class people than at the malnutrition of marginalized people. If the system cannot (or chooses not to) see the problem of childhood malnutrition it is not going to fix it. While many important elements are present in the United States, they are not integrated into a single system directed toward the goal of ending malnutrition. The point is not simply to monitor, but to firmly link the results of monitoring to goal-directed action. There is not much point to keeping your eyes on the road if your hands are not on the steering wheel. The opposite is true as well.

Existing programs should be used wherever feasible. In the United States, children's right to adequate nutrition could be established by providing unambiguous, enforceable rights to Medicaid coverage and WIC, AFDC, Food Stamps and other established programs. Other countries could make more systematic use of whatever monitoring and service programs they already have in place. In poor nations as well as rich nations, if entitlements are capped and existing service programs are used, recognizing and implementing the right of children to adequate nutrition need not be costly. Indeed, focusing the effort could result in more efficient use of existing programs.

Many developing countries have nutrition programs in place which could be adapted to acknowledge children's nutrition rights. In the state of Tamilnadu in India, for example, the Tamilnadu Integrated Nutrition Program (TINP) was introduced in October 1980. It focuses on feeding children at nutritional risk as demonstrated by growth faltering based on weight-for-age. In July 1982 the government introduced the noon meal program, covering all children between two and five years of age regardless of their nutritional status. In September 1984 coverage was expanded to include all poor children going to school, up to the age of 15. The new service protocol, based on careful targeting of services, has proven effective:

Children ages 6–36 months were weighed each month.... Supplementary feeding was provided immediately to those who were severely malnourished, and feeding for children with faltering growth was provided after one month (for children ages 6–12 months) or three months (for children ages 12–35 months). The children selected were fed for at least ninety days. If they failed to gain at least 500 grams in weight, they were referred to health care, and feeding was continued for up to 180 days. Intensive nutrition education was directed at mothers of at-risk children. Food supplementation was also offered to women whose children were being fed, to those who had numerous children, and to those who were nursing while pregnant.

The project cut severe malnutrition in half and prevented many at-risk children from becoming malnourished.[22]

Participants were fed only when required, with the result that food was only 13% of the project's total cost.

In the view of Dr. Anuradha Khati Rajivan, Collector in the Pudukkottai District:

> In the State of Tamilnadu, India, it is now possible to think of the feeding programs for children as entitlement programs. Here the term entitlement is being used in the sense of a right, something accepted by the society and political leadership and which is unlikely to be questioned for reasons of resource constraints.... Budgetary pressures have not led to cutbacks for the feeding program.... The noon meal program now has a first call on the state budget along with food subsidies of the public distribution system and electricity subsidies.

It is still not a hard right because there are no explicit laws assuring children of this entitlement and providing some recourse in case the right is not fulfilled. However, it might not be difficult to make those adaptations. The number of beneficiaries has been increasing steadily, straining the budget. If it becomes necessary to limit the categories of those eligible, it may at the same time be feasible to provide legal assurances for those who are designated as eligible.

Nutrition rights should not be promoted as a replacement or substitute for other means of alleviating malnutrition. Rather, the rights approach complements and indeed reinforces the necessity for a variety of actions to alleviate malnutrition. Reorganizing existing programs within a rights framework could make them more streamlined and efficient, and thus result in more cost-effective service.

GOALS AS RIGHTS

The people of different nations suffer from different types, intensities, and distributions of malnutrition, with differing causes. Moreover, they have different resource bases, and they all have many other concerns. Thus they will set their goals for dealing with malnutrition differently. However, there is now a broad global consensus on how these goals should be framed. At the World Summit for Children held at the United Nations in New York in September 1990, most heads of state signed the *Plan of Action for Implementing the World Declaration on the Survival, Protection and Development of Children.* Among the Major Goals specified in the plan was: 'Between 1990 and the year 2000, reduction of severe and moderate malnutrition among under-5 children by half.' Supporting goals specifically related to nutrition were:

(i)   Reduction in severe, as well as moderate malnutrition among under-5 children by half of 1990 levels;

(ii)   Reduction of the rate of low birth weight (2.5 kg or less) to less than 10 percent;

(iii)   Reduction of iron deficiency anemia in women by one third of the 1990 levels;

(iv)   Virtual elimination of iodine deficiency disorders;

(v)   Virtual elimination of vitamin A deficiency and its consequences, including blindness;

(vi)   Empowerment of all women to breast-feed their children exclusively for four to six months and to continue breast-feeding, with complementary food, well into the second year;

(vii)   Growth promotion and its regular monitoring to be institutionalized in all countries by the end of the 1990s;

(viii)   Dissemination of knowledge and supporting services to increase food production to ensure household food security.

These eight 'supporting goals' have merit in themselves and also can be viewed as important means toward achievement of the major goal. These goals have been endorsed repeatedly, both before and after the World Summit for Children, by many international bodies including the World Health Organization Assembly in 1990, the UNICEF Board Session of 1990, the United Nations Conference on Environment and Development in 1992, and the International Conference on Nutrition in 1992. The International Conference on Nutrition also added two more goals:

To end famine and famine-related deaths; and
To end starvation and nutritional deficiency diseases in communities afflicted by natural and man-made disasters.

The goals have been supported by many nations in their National Programmes of Action prepared in fulfillment of their commitments at the World Summit for Children.

Many nations do not have adequate baseline data for 1990, and in any case have little hope of achieving the goal of reducing severe and moderate malnutrition to half the 1990 level by the year 2000. Nevertheless, the basic form of the language can be retained, with a fresh start and a new commitment. Any nation could reasonably take as its primary nutrition goal *the reduction of severe and moderate malnutrition among under-5 children by half over the next ten years.*

Consider now a transformation in thinking. Imagine that the nation's commitment to the goal of *the reduction of severe and moderate malnutrition among under 5 children by half over the next ten years* is so serious that it is willing to assure its citizens that they had a right to its achievement. Imagine that the government was willing to take on the achievement of this goal as a real duty, one on which it could be called to account for its performance. What would this imply? How would taking this goal as a right be acted out?

Of course it may be that the goal is too demanding, and the government is not willing to make such a firm commitment. Other formulations could be substituted. For example, the government might be willing to make such a strong commitment only if it was limited to children under two years of age, or only if it was limited to severe malnutrition, or only if it had twelve years to achieve the goal. The specifics are open to discussion. The point is that, whatever the details of its formulation, one way to interpret nutrition rights is in terms of a firm commitment to a specific nutrition goal. Rights can be defined not only in terms of current conditions but also in terms of the direction in which individuals and the society as a whole are heading.

This perspective meshes nicely with the argument that poor countries are not to be excused from assuring nutritional and other economic, social, and cultural rights on the grounds that they can't afford it. Instead, there is a positive requirement for *progressive realization* of the goals based on clear plans and the commitment of resources commensurate with the nation's capacity. In the language of the *Limburg Principles on the Implementation of the International Covenant on Economic, Social and Cultural Rights*:

The obligation 'to achieve progressively the full realization of the rights' requires States parties to move as expeditiously as possible towards the realization of the rights. Under no circumstances shall this be interpreted as implying for States the right to defer indefinitely efforts to ensure full realization. On the contrary, all States parties have the obligation to begin immediately to take steps to fulfill their obligations under the Covenant.[23]

The goal can be used as the basis for designing a specific goal-directed program of action. The first step would be further clarification of the goal until it is well concretized, typically in terms of a particular level to be reached on a specified indicator by a definite time. For example, it might be agreed that 'moderate and severe malnutrition' would be taken to refer to protein-energy malnutrition as measured by *wasting*, the degree to which children's weights are 'excessively low' in relation to the reference standards for their heights (or lengths). More specifically, excessively low could be taken to mean more than two standard deviations below the standard.[24]

Programs of action for achieving the goal would be needed at community, district, province, and national levels, with systematic multi-layering. There would be separate targets and programs for each sub-sector.

A decisively goal-directed program of action would be based on a clear strategy, that is, the projection of an orderly series of actions that would move systematically toward achievement of the goal. There needs to be planning, action, reinforcement of effective action, corrections for off-target action, and frequent re-planning. There should be clarity about who is to carry out the actions and what will motivate them to carry the actions out.

In a goal-directed campaign, the monitoring of nutrition status would be carried out not only to measure conditions at particular moments in time but also to assess the effectiveness of the campaign in bringing about changes in that status. Suppose, for example, that the goal was defined in terms of reducing the proportion of children under three years of age whose weights were excessively low. Then, for the purposes of the campaign, any nutrition-related program would be viewed as useful only to the extent that it contributed to reduction of that figure. Resources would be shifted toward those programs that were demonstrably more effective. Of course there could be many nutrition-related programs outside the campaign, serving other purposes.

In this goals-as-rights approach, honoring nutrition rights means making a serious commitment to very specific nutrition goals and then honoring the commitment by devoting the resources and taking the actions that are required to fulfill that commitment. Accountability is based on monitoring to see if good progress is being made toward achievement of the goal. If the program is not 'on track' there could be some legal mechanism for calling the government to account and pressing it to take the action that is required.

Campaigns could be launched to strengthen children's nutrition rights in every nation. Participants in the initial planning meeting should include officials from the relevant ministries and government agencies, representatives from non-governmental organizations concerned with law, human rights, children, and nutrition, and representatives of key governmental and non-governmental international organizations. All will have roles to play in the effort. The purpose of the campaign would be to put an end to malnutrition among the nation's children through the establishment and effective implementation of clear laws regarding children's nutrition rights.

The planning process could have three major components: a review of the existing situation with regard to children's nutrition rights; goal-setting; and the formulation of a strategy for meeting the goal.

Goal-setting should be informed by the nutrition goals set out in a nation's *Plan of Action for Children* and other relevant national and international documents. Alternative formulations should be considered, and then one or more selected as appropriate and feasible to be elevated to the status of a right in the law.

The implications of adopting a particular nutrition goal as a right should then be worked out in terms of the *strategy*, the program of action that would lead to its achievement. What management structure would work to line up the many different kinds of resources that must be brought to bear? What monitoring and steering mechanisms would keep the effort on track? What mechanisms of accountability should be devised? The legislature should not be presented only with a vague goal, but should be asked to make a firm commitment to the complete package, the goal together with the program of action needed to achieve the goal.

A radical approach to strategy formulation could be based on semi-privatization of the effort. If the government decides it really wants to end malnutrition among children it could have that effort managed by a semi-private organization under contract with the government. The operators of this 'Nutrition Rights Corporation' would have a performance-based contract such that they would be fully compensated only if they were successful. The government could specify the goals and set out detailed groundrules, and then put out a formal request for proposals for providing the service, in effect putting the task out to bid. This method could be tested and refined in two or three states with strong support from the central government. In time, a full multi-layered system could be established, with separate management corporations for each state, all functioning under the guidance of a central headquarters office. While the goal-setting and operational guidelines would be established centrally, much of the planning and execution could be decentralized and highly participatory. The bidders would have room for creativity regarding these issues.[25]

Even if it is politically infeasible, thinking in this way suggests the sort of business-like thinking that is needed. Close attention must be given to the 'bottom line' of achieving reductions in malnutrition, much as any business venture must give close attention to the bottom line of profitability. Clear and strong incentives need to be established to assure that the goal is pursued efficiently and effectively.

Many nations have excellent nutrition programs 'on the ground' and devote substantial resources to the alleviation of malnutrition. However, the purposes of these programs vary a great deal. As any military commander knows, assets on the ground become more effective if they are coordinated and goal-directed, all pointing in the same direction. Any nation's resources for alleviating malnutrition could be used more efficiently and effectively if they were organized in a goal-directed program based on clear nutrition rights.

NUTRITION RIGHTS ADVOCACY

Local, national, and international nongovernmental organizations have been working on the problem of malnutrition in many different ways for decades. Some have now emerged specifically to press the view that people should be adequately nourished as a matter of human rights. In December 1992 several international nongovernmental organizations agreed to work together under the umbrella of the *World Alliance for Nutrition and Human Rights*.[26]

A number of distinct but overlapping ways of dealing with nutrition as a human right have emerged. A comprehensive analytic approach has been developed by Asbjørn Eide, Arne Oshaug, and Wenche Barth Eide in their work at the Norwegian Institute of Human Rights and the Nordic School of Nutrition at the University of Oslo in Norway. It is based on a detailed analysis of the root causes of malnutrition, and treats the alleviation of malnutrition not as something held in isolation but as an integral part of the challenge of national development. Their analysis shows, in a matrix format, that there are specific national obligations to *respect, protect*, and *fulfill* the right to adequate nutrition. These obligations apply to food security, adequate care, and adequate prevention and control of diseases.[27]

FIAN is the acronym for the *Foodfirst Information & Action Network,* an 'International Human Rights Organization for the Right to Feed Oneself.' It focuses on the international dimension, calling attention to what it identifies as violations of the right to feed oneself. Through its international newsletter and its chapters in several countries around the world, it organizes 'FIAN Urgent Actions' to correct these violations. At the World Conference on Human Rights in Vienna in June 1993, FIAN took the lead in advocating an *Optional Protocol to the International Covenant on Economic, Social, and Cultural Rights* that would allow individuals to bring complaints to the United Nations Committee on Economic, Social, and Cultural Rights.[28]

Several Task Forces under WANAHR pursue particular themes. The *Task Force on the Use of Food as A Weapon of War or For Political Purposes* promotes compliance with the prohibition of food deprivation as a method of war. It advocates a total ban on the withholding of food for political ends when it deprives needy people of food.

The *Task Force on Monitoring and Implementation of the Right to Food,* working closely with FIAN, is promoting three major types of activities. First, it proposes a meeting to further clarify the obligations of States Parties to the International Covenant on Economic, Social, and Cultural Rights. Second, with FIAN it is campaigning for the *Optional Protocol* to the covenant. Third, it proposes strengthened monitoring procedures in relation to the work of the United Nations Committee on Economic, Social, and Cultural Rights and the Committee on the Rights of the Child.

I serve as the coordinator for the *Task Force on Children's Nutrition Rights.* Its premise is that the idea of the right to adequate nutrition is likely to be more acceptable, more politically feasible, if it focuses on children. The Task Force facilitates and encourages a variety of activities such as research and lobbying on the issue, but its work centers on encouraging the organization of national workshops on the theme. The purpose of these workshops is to launch locally-based long-term campaigns to strengthen children's nutrition rights, giving attention both to their articulation in the law and the effective implementation of that law. Individuals from both governmental and nongovernmental organizations are invited to participate.

Workshops have been held in Guatemala, Mexico, and Nigeria. Discussions are underway with potential organizers elsewhere. Organizers are asked to invite individuals to their workshops who might arrange similar programs in other nations in their regions. Hopefully this will lead to an ongoing process of facilitation, networking, and learning. The Task Force is confident that this process will in time lead to increasing recognition of children's right to adequate nutrition.

9 Children's Rights

Nutrition rights of the sort discussed in the preceding chapter illustrate, in one issue area, the broader context of human rights and children rights. Children's rights have been addressed in many different international instruments.[1] The Geneva *Declaration of the Rights of the Child* adopted by the League of Nations in 1924 was revised and became the basis of the *Declaration of the Rights of the Child* adopted unanimously by the United Nations General Assembly in 1959. The declaration enumerates ten principles regarding the rights of the child, but it does not provide any basis for implementation of those principles.[2]

The *Universal Declaration of Human Rights* was approved unanimously by the UN General Assembly in 1948. It was given effect in the *International Covenant on Civil and Political Rights* and the *International Covenant on Economic, Social, and Cultural Rights.* There also was an *Optional Protocol to the International Covenant on Civil and Political Rights.* The two covenants and the protocol were adopted in 1966 and entered into force in 1976. The covenants include specific references to children's rights.[3]

After ten years of hard negotiations in a working group of the Commission on Human Rights, on November 20, 1989 the United Nations General Assembly by consensus adopted the new *Convention on the Rights of the Child.* It came into force on September 2, 1990 when it was ratified by the twentieth nation. Weaving together the scattered threads of earlier international statements of the rights of children, the convention's articles cover civil, political, economic, social and cultural rights. It includes not only basic survival requirements such as food, clean water, and health care, but also rights of protection against abuse, neglect, and exploitation, and the right to education and to participation in social, religious, political, and economic activities. Most of the world's nations have agreed to the convention, and many are now reviewing and strengthening their national laws relating to the rights of children.[4]

The convention is a comprehensive legal instrument, intended to be binding on all nations that accept it. The articles specify what States Parties are obligated to do under different conditions. National governments that agree to be bound by the convention have the major responsibility for its implementation. To provide added international pressure for responsible implementation, Article 43 calls for the creation of a Committee on the Rights of the Child. It consists of ten experts whose main functions are to receive and transmit reports on the status of children's rights. Article 44 requires States Parties to submit 'reports on the measures they have adopted which give effect to the rights recognized herein and on the progress made on the enjoyment of those rights.'[5] Article 46 entitles UNICEF and other agencies to work with the committee within the scope of their mandates.

On September 29–30, 1990, 71 heads of state and government and 88 representatives at the ministerial level participated in the World Summit for Children held at the United Nations. One of its major purposes was to promote the signing and ratification of the new *Convention on the Rights of the Child*. The summit culminated with *a Declaration and Plan of Action* in which national governments made major commitments to take action in behalf of children.[6] The summit promises did not have the force of law, however.

Children enjoy not only the special rights enumerated in the *Convention on the Rights of the Child*, but also, with some exceptions, all other human rights. The articulation of these rights in international instruments represent an important advance, but there is still much more to be done, especially with respect to implementation.

SOFT vs. HARD RIGHTS

A clear distinction should be drawn between the broad notion of children's interests involving many different things such as shelter and a nurturing environment and the more limited subset of those things that are – or should be – formally recognized as rights in law. There are many good things for which there is no acknowledged right. Some things we may feel ought to be recognized as rights have not been codified in written law. Some of what we may agree are rights in principle or a matter of 'natural law' are not yet rights in the written 'black letter' law.

The focus here is on formal rights as explicitly stated in the law. One can pursue interests in, say, preventing sexual abuse or alleviating malnutrition in many different ways, but the position taken here is that to use the language of rights about these interests means that one is going to use the law. Promoting the rights of abused or malnourished children requires that we talk about the creation of new law or the implementation of existing law relating to their rights.

Soft rights are not spelled out in the law, or if they are there is no strong and effective mechanism to assure their implementation. Brazil's constitution, for example, has comprehensive and detailed provisions regarding the rights of children, but they have long been ignored. India, too, has laws regarding children's rights that are ignored. As just one of many possible examples, India's parliament passed a bill to control the distribution of infant formula that is not likely to be implemented effectively.[7] Without good implementation, rights in law are little more than empty promises.

In themselves, the *Convention on the Rights of the Child* and other international human rights instruments establish only soft rights. They can be transformed into hard rights if national and local governments create suitably strong national and local laws along with effective agencies to implement them.

Of course soft rights can be useful in a transitional stage. The articulation of human rights in the law is important even where there are no special means to assure their implementation. The *Universal Declaration of Human Rights*, for example, has been one of the most important statements of international law even though it does not include any implementation mechanism. Its power arises from its cogent articulation of the near universal imperative: *Do the right thing. This is the right thing.*

Hard or *strong* rights are clearly articulated in the law and are accompanied by effective implementation and accountability mechanisms. Hard rights have a history of case law through which the meaning of the right is tested and refined. There is clear recourse in law for individuals whose rights are not fulfilled, and clear public accountability.

The right to something becomes a hard right only if there are clear and detailed laws providing for that thing, there are designated agencies responsible for providing it, and there is adequate funding to do the job. There must also be means for calling the government to account if it fails to provide what it is supposed to provide.

Consider the nutrition example. Governments can do many different things that will enhance the likelihood that their people will be adequately nourished. They can make the economy function smoothly, provide for health and sanitation services, undertake land reform programs, subsidize staple foods, create social security programs, impose legal obligations on parents, and many other things. Such steps are likely to result in adequate nutrition for the great majority of the population. However, there is no hard right unless the government serves as backup, accepting the obligation to fulfill the need in cases of failure of other more indirect means of fulfilling it. *There is no hard right to adequate nutrition unless the government guarantees to meet the need if other means fail.* It would be neither possible nor wise to provide a hard right in this sense for all claimants, but it should be feasible at least to some extent for those who are most vulnerable: small children who are clearly malnourished.

It is not enough to assure that *most* children are well nourished. The right to adequate nutrition should be understood as an individual right and not only as a group right. Every individual should have the potential for making specific claims for service. The framers of the *Convention on the Rights of the Child* recognized that these rights should be recognized for every individual child, and for that reason did not call it the convention on the rights of *children*.

Rights are important because without clear rights, those who are more powerful, more highly educated, or better connected have an advantage in obtaining services. Clearly established rights empower the weak, leveling the playing field a bit so that the weak are not so disadvantaged.

Rights can be truly hard – that is, clearly articulated and effectively implemented – only where there is a strong and effective legal system in place. In many countries there is no such system. However, where the legal system is weak it may nevertheless be worth advocating the hardening of rights as part of the broader effort to pursue a civil society. Even if they are not effectively implemented by government, rights enshrined in the law can provide a strong basis for political action by nongovernmental organizations and others.

Civil society sometimes refers to a distinct political force in the body of the people, apart from the state and its machinery of government. One sign of it is the existence of vigorous and independent political movements. Another is the existence of clear human rights, based on plainly articulated duties of government to the people. The very existence of such duties acknowledges a distinct political entity in the people separate from the state itself. Thus, hard human rights for which governments have clear duties to respect, protect, and fulfill those rights are an important marker of civil society.

Establishing hard rights is not always immediately practicable, but the vision should be kept in view as an ideal, helping to set the course in long term efforts to strengthen children's rights and, more broadly, to establish civil society.

The soft international human rights law can be understood as a guide to the formulation of national-level human rights law. It is there, at the national level, that it likely to be hardened first. Nations will be willing to look after their own most vulnerable children sooner than they would be willing to look after the world's most vulnerable children. In the following chapter, however, I argue that in addition to hardening rights within nations, we also should aspire to hard *international* human rights law.

RIGHTS REQUIRE ACCOUNTABILITY

When a child is abused or is not adequately nourished it is not only the child's family but the society as a whole that have failed that child. There should be mechanisms for calling governments to account and correcting that failure. If the law says that children are entitled to some particular service as a matter of right, that law also should establish an accountability mechanism to assure that the service is provided adequately and effectively.

An *implementation* mechanism for achieving a goal has both monitoring and response components. The monitoring component assesses the distance and direction from the goal, and the response component acts to move toward the goal. An automobile driver, for example, monitors through her eyes, and responds by pressing the pedals and turning the steering wheel. Where the goal is to improve children's nutrition, the monitoring element could use indicators such as food intake or anthropometric measures to assess the location and extent of malnutrition in the society. The response element would involve feeding, health, and care programs targeted to where the monitoring component showed it was needed.

There are many ways in which such a system could go wrong. The monitoring component may measure the wrong things, or it may not be very sensitive. Or the responses may not work well. For example, income transfers to the family may be diverted to uses other than meeting the needs of the child. Government-funded school lunch programs that feed all students may feed many who don't need assistance, and thus may be unnecessarily costly. People who are technically entitled to a particular benefit may not know about it or may have difficulty accessing it. A child who is fed at a centralized feeding program may for just that reason get less to eat at home. An effective system would notice these problems, and make constant course corrections to navigate the system toward the goal. The design of a system for assuring children's right to adequate nutrition would have to be refined over time until it could be shown that it really works.

Social service programs usually reach only some of the needy some of the time. Governments may boast about the number of individuals served, but they tend to be silent about the number of people who are needy but are not served. Accountability means paying attention to that shortfall. The obligation is not simply to provide some service, but to end the problem of abused or malnourished children. Any government that really wants to address children's problems should be willing to make itself accountable for meeting that challenge.

Assurance that services will be provided results not simply from the creation of service programs (e.g., school lunches, nutrition education programs) but from institutionalized mechanisms to establish accountability. An *accountability* (or *compliance*) mechanism watches the implementation mechanism to make sure it does its job well. It is located outside the implementation mechanism, and may have its own separate monitoring procedures. Governments have their legislative auditors and inspectors general to make sure government agencies stay on track. In the United States, there is a compliance monitoring procedure designed to assure that the states provide disabled children the educational services to which they are entitled under the law. If a government wants to assure that it will always be attentive to the concerns of children, it could pay for an independent Children's Ombudsman to handle complaints against the government.[8]

Many different kinds of measures can be used to provide accountability.[9] In a well-designed system of rights there will be specialized government agencies (such as inspectors general) to assure the accountability of implementing agencies. If they are absent or ineffective, nongovernmental agencies can hold the implementing agencies to account. The use or threat of use of the judicial system can be a potent means for keeping implementing agencies on track, but other more political means (such as public information campaigns through the media) may be used as well. In Hawaii, the Children's Rights Coalition launched and won a suit against the state government for its failure to provide mandated educational services for learning disabled children. If there were a right to adequate nutrition on the books, such a coalition also could bring action against the government for failing to prevent or remedy malnutrition.

In general, if the system threatens to go off the tracks, the compliance or accountability mechanism sounds an alarm and takes action to correct the implementation mechanism. Accountability means there are independent observers of the implementation mechanism that have some capacity to take or call for corrective action if the system is not operating well. Ideally there should be explicit standards against which the accountability agency evaluates the performance of the implementing agency. The accountability agency is in effect a permanent auditor.

In a negative approach to accountability, a government agency assigned the duty of preventing abuse or ending malnutrition could be sued or fined in some way for each abused child or malnourished child that is discovered, thus increasing its incentive to end abuse or malnutrition. (Comparable devices may be found in the right of California's courts to sue the state government when prisons are overcrowded, or in the United

States Clean Water Act which allows private citizens to sue the government for violations.) In a more positive approach, the government could give designated nongovernmental organizations an award or 'bounty' of a small sum of money for each needy child they find and present for services. This sort of positive approach would engage nongovernmental organizations in a partnership with government in support of their larger common purpose.

One form of accountability mechanism is giving aggrieved parties themselves or their representatives a procedure for complaining and getting some remedy. Human rights in the law rests on the principle *ubi jus ibi remedium* – where there is a right there must be a remedy. Article 8 of the *Universal Declaration of Human Rights* asserts that 'everyone has the right to an effective remedy by the competent national tribunals for acts violating the fundamental rights granted him by the constitution or by law.' Children's nutrition rights, rights to protection from abuse, and other rights should be articulated in the law, together with a description of the means of legal recourse that are available if even a single individual's rights are violated. If you or your child don't get what you feel you are entitled to under the law, there should be effective means for pressing your claims. This legal recourse is essential for assuring the government's compliance with the law.

The implementation of children's rights is ultimately the responsibility of government at different levels, but it is also the responsibility of the community at local, national, and international levels. Interested groups both within and outside government can watch the performance of service delivery agencies and call them to account as necessary, even if there is no explicit provision in the law for their playing that role. If the law says, for example, that children have a right to be protected from physical abuse, anyone who is concerned could help to see that the right is honored.

The meaning of hard rights, duty, and accountability can be understood by recalling the nature of contracts. Suppose you have a contract with me in which I promise to provide goods or services in exchange for a specified amount of money. If I provide the goods or services, it is my right to receive and your obligation (responsibility, duty) to give me the money. I am entitled to it. The contract is not simply an articulation of claims; if it is legally binding it represents *enforceable* claims. If one of us is not satisfied, there is some third party to whom we can go to press for fulfillment of the contractual obligations. Similarly, a human rights regime can be understood as representing an implicit contract between citizens and government, comparable to that described by Rousseau in *The Social*

Contract of 1762. To the extent that citizens have rights plainly articulated in the law, governments should have plainly articulated legal obligations to respect, protect, and fulfill those rights. The limits of those obligations should be clarified as well. Clarity with regard to the obligations of governments corresponding to the rights of citizens may be obtained through legislation and through the evolving interpretations that come with case law. Beyond clarity regarding the nature of the obligations, there also must be some means of accountability, some basis on which claims against the government can be enforced.

   Those in power may resist the articulation of specific rights of the people because rights imply specific obligations and accountability on the part of government. Nevertheless, if human rights are to advance there must be clear articulation not only of citizens' rights but also of the corresponding obligations of government. Also, effective mechanisms must be established to assure that the obligations are in fact fulfilled. This articulation of the obligations of government and insistence on government's accountability continues the transition described earlier, in Chapter 1, under which the function of government is not to serve the sovereign but to serve the people. It is a mark of the evolution toward civil society.

MONITORING AND REPORTING ON RIGHTS

In some quarters, human rights are little more than lofty aspirations. Monitoring is an important part of making rights operational. Where there is a human right, government has an obligation under the law to provide services to assure fulfillment of that right. Monitoring, as used here, means *compliance monitoring*, assessing the effectiveness with which the government fulfills its obligations under the law. To illustrate, where there is a right to free speech, the fact that many people are seen to speak freely is not enough to assure us that the right is being effectively implemented. There may be a minority that is not able to speak freely. Tomorrow the government might find a reason to crack down on free speech, or it might simply ignore the disruption by some individuals of the free speech of others. To know that there is an effective right to free speech, and not just the existence of some free speech, one has to know that there are mechanisms in place to assure that the right is fulfilled under different circumstances. Is there a clear law asserting the right? Does the government have clear obligations for enforcing the right? Is there a record of enforcement by the government? Is there some mechanism by which concerned individuals and organizations can call the government to account if it does not enforce the right?

Systematic assessment of the status of particular human rights is an important tool of human rights advocacy within nations and internationally. It is not only the precision of the numbers, the measures, that is important, but also the clarity with regard to concepts that comes from systematic assessment. These perspectives will be illustrated here through consideration of ways in which the fulfillment of nutrition rights can be assessed. The discussion of techniques for monitoring nutrition rights should lead to greater clarity as to the meaning of those rights. The analysis should have clear implications for other rights arenas as well.

Measuring and publicizing things can make them more prominent, more important in people's consciousness. If clear and simple methods can be found to identify individuals who are seriously malnourished, they would be likely to get more attention and care even if no new nutrition programs were created. Systematic assessment could help to improve nutrition conditions even in poor countries where no new service programs can be implemented. 'Monitoring informs policy, introduces accountability, galvanizes and rewards effort, and is a means by which sustained pressure can be brought to bear for the fulfillment of political promises.'[10]

Another reason for monitoring nutrition rights is that it is required. Nations that are parties to the *International Covenant on Economic, Social, and Cultural Rights* or the *Convention on the Rights of the Child* are obligated to provide regular reports to the corresponding United Nations treaty bodies. Since each of these agreements includes nutrition rights, they are required to document the status of nutrition rights as part of their larger reports.

According to Article 16 of the covenant, States Parties agree to submit reports 'on measures which they have adopted and the progress made in achieving the observance of the rights recognized herein.' The reports are to be transmitted to the Secretary General of the United Nations, who then transmits copies to the Economic and Social Council (ECOSOC) and to other specialized agencies of the United Nations. Article 17 provides that ECOSOC should establish a program for reporting. ECOSOC has in effect subcontracted its responsibilities for implementation of the covenant to the United Nations Committee on Economic, Social, and Cultural Rights (CESCR). This committee held its first session in 1987.

Methods for reporting are still evolving. At its fifth session, held in 1990, the CESCR adopted new guidelines. These guidelines are likely to elicit much useful information for consideration by the committee. However, they are very extensive, place a great burden on the reporting nations, and may miss some important categories of information. I want to propose a more systematic conceptual basis for reporting on the right to adequate nutrition.[11]

In my view, reporting on the status of nutrition rights should cover four distinct but interrelated components: (a) the nutrition *problems*; (b) the *law* relating to nutrition rights; (c) the government's *service programs* for responding to the problems, and (d) the *accountability mechanisms*. This four-part outline is likely to be useful for assessing the status of other kinds of rights as well.

Assessing Nutrition Problems

It is important to know what categories of individuals suffer from what sorts of malnutrition problems. The varieties of malnutrition were sketched out in Chapter 7. As pointed out there, the most important form, protein-energy malnutrition, can be gauged by measuring the heights and weights of children and comparing them with the heights and weights of well nourished children. Systematic programs to identify malnourished children can be launched by requiring regular collection and analysis of such data.

Nutrition rights can be developed for different kinds of malnutrition. For example, in countries known to suffer from marked iodine deficiency, laws could be established to require government to assure that salt is iodized and other measures are taken for those who show signs of iodine deficiency. However, since it is the single most serious form of malnutrition worldwide, the focus here is on protein-energy malnutrition, particularly in small children.

Assessing the Law

Some human rights studies focus on data related to human suffering.[12] Care should be taken with this, however, because not all human suffering violates human rights. Poverty, for example, is not in itself a violation of human rights. While there is an international agreement prohibiting genocide, there is no international prohibition against murder. I take the view that if one wants to say that a particular action is a violation of human rights, one should be able to point to a specific, clear, authoritative legal document asserting the relevant right. Strengthening human rights is not the same as railing against human suffering. It is about strengthening the explicit law under which people are protected from suffering. One's nutrition rights are different from one's nutrition status. People may be well nourished and still have no nutrition rights.

There may be natural or inherent human rights, but I feel that to be effective human rights must be enshrined in the law. In my view, articulation in the law is a necessary condition but certainly not a sufficient condition for effective implementation of human rights. If the right is not yet in the law, or if it is not clear enough, political work should be undertaken to strengthen the law. Human rights work needs to be done in legislatures as well as out in the field. As suggested earlier in this chapter, human rights can be understood in terms of a social contract between citizens and their government. Hard rights are based on an *explicit* contract in the sense that the citizens' rights and the government's obligations are plainly spelled out in the law. Thus, in assessing the status of particular rights, the first place to look is the law books. According to the law, what are the rights? what are the obligations?

Rights should be spelled out in the law with as much clarity and detail as possible, specifying not only the rights of the people but also the specific obligations of government for fulfilling those rights. The government's obligations to respect, protect, and fulfill nutrition rights should be acknowledged and should be elaborated to specify the details of these obligations.

Nutrition rights are affirmed in some of the major international human rights instruments, but they are not elaborated. They are also affirmed in the constitutions of some nations. Nutrition rights signify that government has specific obligations, and can be held accountable if those obligations are not fulfilled. Nutrition rights may protect all individuals, certain categories of individuals (e.g., women, the elderly, children), or individuals meeting certain criteria (e.g., children who are more than two standard deviations below the standard weight for their age). As argued earlier, nutrition rights should be based on the clear and effective assurance *in the law* that if all other means fail, the government will do what is necessary to assure that each individual meeting the criteria is adequately nourished.

Upon becoming parties to the international human rights agreements, states parties are expected to modify their national laws to take account of the commitments upon becoming party to the agreements. Thus, reports to these United Nations treaty bodies should include information on the ways in which these adaptations in domestic law have been or are in the process of being made. Over time these rights should be elaborated in statutes and regulations, and there should be a body of case law associated with them. This applies not only to nutrition rights but to the full range of rights affirmed in these agreements.

The law should specify its own implementation mechanism. It should say not only what outcomes are desired but also what agency is to be responsible for bringing about those outcomes, and through what means.

It would be highly desirable if the nutrition rights law went even further, to incorporate specific measurable overall goals. Many countries adopted specific nutrition goals (such as reducing protein-energy malnutrition by half within ten years) at the World Summit for Children in 1990, at the International Conference on Nutrition in 1992, and in other settings, but these commitments did not have the force of law. Incorporating these goals into national law would signal that they are in fact being taken seriously, and compel the allocation of attention and material resources to them.

Assessing Government's Service Programs

The government's *respecting* nutrition rights means it should not itself do things that interfere with people's capacity to provide for themselves. *Protecting* nutrition rights means stopping other parties from interfering. If such interference is neither frequent nor serious, existing government agencies may be able to handle it. Thus, respecting and protecting nutrition rights require attentiveness on the part of government, but may not require any special institutional arrangements. In contrast, the obligation to *fulfill* nutrition rights under particular circumstances requires specific institutional arrangements for the purpose.

If nutrition rights exist, there must be government-sponsored services to assure that people are adequately nourished. These services should be concerned with the three key factors in good nutrition, food, health, and care. Services should be both preventive, to keep malnutrition from occurring, and remedial, to undo malnutrition after it occurs. Preventive services may include such things as health education, water supply, immunization programs, or programs to keep people from being displaced from their land. Remedial services for those who are malnourished or at risk of malnutrition may include feeding programs, clinics, land reform programs, and so on. If there are real rights, there must be programs that provide services directly when other means for maintaining adequate nutrition fail. The programs may be owned and operated by the government itself, or they may be privately run programs with partial funding or other forms of support from the government.

There may be private nutrition programs for which there is no governmental support. These are not relevant here because in assessing the status of nutrition rights it is important to know how *government* takes on responsibility for assuring that people are adequately nourished.

It is not enough to know that government-support service programs exist. They also should be effective and adequate in coverage. After listing the programs, it would be useful to gather several kinds of information about them.

Character

What sort of nutrition service program is it? What services does it provide? Who runs it? How is it funded? After some work and experience with this, a simple outline or checklist could be developed to characterize the different types of nutrition service programs.

Effectiveness

Do the program's services work? Are preventive services effective so that few become malnourished? Do those who receive remedial services soon become adequately nourished, or do they remain malnourished? Do areas or peoples receiving the program show better nutrition status as a result of the program? Is effectiveness measured? Are there regular efforts to improve effectiveness? Is the service goal directed, or does it just keep doing the same old things without attention to results?

Coverage

Who are the program's *intended* targets? Are there clear and explicit criteria of eligibility, saying who may or must receive the service? For example, some services might be provided to all children under 12 who are severely wasted, and other services might be provided to those who are moderately wasted. Is priority given to those who are most needy?

Who does the program *actually* serve? Typically, not all of those who should get the service actually receive it. Are the programs satisfied with serving *some* of the needy, or do they undertake outreach programs in an effort to find and serve all who meet the eligibility criteria? What percentage of those who are eligible actually participate in the program and receive the service? The size of the gap between the numbers of people who should get the service and the numbers who actually do get the service should be estimated. What are the reasons for the gap? Are efforts made to shrink the gap?

In addition to missing some needy people, and thus having inadequate coverage, there may also be a problem of excessive coverage. Are there some people receiving the service who shouldn't be receiving it? Excessive coverage in this sense can divert scarce resources away from the needy, and thus make the program inefficient.

Beyond estimating its numerical size, it is also important to determine whether gaps in coverage are associated with systematic biases. Does the coverage favor certain groups of needy people, such as city residents or particular ethnic or cultural groups? Do some categories of people have especially great difficulty in obtaining services?

Given the magnitude of the malnutrition problem and the level of resources available, judgments should be made as to whether the eligibility criteria are too high (excluding many who should be served), too low (including many who should not be served), or about right. No matter how effective a service procedure may be for those who are served, it does little good if it fails to reach large numbers of people who should receive it.

Mandate

It is also important to know which of the nutrition-related programs has a clear and direct mandate in fulfilling nutrition rights. A school lunch program, for example, may be organized around the objective of maximizing the number of lunches it can serve for a given amount of money, with no explicit and systematic concern for its nutritional impacts. Nutrition service programs already exist in many countries in which there are no nutrition rights. Some nutrition programs may operate with no explicit mandate relating to nutrition rights. Some may not even be aware of the concept. Thus it is useful to have the specific service programs that are to be responsible for the implementation of nutrition rights named in the law.[13]

Beyond assessing the nutrition service programs individually, in terms of their own objectives, it is important to examine them collectively to judge whether, taken together, they are effective and adequate in addressing the entire nation's nutrition problems. It may be that, even with each program doing its job, some geographical areas or marginalized groups do not get enough attention or that some important types of malnutrition are neglected.

Assessing Accountability Mechanisms

What institutional arrangements are there for calling the government to account? Are there arrangements established by government itself, such as auditors or inspectors general? Apart from the direct service programs, there is a need for effective institutional arrangements to assure that the government is held accountable for fulifling its obligations with reference to the nutrition rights law.

Many countries have means for identifying malnourished individuals and have programs for providing services, but if people are to have meaningful nutrition rights there must also be strong mechanisms of accountability established by law. Of course there may also be some informal monitoring of government performance by the mass media or by interested nongovernmental organizations, but hard nutrition rights would require that the government itself establishes means to hold itself accountable.

In addition to asking whether there are government agencies which regularly assess the performance of the nutrition service programs, one should also inquire where there is a provision for *clear legal recourse* for individuals who do not get the services to which they are entitled. Are there means to assure that individuals with nutrition rights can in fact obtain the services that are due them? Is there an *ombudsman* or some other designated individual to whom complaints may be taken? Is the complaint procedure straightforward, simple, accessible, inexpensive, fair, and safe to use? Is there a record of cases in which complaints have been made and government has been legally required to respond to the needs of those who are eligible for services? Are these complaint mechanisms effective and adequate?

Ideally, the government should view mechanisms of accountability as helping it to accomplish what it wants to accomplish. Accountability is a corrective that helps to keep government on track. Governments recognize the importance of such services when they hire auditors, ombudsmen, and inspectors general. A negative approach to holding the government accountable, such as lawsuits, should be invoked only if and when the friendlier, dialogical approaches have failed.

Reports to the United Nations Committee on the Rights of the Child or the Committee on Economic, Social and Cultural Rights relating to the status of nutrition rights should address all four of these dimensions: nutrition problems, law, service programs, and accountability mechanisms. The real importance of developing clarity with regard to these dimensions, however, is that doing so can help guide efforts to strengthen nutrition rights.

INTERNATIONAL NUTRITION MONITORING

Information in these four categories is needed to assess the status of nutrition rights within a nation, a province, a prison, a refugee camp, or any other administrative unit. Nutrition monitoring can take on international dimensions in several different ways. One important issue, for example is international comparability. It is useful to have common methods of monitoring across nations to facilitate reporting to the international treaty bodies and to make comparisons across countries more meaningful.

For most purposes, however, the United Nations treaty bodies will focus not on international comparisons but on conditions within individual nations and their changes over time. Every nation should demonstrate steady improvements in nutrition status until virtually all malnutrition is abolished. In wealthy nations, the great majority of the population may be well nourished, but if there are marginalized groups whose nutrition status is poor, and it remains poor over time, and the government does nothing about it, one would have to say nutrition rights are weak. There may be many groups with nutrition problems in poor nations, but where the government is attentive to these problems, providing service programs to the limits of its capacity, and providing legal protections to assure that those who need the services obtain them in fact, one would have to say that in such nations nutrition rights were quite strong. Nutrition rights are multi-dimensional, so there is no mechanical way to produce a simple score describing the status of nutrition rights in any particular country. But with good information on the situation with respect to the four dimensions of nutrition rights described here, it is possible to make clear overall judgments, and thus know where nutrition rights are strong and where they need to be strengthened.

Agencies of the United Nations system regularly publish data relating to nutrition status throughout the world. It would be useful to also assess nutrition *rights* globally. The first stage of this analysis might be understood as the simple aggregation of the status of nutrition rights within nations, perhaps as a global average of sorts. However, this would miss the *inter*-national dimension. As argued in the following chapter, there is responsibility for implementing nutrition rights not only by national governments but also by the international community as a whole. There are obligations not only within nations but also across nations, a dimension that is not systematically assessed in current reporting procedures. The international community acts to deal with global malnutrition through its international organizations, particularly the international governmental organizations, globally and regionally. They too should be held to account for fulfilling responsibilities for ending malnutrition worldwide.

10 International Children's Rights

People often need help desperately, and sometimes that help is not or cannot be provided from within their own countries. At times international assistance is provided in spectacular ways. On April 5, 1991 the Security Council of the United Nations passed a resolution condemning Iraq's repression of the Kurds and calling for humanitarian assistance. On the same day the U.S. president ordered the U.S. military to begin airdropping humanitarian supplies to Kurds camping along the Iraq-Turkey border. In December 1992 the United States Marines, acting under United Nations cover, moved into Somalia to rescue a faltering humanitarian assistance program. The airdrop of emergency food supplies to remnants of what had been Yugoslavia was started in March 1993. The problems of providing humanitarian assistance in the midst of armed conflict have been clearly documented in connection with the civil war in the Sudan.[1] Even in non-conflict situations, assistance becomes the victim of all kinds of inefficiencies and political pressures.[2] Often there is no attempt to assist. What principles should guide the provision of humanitarian assistance?

People suffer from many kinds of distress. In this study I have focused on the plight of children and the ways in which they suffer from excessive mortality, armed conflict, abusive working conditions, and inadequate food, care, and health services. I have highlighted the problem of malnutrition to show how the human rights approach can be used to address some of these problems within nations. This chapter extends the analysis to show how the rights approach can be used internationally, again using malnutrition to illustrate the possibilities. Malnutrition provides good opportunities for strengthening international rights because it is so unambiguous and because it is so inexpensive and – usually – politically safe to address. If clear principles can be established in this arena, they might then be adapted to addressing other more difficult humanitarian problems.

Some lawyers reserve the term *humanitarian* law to refer to international humanitarian law as described in the Geneva conventions, and thus take it to refer to armed conflict situations. For some, humanitarian assistance refers to attempts to prevent gross violations of human rights such as genocide or torture. Here, however, the term refers

157

generally to assistance to people in great need whether or not the situation is one of armed conflict and regardless of the causes of the problems. Humanitarian assistance is motivated not so much by the donor's self-interest as by concern for the well-being of the needy. It also could be described as compassionate assistance.[3]

The thesis here is that the provision of humanitarian assistance of different kinds will become more orderly and effective if we acknowledge that under some specified conditions the needy – children and others – have a *right* to humanitarian assistance. The purpose is not simply to press for more assistance but, more importantly, to find ways to make better use of the assistance that is provided. Let us first look at the nature of humanitarian assistance in general and then at its character at the international level.

RIGHTS TO ASSISTANCE

Assistance may be understood to mean charity, something given voluntary by a donor, without compulsion of any kind. The idea that anyone might have a *right* to assistance, an entitlement of some sort, thus may seem oxymoronic, contradictory, absurd. It is a troubling conjunction of concepts.

If there is a right of those in need to receive assistance under specified conditions, then there must also be an obligation for others to render assistance. (I take obligation to refer to the articulation in law of specific responsibilities for action.) The rights/obligations nexus can be understood as a kind of contract, explicit or implicit, that establishes who is to do what under what conditions. The challenge then, is to determine the nature of the contract: *who should be entitled to what sort of assistance from whom under what conditions at whose expense*? Different sorts of answers would be appropriate for different kinds of situations or needs: poverty, armed conflict, refugees, famine, chronic malnutrition, floods, droughts, terrorism, and so on. Presumably some general principles would apply across broad categories of cases.

Most of us would agree that there are some extreme situations in which needy people should have a clear right to receive help. In any decent social order, if a child falls down a well, there should be a requirement that the child will be rescued. But the idea of the right to assistance has a very checkered history. Mary Glendon points out that the law in the United States is characterized by 'the missing language of responsibility.'[4] In 1964 Kitty Genovese was murdered in New York City while 38 people watched without helping or calling for help. They were not under any legal obligation to help. Under the no-duty-to-rescue principle that prevails in the United States, bystanders are not required to come to the assistance of strangers in peril if they did not cause that peril.

Remarkably, in the U.S. even agents of government such as police officers and firefighters are not legally required to help individuals in trouble. The courts have applied the general principle of tort law according to which one does not have a duty to rescue a stranger in distress:

> One might think that when the potential rescuer is a police officer, whose very job is to protect us, the principle might be different. But that notion was recently described by the California Supreme Court as a 'widely held misconception concerning the duty owed by police to individual members of the general public.' The fact is that, in civil damage actions, most courts apply the same rules to police officers as to private citizens.[5]

Thus individuals cannot claim a clear right to service from their local police force or firefighters in case of emergency. Certainly there is no *constitutional* right to such service. However, there is some variation among the states in the degree and ways in which they acknowledge some duty to provide services. For example, in some places there are requirements to report to authorities in cases of suspected child abuse.

This principle of no-duty-to-rescue is peculiarly American. In contrast, 'most European countries *do* impose a legal duty on individuals to come to the aid of an imperiled person where that can be done without risk of harm to the rescuer. And the constitutions of many other liberal democracies *do* obligate government to protect the health and safety of citizens.'[6] In international law there is no general duty of nations to respond to distress in other nations. However, nations sometimes do make specific agreements to provide assistance under certain circumstances.

THE QUESTION OF CONSENT

International humanitarian *intervention* is understood here as referring to humanitarian assistance provided to people within a nation by outsiders without the consent of the national government. Such assistance has been provided to the Kurds in Iraq, to Bosnians and Croats in what had been Yugoslavia, and to Somalians. Some writers define humanitarian intervention as armed intervention for humanitarian purposes, but this does not recognize the possibility of unarmed coercive measures such as sanctions or non-coercive assistance such as airdrops of food.[7]

Within nations, similar issues arise in regard to assistance by national governments without the consent of local (e.g., state or provincial) governments. Locally they come up in regard to intervention to protect children in the absence of parental consent. The question of whether assistance should be provided despite objections arises in many forms. Should motorcyclists be forced to wear helmets? Should children be forcibly immunized over their objections? Over their parents objections?

Humanitarian intervention pierces the veil of sovereignty, the basis for the integrity of nation-states in the international system. The idea of inviolable national sovereignty has served the international system well since the Treaty of Westphalia of 1648, but times have changed. There have been massive violations of human rights by national governments, especially in this century. Also in this century, there is new international law with regard to human rights, and there are new international mechanisms for implementing and monitoring that law, especially in the United Nations system. There is increasing acknowledgment that the doctrine of non-interference in the internal affairs of nations should be revised. The practice of nations has already moved ahead of international law in this area, as illustrated by the delivery of international humanitarian assistance without the consent of national governments in Iraq, Bosnia and Somalia.

The historical shift from a doctrine of inviolable sovereignty to acceptance of humanitarian intervention under special circumstances has a parallel in the historical evolution of the family. Until late in the nineteenth century, in many places parents could abuse and torture their children, but police would not intervene in 'family matters.' Parents in effect had sovereign control over their families. Now, however, it is widely accepted that when there are gross violations of a child's rights, outside agencies should intervene to protect that child. The rights of supervising adults are not absolute, but must be balanced by consideration of the best interests of the child; under some special circumstances it may be necessary to intervene on behalf of the child. Now that principle is coming to be acknowledged at the societal level.

The question of humanitarian assistance comes up frequently in relation to armed conflict situations (warfare). That is the special province of the International Committee for the Red Cross. In its own terms, the ICRC

... is an independent humanitarian institution. As a neutral intermediary in the event or armed conflict or unrest it endeavours, on its own initiative or on the basis of the Geneva Conventions, to bring protection and assistance to the victims of international and non-international armed conflict and internal disturbances and tensions.

In many conflict situations those in power refuse to allow the ICRC and others to provide humanitarian assistance. However, consent often is obtained if the proposed assistance appears to be even-handed, and if it is directed to non-combatants such as children or the injured. UNICEF, for example, has been successful in negotiating zones of peace, zones of tranquility, or cease fires to allow children to receive immunizations and other kinds of assistance.[8]

Some writers equate humanitarian *intervention* with humanitarian assistance in armed conflict, but as indicated above, here humanitarian intervention is taken to mean assistance *without consent*. Not all humanitarian assistance in armed conflict situations is a matter of intervention. And not all humanitarian intervention occurs in armed conflict situations.

In early 1993 humanitarian assistance was needed in many conflict and non-conflict situations. The *New York Times* listed 49 ongoing ethnic conflicts,[9] and people were also suffering for other reasons in many parts of the world. Why were only Bosnia and Somalia given extensive international attention? One hypothesis was offered in reference to the conflict between Kasai and Katangans in Zaire:

> Many diplomats and missionaries voice anger and frustration over how little attention the world has paid to the crisis here. The phrase that is often heard here about the reprisals against the Kasai from the Katangans is 'ethnic cleansing, African style.'

> 'What's happening here is the same as what's happening in Yugoslavia,' said a missionary here with more than 30 years experience in Africa. 'The only difference is that the European victims are white, and the Africans are black.'[10]

The question of consent often comes up in situations in which there is no armed conflict. For example, there have been many cases of mass murder by governments or nongovernmental entities in which there was little or no intervention from the outside, and not even a call for intervention.[11] The Kitty Genovese case is repeated over and over again on a global scale. It is not suggested here that the international community should intervene every time, indiscriminately. No one would expect firefighters to take on every blaze, no matter how massive. But we do expect them to show up, assess the situation, and do something, especially for large conflagrations. By the same token, there should be an institutionalized mechanism through which the international community would deal with genocide or other kinds of mass murder.

At the International Conference on Nutrition held in Rome in December 1992 there was a debate over humanitarian intervention. While people of Third World nations would be the primary beneficiaries of nutrition assistance, their governments resisted because of their concern with guarding their sovereignty. They fear that humanitarian intervention might be used against them for political purposes. In discussion of Article 9 of the *World Declaration on Nutrition*, Mexico voiced the position of many Third World governments when it argued that humanitarian assistance should be provided only under the terms of United National General Assembly Resolution 46/182 of December 19, 1991, on *Strengthening of the Coordination of Humanitarian Emergency Assistance of the United Nations*, and not simply according to the views and desires of the intervening nation. Third World governments do not want developed nations, which might have ulterior political motives, intervening without their consent under the pretense of providing assistance.

Humanitarian intervention may sometimes be used to serve the political purposes of the assisting nation, but those purposes may be good or bad. In some cases the intervening nation may want to protect a population from an oppressive government. When governments withhold consent, that is likely to reflect real differences in interests between governments and their people.

More systematic procedures need to be developed for providing humanitarian assistance in extreme situations in the absence of consent by those in power. These will often be situations of armed conflict, but humanitarian intervention also may be needed from time to time in other kinds of situations.

The determination of when humanitarian intervention is legitimate should not be made by individual nations that may have other, ulterior motives for intervening. To the extent possible, intervention should be depoliticized, which means that it should be carried out under clear rules by appropriate international bodies, usually the United Nations and its agents. When intervention is wholly discretionary it is subject to abuse.

The widespread preoccupation with the issue of humanitarian intervention may suggestion that humanitarian assistance is problematic only where there is a lack of consent. But even with consent, the international community is still not very good at it. There is little consensus about when and how humanitarian assistance should be provided. Hereafter my concern is with the conditions under which humanitarian assistance should be provided in cases where consent is not a problematic issue. In particular, are there conditions under which there should be a *duty* to provide assistance?

Most current discussions regarding humanitarian intervention are about the *right* of outside parties to provide humanitarian assistance; they are not about a *duty* to provide such assistance. Rights of the needy to receive international assistance, as distinguished from rights of outsiders to provide assistance, are rarely discussed in the legal literature.[12] Where it is discussed it seems it is mainly to clarify the conditions under which intervention may be undertaken.[13] In practice, there is no recognized duty to provide international assistance based on clear rights of the needy to receive assistance. Establishing clear rights of international agencies and humanitarian organizations to deliver humanitarian assistance would be an advance–but that is not the same as acknowledging that the needy should have a right to assistance. There should be not only a right but also a duty of international humanitarian assistance under some circumstances.[14]

PROGRESSIVE REALIZATION

The idea of establishing rights to humanitarian assistance is idealistic, especially at the international level. It can be approached slowly, in relation to restricted sets of issues. Recent resolutions adopted by the United Nations show clear support for regularizing international humanitarian assistance:

General Assembly Resolution 2816 of December 14, 1971 created the Office of the United Nations Disaster Relief Coordinator, UNDRO.

General Assembly Resolution 43/131 of December 8, 1988 was on *Humanitarian Assistance to Victims of Natural Disasters and Similar Emergency Situations.*

General Assembly Resolution 44/236 of December 22, 1989 declared the 1990s the International Decade for Natural Disaster Reduction (IDNDR).

General Assembly Resolution 45/100 of December 14, 1990 proposed consideration of relief corridors to facilitate access to victims of armed conflict.

Security Council Resolution 688 of April 5, 1991 provided for humanitarian assistance to Kurds in Iraq.

General Assembly Resolution 46/182 of December 19, 1991 was on *Strengthening of the Coordination of Humanitarian Emergency Assistance of the United Nations.*

A series of repetitive Security Council resolutions in 1992 and 1993 relating to assistance for the people of Somalia underscored the need for more orderly handling of international humanitarian assistance.

The international community is not legally required to assist nations suffering from natural disasters, but assistance has been generous and effective, especially from the United States. Relief has been handled mainly on an *ad hoc* basis, with much of it provided through the Office of the United Nations Disaster Relief Coordinator (UNDRO) and USAID's Office of Foreign Disaster Assistance (OFDA). The coverage remains selective and uneven, however. Through Res. 44/236 of December 22, 1989 the United Nations has taken up the issue and declared the 1990s the International Decade for Natural Disaster Reduction. Thus recent developments show that progress can be achieved in regularizing humanitarian assistance.

Around the world, training and logistical arrangements for providing relief from natural disasters are improving steadily. Emphasis is placed on preparing national governments to make effective use of their own resources to deal with disasters. It is also recognized that sometimes national resources are inadequate, and it is necessary to call in outsiders. The world is moving toward the institutionalization of a global rescue squad.

The movement toward providing humanitarian assistance in a more orderly and effective manner is being facilitated by Resolution 46/182 on *Strengthening of the Coordination of Humanitarian Emergency Assistance of the United Nations.* It articulates a list of 42 *Guiding Principles*, the first of which are:

1.   Humanitarian assistance is of cardinal importance for the victims of natural disasters and other emergencies.
2.   Humanitarian assistance must be provided in accordance with the principles of humanity, neutrality and impartiality.
3.   The sovereignty, territorial integrity and national unity of States must be fully respected in accordance with the Charter of the United

Nations. In this context, humanitarian assistance should be provided with the consent of the affected country and in principle on the basis of an appeal by the affected country.

Until full rights can be articulated in any specific issue area, it is useful to spell out guiding principles. An intermediate step toward the achievement of a full regime of rights in connection with disaster relief is the formulation of a widely accepted international code of conduct for disasters. Resolution 46/182 is an important step in this direction. In addition to stating general principles it establishes a locus of responsibility for promoting those principles. As the new Under Secretary General for Humanitarian Affairs explained:

> The Department will have offices in New York and in Geneva. It will bring together a strengthened UNDRO with other *ad hoc* mechanisms that have recently been established for specific complex emergencies to create a more effective and streamlined emergency management capacity. Political co-ordination and leadership will be excercised in New York, with special emphasis on those grey areas where humanitarian and political issues are closely intermingled. ... From New York ... the Department of Humanitarian Affairs will attempt to ensure that there is no gap remaining between humanitarian issues and political issues which may cause undue suffering to innocent human beings. ... the technical and operational part of emergency management will be carried out in Geneva, where the relief co-ordination and disaster mitigation activities of UNDRO will be strengthened in the framework of the Department of Humanitarian Affairs.[15]

Several nongovernmental organizations are looking at the policy questions raised by the need for humanitarian assistance in particular kinds of circumstances. The needs of refugees are the focus of the Refugee Policy Group based in Washington, D.C. This group and the Thomas J. Watson Jr. Institute for International Studies at Brown University are together examining ways of improving humanitarian action in armed conflict situations.[16] The Swedish Red Cross has been looking at what should be done for children in situations of armed conflict. Other groups and organizations are examining the ways in which assistance is provided in other kinds of circumstances.

Different kinds of rights/obligations packages can be designed for different issue areas. Some, such as limited rights to emergency disaster relief for poor nations might be widely acceptable. Others, such as requirements for intervention to suppress mass murder, may not be as easy to implement. Through the international humanitarian law articulated in the Geneva conventions, the international community has acknowledged some duties to assist civilians in armed conflict situations. So far there are no clear duties for providing international assistance in non-conflict situations. In the following sections I look into possibilities for creating programs of obligation for dealing with serious malnutrition. Broadly, the question is the same as it would be for any other issue area: *who should be entitled to what sort of assistance from whom under what conditions at whose expense?*

CHRONIC CONDITIONS

Orderly arrangements need to be made for providing humanitarian assistance not only in conflict and acute disaster situations but also to deal with intense chronic problems. Indeed, the places on earth that are now suffering the most extreme forms of poverty and hunger can be viewed as disaster areas. Prince Sadruddin Aga Khan, co-chair of the Independent Commission on International Humanitarian Issues, recognizes that 'disaster relief is needed most in the South by the poorest of the poor. Famine and starvation are only the most obvious of these emergencies.'[17]

The situations in Ethiopia and Somalia came to the attention of the West through television because they had intense famines resulting from collapse of the normal food supply systems. Sudan has had many deaths due to hunger as well, but its civil war is more than a decade old, and apparently no longer of much interest to the West. In Malawi, high rates of malnutrition and of children's mortality are so constant that for the West they become part of the steady-state background. Worldwide, famine – episodic hunger – accounts for only about ten percent of all hunger-related deaths. The other ninety percent rarely shows up on television news. The situations in places like Malawi are not regarded as news.

In the Indian state of Orissa, hunger has become so intense that families are selling their children for small sums of money.[18] Obviously this reflects a failure of the Indian government, but we must also ask what the international community is doing about this. The international community has failed to intervene in many situations of great human suffering where there is little physical or political risk to those who might assist. How can we expect outsiders to intervene to prevent slaughters if we don't step in to prevent starvation and the sale of children? The international community turns away not only from bloody scenes of mass murder but also from the quiet suffering of children.

It seems strange that the suggestion of a duty to provide international humanitarian assistance has arisen only in connection with armed conflict situations. These are situations that are especially difficult because of the likelihood of hostile responses from the conflicting parties. Human suffering is often greater outside armed conflict situations. Why is there no duty to provide assistance in non-conflict situations where there is no risk of attack and consent is not an issue? Why isn't there even discussion of such a duty?

Internationally, the record of humanitarian assistance is quite good in relation to episodic events such as famines and natural disasters, at least those not associated with armed conflicts. Ongoing chronic problems, however, do not get comparable attention. Assistance arrangements should be rationalized for chronic problems as well as for acute emergency conditions.

DEVELOPMENT ASSISTANCE vs. HUMANITARIAN ASSISTANCE

The book *Lords of Poverty* suggests that only a small share of the approximately $60 billion provided in official development assistance every year actually reaches the needy. As pointed out in Chapter 2, the United Nations Development Programme says that 'the richest 40% of the developing world population receives more than twice as much aid per capita as the poorest 40%'[19] Much international assistance is handled wastefully or is used for political purposes rather than for meeting needs.[20] International assistance is intended to serve a wide range of purposes, and not just helping the needy. UNICEF observes that

> ... to a large extent, the size and shape of today's aid programmes remain frozen in the pattern of the cold war era. About 25% of United States foreign assistance is military aid and for fiscal year 1994 more than 25% of non-military aid is earmarked for Egypt, Israel, and the nations of the former Soviet Union – leaving only about $6.5 billion for the rest of the developing world. ... Only about 25% of all aid ... goes to the ten countries in the world that are home to 75% of the world's poor.[21]

Careful distinctions must be made. Most assistance does in fact go to poorer countries, and it is not based simply on the donor's interest in the receiving countries as trading partners. A recent study shows that 'the concentration of aid on the [least developed countries], and on poorer states generally, reflected a choice to send aid to poor states rather than to economically important ones, and it was apparent in the aid programs of virtually all donors.'[22] But the aid does not necessarily go to the extremely poor people in those poor countries. There has been a strong trend away from direct relief for those in need and in favor of development assistance. The development agencies focus on entrepreneurial activities and projects that benefit middle and upper classes. When development assistance is specifically focused on relieving poverty, it usually goes to those among the poor who are most capable of succeeding in development projects. Assistance is viewed as a kind of investment, and thus moves toward the more powerful among the poor rather than the more needy. Thus, those who are the worst off get little benefit from programs of international assistance. The developmentalist response, while useful, does not address urgent current needs. The result is a form of global *triage*, with those least able to help themselves being abandoned to their fates.

The same sort of issue arises with regard to social welfare programs within nations. Many of us agree that people who are down and out should be given temporary assistance so that they can get back on their own feet. At the same time, we don't like to see families permanently on welfare, 'on the dole,' and certainly no one wants to see welfare continue in families generation after generation. Thus there is an emphasis on schooling, employment training, and limiting the length of time for which people can collect welfare payments. This is the basis of President Clinton's efforts to 'end welfare as we know it.' This attempt to build self-sufficiency corresponds to the developmentalist approach internationally. The slogans are familiar: A 'hand up' is preferable to a 'handout.' Rather than give a needy person a fish, it is better to teach that person how to fish.

Of course. But while agreeing with the merits of the developmentalist approach, we should remember that there are some people who do not have the capacity for self-sufficiency. There are some people who are blind or crippled or severely retarded who cannot take care of themselves. There are some people who live in social circumstances in which they do not have decent opportunites, as in cases in which peasants have been forced off land that is now controlled by and for foreign corporations. It is not always the case that with some education and good motivation, people will be able to 'make it.' Many poor people, in the United States as well as in poor countries, are employed and work very hard, but for meager wages.

Certainly the failures are sometimes in individuals, but they are sometimes at least in part in their social circumstances as well. One should not be too quick to 'blame the victim.'[23] The weak and those who do not have decent opportunities should not be abandoned in the rush to celebrate the virtues of self-sufficiency. Society should be prepared to help care for its weakest members without imposing performance requirements on them. There is a humanitarian element in assistance programs both within nations and internationally, but the strong urge to promote self-sufficiency often limits its reach.

Globally, there are efforts such as the World Food Programme's emergency measures, the United States Agency for International Development's (USAID) child survival program, and various programs sponsored by UNICEF that reach the most needy with assistance, but they are inadequately funded, and come nowhere close to meeting the needs. The proportion of international assistance that is used to meet needs directly is very small. When such assistance is provided it is usually in acute crisis situations such as famines, natural disasters, and armed conflicts. Most international assistance bypasses those who are chronically needy, or reaches them only indirectly.

International humanitarian assistance programs might become more orderly and effective if they were based on the principle that under specified conditions the needy have a *right* to humanitarian assistance. There may be objections to the idea that people should have a right to assistance, but surely no one wants assistance to be provided in ways that are chaotic, ineffective, and inefficient. In place of the current system for providing international assistance, it might be possible to design programs, using far less money, to assure that those who are most needy receive assistance *as a matter of right*. That would probably alleviate chronic misery far more effectively than the present system.

THE PRINCIPLE INTERNATIONALLY

The master question – *who should be entitled to what sort of assistance from whom under what conditions at whose expense?* – can be raised not only with respect to assistance within nations but also with respect to international assistance. What should the international community do in case of a severe flood in the Netherlands, a plane crash in Bangladesh, an epidemic in Peru, or genocide anywhere? What *may* the international community do? Should there be some conditions under which the international community *must* provide humanitarian assistance?

There is much discussion of international protection of human rights, but what does that mean? A 1990 brochure from UNICEF and the UN

Centre for Human Rights says in its title that *Children's Rights Need International Protection* and suggests that the new Convention on the Rights of the Child responds to that need. I don't agree that the convention establishes *international* rights – certainly not hard international rights. If one party has a hard right to something, some other party must have the duty to provide it. Children's rights would really be international only if, upon failure of a national government to do what needed to be done to fulfill those rights, the international community was *obligated* to step in to do what was necessary – with no excuses. There is now no mechanism and no commitment to do that. The international community provides humanitarian assistance in many different circumstances, but it is not required to do so. Currently, 'international law imposes no obligation on States to respond to requests for assistance or to make offers of contributions for relief operations in other countries.'[24] And 'there is still no international convention setting out obligations of States concerning the donation or acceptance of humanitarian assistance or regulating the coordination of relief in peacetime.'[25]

The international human rights instruments are concerned primarily with the responsibilities of States Parties to their own people, not to people elsewhere. Article 11 of the *International Covenant on Economic, Social, and Cultural Rights* does require States Parties individually and through international cooperation to take the measures needed to implement 'the fundamental right of everyone to be free from hunger,' so the language does in fact speak of international obligations. In practice, however, there is no clear, hard duty with corresponding measures to assure accountability. There is no international history of case law with respect to nutrition rights. There is no hard international law with respect to nutrition rights.

The international community should take responsibility and not allow small children to be sacrificed when their governments are unwilling or unable to fulfill their needs. The principle advocated in Chapter 8 should apply globally as well as locally: *There should be a recognized legal obligation of the international community to provide services to assure that every child is adequately nourished.* After all, children of particular nations are also children of the world. There could be an international agreement that certain kinds of international assistance programs *must* be provided, say, to children in nations in which children's mortality rates exceed a certain level.

This international obligation to provide assistance should stand unconditionally where national governments, or more generally, those in power, consent to receiving the assistance. The obligation must be mitigated, however, where those in power refuse the assistance and delivering the assistance would require facing extraordinary risks.

In the rings of responsibility image described in Chapter 1, the international community is the outer ring, the last resort in looking after the well-being of children. The very outermost ring is comprised of the international governmental organizations (IGOs). Just inside that ring are the international nongovernmental organizations (INGOs). The international bodies' task is not to deliver services to children directly but, to the extent possible, to empower agencies in the inner rings. What can the international community do practically to help assure that all agencies in the inner rings do what they can to assure that children are adequately nourished?

INTERNATIONAL NUTRITION RIGHTS

International humanitarian law clearly asserts that hunger is not to be used as an instrument of warfare.[26] As we know from Bosnia, Cambodia, Ethiopia, Nigeria, Somalia, Sudan, and many other places, nutrition rights have not been honored in conflict situations. In his opening address at the International Conference on Nutrition, Pope John Paul II articulated the duty that should be acknowledged:

Wars between nations and civil conflicts should not be allowed to condemn defenceless civilians to die of hunger for selfish or partisan reasons. In such instances, we must in any case ensure that food and health aid get through, by removing all obstacles, including those arising from arbitrary recourse to the principle of non-interference in a country's internal affairs. The conscience of humanity, now backed by the provisions of international humanitarian law, demands compulsory humanitarian intervention when the survival of entire ethnic groups and populations is seriously compromised: this is a duty for nations and for the international community ...

The idea of *compulsory* humanitarian intervention is very new, one that is yet to be considered seriously by the international community. Before insisting on such intervention in difficult conflict situations, however, the international community should first learn how to intervene in orderly ways in non-conflict situations.

Consider the recent history of arrangements for providing food supplies in emergencies. In 1975 the United Nations General Assembly established the International Emergency Food Reserve (IEFR) to provide a rapid-response facility. The minimum annual target for the IEFR was set at 500 000 tons of cereals, to be placed at the disposal of the World Food Programme for urgent, unconditional use in emergencies:

> In actual practice, however, the IEFR has been seriously circumscribed by (among other things) donors too often pledging *ad hoc*; earmarking for specific countries only; and designating the source of purchase and/or type of commodity from which WFP must procure against a pledge. The further requirement of a number of donors for case-by-case approval of use of their IEFR pledges causes serious delays in even starting to move food towards an emergency. Average response time now often exceeds three months. WFP has repeatedly had to resort, in emergencies, to borrowing money from shipments intended for food for development (including school-feeding) with disastrous consequences for those projects.
>
> Another very serious handicap is that the IEFR does not receive enough straight cash to cover anything like the full needs in two other vital elements of emergency food aid – ability to buy supplementary commodities from wherever needed to ensure that recipients have a minimally balanced diet, and money enough to actually transport food to them.[27]

These difficulties might be overcome if IEFR supplies were to be provided on the basis that under certain explicitly specified conditions the needy had a right to assistance. The entire program could be rationalized on a contractual basis, with donors asked to subscribe over a sustained period. Through this contract, they would forego direct operational control, and would instead be asked to agree to the specified principles of operation.

Nations that wanted to maintain control over their contributions would have to give directly to the receiving nations without going through the IEFR system. Some current contributors, seeing that they would have less direct control under this new method for providing emergency food supplies, might be less willing to donate to the effort. However, their withdrawal might be more than compensated by a new willingness of nations to support a program that is well managed and truly effective.

A new regime of international nutrition rights would not involve massive international transfers of food. Its main function would be to assure that nations become willing and able to address the problem of malnutrition among their own people using the resources within their own nations.

IMPLEMENTATION INTERNATIONALLY

If the idea that there should be international nutrition rights is accepted in principle, we must attend to the issue of implementation: how do we make it happen?

In advancing nutrition rights within nations it is wise to work with nutrition programs that are already in place. In many cases the rules under which people have access to these programs can be revised to guarantee that those who are most needy are assured of receiving services. Similarly, we should recognize that there already are institutional arrangements for dealing with nutrition issues at the global level and see how their methods of work can be adapted to advance nutrition rights.

The most prominent IGOs concerned with nutrition are the Food and Agriculture Organization of the United Nations (FAO), the World Food Council (WFC), the World Food Programme (WFP), the International Fund for Agricultural Development (IFAD), the World Health Organization (WHO), and the United Nations Children's Fund (UNICEF). They are governed by boards comprised of member states. Responsibility for coordinating nutrition activities among these and other IGOs in the United Nations system rests with the Administrative Committee on Coordination/Subcommittee on Nutrition (ACC/SCN). Representatives of bilateral donor agencies such as the Swedish International Development Authority (SIDA) and the United States Agency for International Development (USAID) also participate in ACC/SCN activities. There are also numerous international nongovernmental organizations (INGOs) concerned with nutrition.

The main role of the IGOs is not to feed people directly but to help nations use their own resources more effectively. In much the same way, a new regime of international nutrition rights would not involve massive international transfers of food. Its main function would be to press and help national governments address the problem of malnutrition among their own people using the food, care, and health resources within their own nations. There may always be a need for a global emergency food facility to help in emergency situations that are beyond the capacity of individual nations, but a different kind of design is needed for dealing with chronic malnutrition. Moreover, as chronic malnutrition is addressed more effectively, nations would increase their capacity for dealing with emergency situations on their own. Over time the need for emergency assistance from the outside would decline.

The IGOs could use their leverage to press for the establishment of nutrition rights within the nations they serve. For example, the World

Food Programme could make it known that in providing food supplies for development it will favor those nations that are working to establish clear nutrition rights for the most needy in their nations.[28] All of the IGOs could be especially generous in providing assistance to those nations that create national laws and national agencies devoted to implementing nutrition rights. Poor nations, relieved of some of the burden of providing material resources, would be more willing to create programs for recognizing nutrition rights. Such pledges by international agencies could be viewed as a precursor to recognition of a genuine international duty to recognize and effectively implement rights to adequate nutrition.

The IGOs could encourage and support nations in conducting national workshops on children's nutrition rights of the sort described in Chapter 8. With very modest incentives, many nations might be willing to review their existing nutrition programs to determine ways in which the rules governing access to those programs might be improved through careful use of the law.

A GLOBAL ACTION PLAN

The IGOs are concerned with the problems of famine and chronic malnutrition, but these are only a part of their broad agendas. For example, the FAO gives a great deal of attention to the interests of food producers, and WHO deals with the full range of health issues. UNICEF, too, addresses a very broad range of subjects. Moreover, the division of responsibilities among the IGOs for dealing with nutrition has not yet been worked out adequately. Thus malnutrition has not yet gotten the commitment of attention and resources needed to really solve the problem. The concept of moving progressively toward a global regime of nutrition rights could be the basis for working out *a global program of concerted action by the IGOs.*

How can the world deal decisively with the problem of widespread chronic malnutrition? Imagine that a global meeting was held in which all governments and concerned international organizations were represented. Imagine further that they were determined to end malnutrition in the world and wanted to draw up concrete action plans toward that end. We can also suppose that they agreed to commit resources to the effort at a rate up to, but no greater than, the overall amounts now spent on food- and nutrition-related international assistance programs.

What might the action plan look like? In some respects it would echo the *World Declaration on Nutrition* and the *Plan of Action for Nutrition* approved by the world's governments in Rome in December 1992.

Certainly the early parts of those texts describing the nature of the problem and the seriousness of the governments' concerns would be similar. The big differences would be in the operational sections specifying who exactly is making what commitments to do what, in what time frame, with what sorts of accountability. The conference participants in 1992 went as far as they could go, but in the new agreement contemplated here we would look for a business-like contract, with clearly elaborated responsibilities and commitments.

At the 1992 meeting the major parties were the nations of the world, and the concerned IGOs stood to the side as facilitators of the meeting. The focus was on the formulation of national plans of action, not a global plan of action. In the new negotiations envisioned here the IGOs would be at center-stage, working out *their* roles in the new nutrition rights regime. They would have to work out the division of responsibilities among them so that each could make its own best contribution to assuring that people are adequately nourished. Of course it would always have to be recognized that the IGOs are not independent agents, but are instruments of, and accountable to, their member nations.

Strategically, the program of action would begin the work of alleviating malnutrition with the very worst cases, and then as those problems were solved, move to dealing with less severe situations. Rules would be established so that the targets of action would be selected on the basis of clear measures of need, thus reducing the possibilities for making politicized selections. The IGOs could continue to carry out other functions, but with regard to the challenge of addressing serious malnutrition their actions would be coordinated under the new global program of action, the contract adopted at the meeting.

At the core of the new arrangement would be the establishment of a new global body that had responsibility for seeing to it that the terms of the contract negotiated at the meeting were carried out. This new agency, created by national governments working together with the IGOs, would see to it that those that made agreements, and thus incurred obligations, carried out their obligations in fact.

The IGOs would support national governments in dealing with malnutrition among their own people. Local and international nongovernmental organizations would be a part of the system in that they would help to identify and report serious cases of malnutrition, they would help to provide services, and they would monitor to make sure that national and local agencies carried out their work of alleviating malnutrition.

It would be agreed that where there was serious malnutrition and national agencies could not or would not solve the problem, the IGOs would have the authority and the duty to become directly involved. The nature of that involvement would have to be worked out. Concrete programs of action would have to be designed to fit particular cases, but the planning exercise would establish general procedures and guidelines for action. Consideration would have to be given to issues of consent, costs, logistics, risks, and so on. Intervention would not be automatic and indiscriminate, but there would be an agency in place that would be prepared to assess the situation and act under suitable internationally accepted guidelines. Initially, the international community would have a firm duty to assist only where there was consent from governments of the nations receiving assistance.

There have been comparable global planning efforts before, not only the *World Declaration* and *Plan of Action on Nutrition* formulated at the International Conference on Nutrition held in Rome in December 1992, but also the *International Undertaking on World Food Security* of 1974, the *Plan of Action on World Food Security* of 1979, the *Agenda for Consultations and Possible Action to deal with Acute and Large-scale Food Shortages* of 1981, and the *World Food Security Compact* of 1985.[29] The major differences between these earlier efforts and the Global Action Plan outlined here are the prominent roles of the international governmental organizations as actors, the sharply focused purpose and program of action, the clear contractual commitments, and most importantly, the creation of a central agency responsible for assuring that the commitments are honored. Moreover, while previous plans had somewhat obscure and difficult purposes, the objective of reducing malnutrition among children worldwide to virtually zero is a clear and achievable objective.

Of course the idea of ending serious malnutrition in the world through establishment of a regime of hard international nutrition rights is idealistic. Nevertheless, the idea can be useful in setting the direction of action. We can think of the IGOs as having specific duties with regard to the fulfillment of nutrition rights. We can move progressively toward the ideal by inviting IGOs to establish clear rules and procedures which they would follow *as if* they were firm duties.[30]

SOVEREIGNTY AND CIVILIZATION

I have argued that as a matter of principle, there should be a recognized legal obligation of the international community to provide services to assure that children are adequately nourished. Some may feel that accepting such a principle would be an unacceptable derogation of national sovereignty; that it would compromise the integrity of nations and the very foundation of the international system.

This objection is based on an inappropriate interpretation of sovereignty. Sovereign entities often have good reasons to make commitments, and thus constrain their own freedom of action. Garrett Hardin, in the *Tragedy of the Commons*, makes it clear that effective management of the commons requires mutual constraints, mutually agreed upon.[31] Any negotiated contract involves accepting limitations on one's freedom of action in exchange for some larger good. The basis of citizenship is that there are real advantages to accepting duties. There should be duties and accountability at the highest levels as well as the lowest.

Internationally recognized and implemented rights and duties cannot be imposed. They must be established through agreement of the nations of the world. Reaching such agreement would be action not against sovereignty but against global anarchy. It is important to move toward a global rule of law under which there is acknowledged global responsibility.

Where humanitarian assistance is provided on a purely discretionary basis, there is no acknowledgment of a responsibility to assist, and the assistance that is provided is likely to be handled politically and wastefully. However, the gradual regularizing of assistance as reflected in United Nations resolutions is a mark of 'the development of what we may call global civil society, in which members of global society are starting to try to make the state system responsible.'[32] Regularized assistance to the needy under the law is a mark of civilization *within* nations. If we are to civilize relations *among* nations, international humanitarian assistance also should be regularized under the law.

In a new and better world order, in a global civil society, the international political economy will treat its weakest members in a more civilized way. It should be recognized that children everywhere have a right to adequate nutrition, and that consequently the international community has a positive obligation, recognized in law, to help fulfill that right. Critics will find a thousand reasons for arguing that international nutrition rights cannot work, but one consideration – malnourished children – is reason enough to make it work. Looking after our children internationally could be the leading edge of the project of civilizing the world order.

Appendix: Data on Children

The following data tables are drawn, with permission, from James P. Grant, *The State of the World's Children 1994* (New York: Oxford University Press, 1994), pp. 64–71. '..' means data not available. 'x' indicates data that refer to years or periods other than those specified in the column heading, differ from the standard definition, or refer to only part of a country. Key terms are defined as follows:

Under-five mortality rate

Number of deaths of children under five years of age per 1 000 live births. More specifically, this is the probability of dying between birth and exactly five years of age.

Infant mortality rate

Number of deaths of infants under one year of age per 1 000 live births. More specifically, this is the probability of dying between birth and exactly one year of age.

GNP

Gross national product, expressed in current United States dollars. GNP per capita growth rates are average annual growth rates that have been computed by fitting trend lines to the logarithmic values of GNP per capita at constant market prices for each year of the time period.

Life expectancy at birth

The number of years newborn children would live if subject to the mortality risks prevailing for the cross-section of population at the time of their birth.

Adult literacy rate

Percentage of persons aged 15 and over who can read and write.

Primary and secondary enrollment ratios

The gross enrollment ratio is the total number of children enrolled in a schooling level – whether or not they belong in the relevant age group for that level – expressed as a percentage of the total number of children in the relevant age group at that level. The net enrollment ratio is the total number of children enrolled in a schooling level who belong in the relevant age group, expressed as a percentage of the total number in that age group.

Income share

Percentage of private income received by the highest 20% and lowest 40% of households.

Low birth weight

Less than 2500 grams.

Underweight

Moderate and severe – below minus two standard deviations from median weight for age of reference population;
Severe – below minus three standard deviations from median weight for age of reference population.

Wasting

Moderate and severe – below minus two standard deviations from median weight for height of reference population.

Stunting

Moderate and severe – below minus two standard deviations from mediate height for age of reference population.

Total goiter rate

Percentage of children aged 6–11 with palpable or visible goiter. This is an indicator of iodine deficiency, which causes brain damage and mental retardation.

Access to health services

Percentage of the population that can reach appropriate local health services by the local means of transport in no more than one hour.

DPT

Diphtheria, pertussis (whooping cough) and tetanus.

ORT use

Percentage of all cases of diarrhea in children under five years of age treated with oral rehydration salts or an appropriate household solution.

Children reaching final grade of primary school

Percentage of the children entering the first grade of primary school who eventually reach the final grade.

Table A1: Basic indicators

	Under 5 mortality rate 1960	Under 5 mortality rate 1992	Infant mortality rate (under 1) 1960	Infant mortality rate (under 1) 1992	Total population (millions) 1992	Annual no. of births (thousands) 1992	Annual no. of under-5 deaths (thousands) 1992	GNP per capita (US$) 1991	Life expectancy at birth (years) 1992	Total adult literacy rate 1990	% of age-group enrolled in primary school (gross) 1986-91	% share of household income of 1980-91 lowest 40%	% share of household income of 1980-91 highest 20%
1 Niger	320	**320**	191	191	8.3	428	137	300	46	28	29	..	..
2 Angola	345	**292**	208	170	9.9	514	150	610x	46	42	95	..	..
3 Mozambique	331	**287**	190	167	14.9	683	196	80	47	33	58	..	..
4 Afghanistan	360	**257**	215	165	19.1	1031	265	280x	43	29	24	..	..
5 Sierra Leone	385	**249**	219	144	4.4	213	53	210	43	21	48	..	..
6 Guinea-Bissau	336	**239**	200	141	1.0	43	10	180	43	37	59	..	..
7 Guinea	337	**230**	203	135	6.1	313	72	460	44	24	37	..	..
8 Malawi	365	**226**	206	143	10.4	567	128	230	44	..	71	..	..
9 Rwanda	191	**222**	115	131	7.5	396	88	270	46	50	69	23	39
10 Mali	400	**220**	233	122	9.8	504	111	280	46	32	24	..	..
11 Liberia	288	**217**	192	146	2.8	132	29	450x	55	40	40x	..	..
12 Somalia	294	**211**	175	125	9.2	469	99	150x	47	24	15x	..	..
13 Chad	325	**209**	195	123	5.8	258	54	210	47	30	57	..	..
14 Eritrea	294	**208**	175	123	3.3	140	29	120	47	..	..	..	..
15 Ethiopia	294	**208**	175	123	53.0	2627	547	120	47	24x	38	..	41
16 Mauritania	321	**206**	191	118	2.1	100	21	510	48	34	51	40	..
17 Zambia	220	**202**	135	113	8.6	403	81	420x	45	73	93	11x	61x
18 Bhutan	324	**201**	203	131	1.6	65	13	180	48	38	26	..	..
19 Nigeria	204	**191**	122	114	115.7	5259	1004	340	52	51	72	21	..
20 Zaire	286	**188**	167	121	39.9	1912	359	230x	52	72	78	..	..

Table A1: Basic indicators continued

	Under 5 mortality rate		Infant mortality rate (under 1)		Total population (millions) 1992	Annual no. of births (thousands) 1992	Annual no. of under-5 deaths (thousands) 1992	GNP per capita (US$) 1991	Life expectancy at birth (years) 1992	Total adult literacy rate 1990	% of age-group enrolled in primary school (gross) 1986–91	% share of household income of 1980–91	
	1960	1992	1960	1992								lowest 40%	highest 20%
21 Uganda	218	185	129	111	18.7	960	178	170	42	48	76	21	42
22 Cambodia	217	184	146	117	8.8	349	64	200x	51	35	:	:	:
23 Burundi	255	179	151	108	5.8	271	48	210	48	50	72	:	:
24 Central African Rep.	294	179	174	105	3.2	142	25	390	47	38	67	:	:
25 Yemen	378	177	214	107	12.5	611	108	520	52	39	78	:	:
26 Tanzania, U. Rep. of	249	176	147	111	27.8	1351	238	100	51	:	63	8	63
27 Ghana	215	170	128	103	16.0	671	114	400	56	60	75	18	44
28 Madagascar	364	168	219	110	12.8	589	99	210	55	80	92	:	:
29 Sudan	292	166	170	100	26.7	1128	187	420x	52	27	49	:	:
30 Gabon	287	158	171	95	1.2	53	8	3780	53	61	:	:	:
31 Lesotho	204	156	138	108	1.8	64	10	580	60	:	107	11	61
32 Burkina Faso	318	150	183	101	9.5	449	67	290	48	18	36	:	:
33 Benin	310	147	184	88	4.9	243	36	380	46	23	61	:	:
34 Senegal	303	145	174	90	7.7	334	48	720	49	38	58	:	:
35 Lao Peo. Dem. Rep.	233	145	155	98	4.5	205	30	220	51	84x	104	:	:
36 Pakistan	221	137	137	95	124.8	5117	701	400	59	35	37	21	40
37 Togo	264	137	155	86	3.8	169	23	410	55	43	103	:	:
38 Haiti	270	133	182	87	6.8	240	32	370	56	53	84	6x	48x
39 Nepal	279	128	186	90	20.6	778	100	180	53	26	86	22	40
40 Bangladesh	247	127	151	97	119.3	4623	587	220	53	35	73	23	39

Table A1: Basic indicators continued

		Under 5 mortality rate		Infant mortality rate (under 1)		Total population (millions) 1992	Annual no. of births (thousands) 1992	Annual no. of under-5 deaths (thousands) 1992	GNP per capita (US$) 1991	Life expectancy at birth (years) 1992	Total adult literacy rate 1990	% of age-group enrolled in primary school (gross) 1986–91	% share of household income of 1980–91	
		1960	1992	1960	1992								lowest 40%	highest 20%
41	Côte d'Ivoire	300	124	165	91	12.9	650	81	690	52	54	75x	19	42
42	India	236	124	144	83	879.5	25900	3212	330	60	48	97	21	41
43	Bolivia	252	118	152	80	7.5	261	31	650	61	78	82	12	58x
44	Cameroon	264	117	156	74	12.2	499	58	850	56	54	101	..	..
45	Myanmar	237	113	158	83	43.7	1431	162	220x	57	81	127	..	..
46	Indonesia	216	111	127	71	191.2	5146	571	610	62	82	117	21	42
47	Congo	220	110	143	82	2.4	107	12	1120	52	57	..	..	..
48	Libyan Arab Jamahiriya	269	104	160	70	4.9	206	21	5310x	63	64	..	..	..
49	Turkmenistan	..	91	..	72	3.9	140	13	1700	66	..	..	23	..
50	Turkey	217	87	161	70	58.4	1653	144	1780	67	81	110	11x	55x
51	Zimbabwe	181	86	109	60	10.6	434	37	650	56	67	117	..	..
52	Tajikistan	..	85	..	65	5.7	229	19	1050	69	..	..	23	..
53	Iraq	171	80	117	64	19.3	753	60	1500x	66	60	96	..	..
54	Mongolia	185	80	128	61	2.3	79	6	780x	63	..	98	..	..
55	Namibia	206	79	129	62	1.5	66	5	1460	58	..	94	..	..
56	Papua New Guinea	248	77	165	54	4.1	136	11	830	56	52	71	..	..
57	Guatemala	205	76	137	55	9.7	380	29	930	64	55	77	8	63
58	Nicaragua	209	76	140	54	4.0	163	12	460	66	..	98	12x	58x
59	Kenya	202	74	120	51	25.2	1111	82	340	59	69	94	9	61
60	Algeria	243	72	148	60	26.3	901	65	1980	66	57	95	..	..

Table A1: Basic indicators continued

		Under 5 mortality rate		Infant mortality rate (under 1)		Total population (millions) 1992	Annual no. of births (thousands) 1992	Annual no. of under-5 deaths (thousands) 1992	GNP per capita (US$) 1991	Life expectancy at birth (years) 1992	Total adult literacy rate 1990	% of age-group enrolled in primary school (gross) 1986–91	% share of household income of 1980–91	
		1960	1992	1960	1992								lowest 40%	highest 20%
61	South Africa	126	**70**	89	53	39.8	1253	88	2560	63	76x	..	..	..
62	Uzbekistan	..	**68**	..	56	21.5	736	50	1350	69	..	..	22	..
63	Brazil	181	**65**	118	54	154.1	3626	236	2940	66	81	108x	7	68
64	Peru	236	**65**	143	46	22.5	658	43	1070	64	85	126	14	51
65	El Salvador	210	**63**	130	47	5.4	182	11	1080	66	73	78	8x	66x
66	Morocco	215	**61**	133	50	26.3	854	52	1030	63	50	68	17	46
67	Kyrgyzstan	..	**60**	..	49	4.5	135	8	1550	66	..	..	21	..
68	Philippines	102	**60**	73	46	65.2	1992	120	730	65	90	111	17	48
69	Ecuador	180	**59**	115	47	11.1	332	20	1000	66	86	118	..	..
70	Botswana	170	**58**	117	45	1.3	51	3	2530	61	74	110	6	66
71	Honduras	203	**58**	137	45	5.5	205	12	580	66	73	108	9	64
72	Iran, Islamic Rep. of	233	**58**	145	44	61.6	2473	143	2170	67	54	112	..	..
73	Egypt	258	**55**	169	43	54.8	1732	95	610	61	48	98	21x	41x
74	Azerbaijan	..	**53**	..	37	7.3	189	10	1670	71	..	..	..	..
75	Dominican Rep.	152	**50**	104	42	7.5	214	11	940	67	83	95	12	56
76	Kazakhstan	..	**50**	..	43	17.0	351	18	2470	69	..	..	..	..
77	Viet Nam	219	**49**	147	37	69.5	2039	100	240x	64	88	102x	..	..
78	Lebanon	91	**44**	68	35	2.8	78	3	2150x	68	80	100x	..	..
79	China	209	**43**	140	35	1188.0	25057	1077	370	71	73	135	17	42
80	Saudi Arabia	292	**40**	170	35	15.9	574	23	7820	69	62	78	..	..

186

Table A1: Basic indicators continued

		Under 5 mortality rate 1960	1992	Infant mortality rate (under 1) 1960	1992	Total population (millions) 1992	Annual no. of births (thousands) 1992	Annual no. of under-5 deaths (thousands) 1992	GNP per capita (US$) 1991	Life expectancy at birth (years) 1992	Total adult literacy rate 1990	% of age-group enrolled in primary school (gross) 1986–91	% share of household income 1980–91 lowest 40%	highest 20%
81	Syrian. Arab Rep.	201	40	136	34	13.3	569	23	1160	67	65	109	:	:
82	Tunisia	244	38	163	32	8.4	230	9	1500	68	65	116	16	46
83	Moldova	:	36	31	4.4	4.4	69	2	2170	68	:	:	23	:
84	Albania	151	34	112	28	3.3	76	3	790x	73	:	98	:	:
85	Armenia	:	34	:	29	3.5	79	3	2150	72	:	:	22	:
86	Paraguay	90	34	66	28	4.5	151	5	1270	67	90	107	:	:
87	Korea, Dem. Peo. Rep.	120	33	85	25	22.6	553	18	970x	71	:	106	:	:
88	Mexico	141	33	98	28	88.2	2491	82	3030	70	88	112	12	56
89	Thailand	146	33	101	27	56.1	1176	39	1570	69	93	85	16	51
90	Russian Federation	:	32	:	28	148.3	1809	58	3220	69	:	:	:	:
91	Oman	300	31	180	24	1.6	67	2	6120	69	:	103	:	:
92	Jordan	149	30	103	25	4.3	171	5	1050	68	80	104	:	:
93	Georgia	:	29	:	25	5.5	84	2	1640	73	:	:	21	:
94	Romania	82	28	69	23	23.3	363	10	1390	70	:	91	:	:
95	Latvia	:	26	:	22	2.7	37	1	3410	71	:	:	:	:
96	Ukraine	:	25	:	21	51.9	633	16	2340	70	:	:	21	:
97	Argentina	68	24	57	22	33.1	673	16	2790	71	95	111	14x	51x
98	Estonia	:	24	:	20	1.6	22	1	3830	71	100x	:	20	:
99	Mauritius	84	24	62	20	1.1	20	0	2410	70	:	106	12x	46x
100	Venezuela	70	24	53	20	20.2	531	13	2730x	70	88	92	14	50

Table A1: Basic indicators continued

	Under 5 mortality rate		Infant mortality rate (under 1)		Total population (millions) 1992	Annual no. of births (thousands) 1992	Annual no. of under-5 deaths (thousands) 1992	GNP per capita (US$) 1991	Life expectancy at birth (years) 1992	Total adult literacy rate 1990	% of age-group enrolled in primary school (gross) 1986–91	% share of household income of 1980–91	
	1960	1992	1960	1992								lowest 40%	highest 20%
101 Belarus	..	23	..	20	10.3	136	3	3110	71	..	..	22	..
102 Trinidad and Tobago	73	22	61	19	1.3	30	1	3670	71	95x	95	13x	50x
103 United Arab Emirates	240	22	160	18	1.7	35	1	19860x	71	..	116	..	..
104 Uruguay	47	22	41	20	3.1	54	1	2840	72	96	106	18x	44x
105 Yugoslavia (former)	113	22	92	19	23.9	338	7	3060x	72	93	95	16	44
106 Colombia	132	20	82	17	33.4	809	16	1260	69	87	110	13	53
107 Lithuania	..	20	..	17	3.8	56	1	2710	73	98x	..	..	..
108 Panama	104	20	67	18	2.5	63	1	2130	73	88	107	8	60
109 Bulgaria	70	20	49	16	9.0	111	2	1840	72		96		
110 Sri Lanka	130	19	90	15	17.7	371	7	500	71	88	107	13	56
111 Malaysia	105	19	73	14	18.8	545	10	2520	71	78	93	13	54
112 Chile	138	18	107	15	13.6	309	6	2160	72	93	98	11	63
113 Kuwait	128	17	89	14	2.0	54	1	16150x	75	73	100	..	..
114 Poland	70	16	62	14	38.4	550	9	1790	72	..	98	23	36
115 Hungary	57	16	51	15	10.5	127	2	2720	70	99x	94	26	34

Table A1: Basic indicators continued

		Under 5 mortality rate		Infant mortality rate (under 1)		Total population (millions) 1992	Annual no. of births (thousands) 1992	Annual no. of under-5 deaths (thousands) 1992	GNP per capita (US$) 1991	Life expectancy at birth (years) 1992	Total adult literacy rate 1990	% of age-group enrolled in primary school (gross) 1986-91	% share of household income of 1980-91	
		1960	1992	1960	1992								lowest 40%	highest 20%
116	Costa Rica	112	16	80	14	3.2	85	1	1850	76	93	102	13	51
117	Jamaica	76	14	58	12	2.5	55	1	1380	73	98	105	16	48
118	Slovakia	..	14	..	12	5.4	79	1	..	72	..		..	..
119	Portugal	112	13	81	11	9.9	114	2	5930	75	85	119	..	..
120	Czech Republic	..	12	..	11	10.4	135	2	..	72	..	..	..	..
121	Cuba	50	11	39	10	10.8	190	2	1170x	76	94	103	..	..
122	Israel	39	11	32	9	5.1	110	1	11950	76	92x	93	18	40
123	Belgium	35	10	31	9	10.0	122		18950	76	..	102	22	36
124	USA	30	10	26	9	255.2	4078	42	22240	76	..	105	16	42
125	New Zealand	26	10	22	8	3.5	60	1	12350	76	..	106	16	45
126	Italy	50	10	44	8	57.8	578	6	18520	77	97	97	19	41
127	Spain	57	9	46	8	39.1	422	4	12450	77	95	109	19	40
128	Greece	64	9	53	8	10.2	106	1	6340	77	93	100	..	..
129	Korea, Rep. of	124	9	88	8	44.2	723	7	6330	71	96	107	20x	42x
130	Austria	43	9	37	7	7.8	91	1	20140	76	..	103	..	..
131	France	34	9	29	7	57.2	773	7	20380	77	..	111	18	41
132	United Kingdom	27	9	23	7	57.7	801	7	16550	76	..	107	17	40
133	Australia	24	9	20	7	17.6	265	2	17050	77	..	105	16	42
134	Switzerland	27	9	22	7	6.8	86	1	33610	78	..		17	45
135	Germany	40	8	34	7	80.3	912	8	23650	76	..	105	20	39

Table A1: Basic indicators continued

		Under 5 mortality rate		Infant mortality rate (under 1)		Total population (millions) 1992	Annual no. of births (thousands) 1992	Annual no. of under-5 deaths (thousands) 1992	GNP per capita (US$) 1991	Life expectancy at birth (years) 1992	Total adult literacy rate 1990	% of age-group enrolled in primary school (gross) 1986–91	% share of household income of 1980–91	
		1960	1992	1960	1992								lowest 40%	highest 20%
136	Canada	33	**8**	28	7	27.4	391	3	20440	77	::	105	18	40
137	Denmark	25	**8**	22	7	5.2	64	1	23700	76	::	98	17	39
138	Norway	23	**8**	19	6	4.3	63	0	24220	77	::	99	19	37
139	Netherlands	22	**7**	18	6	15.2	207	2	18780	77	::	117	20	38
140	Sweden	20	**7**	16	6	8.7	120	1	25110	78	::	107	21	37
141	Hong Kong	52	**7**	38	6	5.8	75	1	13430	78	::	105	16	47
142	Singapore	40	**7**	31	6	2.8	44	0	14210	74	83x	110	15	49
143	Finland	28	**7**	22	6	5.0	64	0	23980	76	::	99	18	38
144	Japan	40	**6**	31	4	124.5	1390	8	26930	79	::	101	22	38
145	Ireland	36	**6**	31	5	3.5	50	0	11120	75	::	100	::	::

Countries listed in descending order of their under-five mortality rates (shown in bold type).

Table A2: Nutrition

	% of Infants with low birth weight 1990	% of children (1986–92) who are:			% of children (1980–92) suffering from:				Total goiter rate (6–11 years) (%) 1980–92	Daily per capita calorie supply as a % of requirements 1988–90	% share of total household consumption (1980–85)	
		exclusively breastfed (0–3 months)	breastfed with complementary food (6–9 months)	still breastfeeding (20–23 months)	underweight (0–4 years) moderate & severe	severe	wasting (12–23 months) moderate & severe	stunting (24–59 months) moderate & severe			all food	cereals
1 Niger	15	:	:	:	49	:	23x	38x	9	95	:	:
2 Angola	19	3	83	53	:	:	:	:	7	80	:	:
3 Mozambique	20	:	:	:	:	:	:	:	20	77	:	:
4 Afghanistan	20	:	:	:	:	:	:	:	20	72	:	:
5 Sierra Leone	17	:	94	41	29	:	18	39	7	83	56	22
6 Guinea-Bissau	20				23x				19	97		
7 Guinea	21	:	:	:	:	:	:	:	19	97	:	:
8 Malawi	20	3	89		27	8	11	62	13	88	30	9
9 Rwanda	17	90	75		29x	6x	9x	58x	49	82	29	10
10 Mali	17	8	45	44	31x	9x	16	34x	29	96	57	22
11 Liberia	:	15	56	26	20x	:	:	:	6	98	:	:
12 Somalia	16	:	:	:	:	:	:	:	7	81	:	:
13 Chad	:	:	:	:	:	:	:	:	15	73	:	:
14 Eritrea	:	:	:	:	:	:	:	:	:	:	:	:
15 Ethiopia	16	74	:	35	48x	16x	12x	63x	22	73	49	24
16 Mauritania	11	12	39	:	48	:	18	65	51x	106	:	:
17 Zambia	13	13	88	34	25	6	10	47	25	87	36	8
18 Bhutan	:	:	:	:	38	:	4x	56x	56x	128	:	:
19 Nigeria	16	2	52	43	36	12	16	54	10	93	48	18
20 Zaire	15	:	:	:	:	:	:	:	9	96	:	:

Table A2: Nutrition continued

	% of Infants with low birth weight 1990	% of children (1986–92) who are exclusively breastfed (0–3 months)	breastfed with complementary food (6–9 months)	still breast-feeding (20–23 months)	underweight (0–4 years) moderate & severe	severe	wasting (12–23 months) moderate & severe	stunting (24–59 months) moderate & severe	Total goiter rate (6–11 years) (%) 1980–92	Daily per capita calorie supply as a % of requirements 1988–90	% share of total household consumption (1980–85) all food	cereals
21 Uganda	:	70	67	39	23x	5x	4x	51x	7	93	:	:
22 Cambodia	:	:	:	:	:	:	:	:	15	96	:	:
23 Burundi		89	66	73	:	10x	10	60x	42	84	:	:
24 Central African Rep.	15	:	:	:	38x	:	:	:	63	82	:	:
25 Yemen	19	15	51	:	30	4	17	49	32	:	:	:
26 Tanzania, U. Rep. of	14	32	59	57	29	7	10	58	37	95	64	32
27 Ghana	17	2	57	52	27	6	15	39	10	93	50	:
28 Madagascar	10	:	:	:	33x	8x	17	56x	24	95	59	26
29 Sudan	15	14	45	44	35x	7x	13x	32x	20	87	60	:
30 Gabon	:	:	:	:	:	:	:	:	5	104	:	:
31 Lesotho	11	:	:	:	16	2	7	23	16	93	:	:
32 Burkina Faso	21x	3	35	:	:	:	:	:	16	94	:	:
33 Benin	11	:	:	:	:	:	:	:	24	104	37	12
34 Senegal	11	7	68	37	22	2	8	30	12	98	49	15
35 Lao Peo. Dem. Rep.	18	:	:	:	37	:	20	44	25	111	:	:
36 Pakistan	25	25	29	52	40	14	11	60	32	99	37	12
37 Togo	20	10	86	68	24x	6x	10	37x	22	99	:	:
38 Haiti	15	:	:	:	37x	3x	17x	51x	4x	89	:	:
39 Nepal	:	:	:	:	:	:	:	:	44	100	57	38
40 Bangladesh	50	:	:	:	66	27	28	65	11	88	59	36

Table A2: Nutrition continued

		% of Infants with low birth weight 1990	% of children (1986–92) who are exclusively breastfed (0–3 months)	breastfed with complementary food (6–9 months)	still breast-feeding (20–23 months)	underweight (0–4 years) moderate & severe	underweight severe	wasting (12–23 months) moderate & severe	stunting (24–59 months) moderate & severe	Total goiter rate (6–11 years) (%) 1980–92	Daily per capita calorie supply as a % of requirements 1988–90	% share of total household consumption (1980–85) all food	cereals
41	Côte d'Ivoire	14x	:	:	:	12	2	17	20	6	111	39	13
42	India	33	:	:	:	63x	27x	:	65x	9	101	52	18
43	Bolivia	12	59	57	30	13x	3x	2	51x	21	84	33	:
44	Cameroon	13	7	77	35	14	3	7	32	26	95	24	7
45	Myanmar	16	:	:	:	32x	9x	:	:	18	114	:	:
46	Indonesia	14	53	76	62	40	:	:	:	28	121	48	21
47	Congo	16	43	:	27	24	:	13	33	8	103	37	16
48	Libyan Arab Jamahiriya	:	:	:	:	:	:	:	:	6	140	:	:
49	Turkmenistan	:	:	:	:	:	:	:	:	20	:	:	:
50	Turkey	8	:	:	:	26	6	:	:	36	127	40	9
51	Zimbabwe	14	11	94	26	12	2	2	31	42	94	40	9
52	Tajikistan	:	:	:	:	:	:	:	:	20	:	:	:
53	Iraq	15	:	:	:	12	2	:	:	7	128	:	:
54	Mongolia	10	:	:	:	12x	:	2x	29x	7	97	:	:
55	Namibia	12	22	65	23	26	6	13	29	35	:	:	:
56	Papua New Guinea	23	:	:	:	35	:	:	:	30	114	:	:
57	Guatemala	14	:	:	44	34x	8x	3	68x	20	103	36	10
58	Nicaragua	15	:	:	:	11	1	0	22	4	99	:	:
59	Kenya	16	24	87	46	14x	3x	5x	32x	7	89	38	16
60	Algeria	9	:	:	:	9	:	7	18	9	123	:	:

Table A2: Nutrition continued

	% of Infants with low birth weight 1990	% of children (1986–92) who are — exclusively breastfed (0–3 months)	breastfed with complementary food (6–9 months)	still breast-feeding (20–23 months)	% of children (1980–92) suffering from — underweight (0–4 years) moderate & severe	underweight severe	wasting (12–23 months) moderate & severe	stunting (24–59 months) moderate & severe	Total goiter rate (6–11 years) (%) 1980–92	Daily per capita calorie supply as a % of requirements 1988–90	% share of total household consumption (1980–85) all food	cereals
61 South Africa	:	:	:	:	:	:	:	:	2	128	34	:
62 Uzbekistan	:	:	:	:	:	:	:	:	18	:	:	:
63 Brazil	11	4	27	13	7	1	3	16	14x	114	35	9
64 Peru	11	40	62	36	11	2	3	46	36	87	35	8
65 El Salvador	11	:	:	:	15	:	3	36	25	102	33	12
66 Morocco	9	48	48	18	16x	4x	6	34x	20	125	38	12
67 Kyrgyzstan	:	:	:	:	:	:	:	:	20	:	:	:
68 Philippines	15	:	:	:	34	5	14	45	15	104	51	21
69 Ecuador	11	31	31	23	17	0	4	39	10	105	30	:
70 Botswana	8	41	82	23	15x	:	:	:	8	97	25	12
71 Honduras	9	:	:	:	21	4	2x	34x	9	98	39	:
72 Iran, Islamic Rep. of	9	:	:	:	:	:	:	:	30	125	37	10
73 Egypt	10	38	52	:	10	3	4	32	5	132	49	10
74 Azerbaijan	:	:	:	:	:	:	:	:	20	:	:	:
75 Dominican Rep.	16	10	23	7	10	2	1	22	:	102	46	13
76 Kazakhstan	:	:	:	:	:	:	:	:	20	:	:	:
77 Viet Nam	17	:	:	:	42	14	12x	49x	20	103	:	:
78 Lebanon	10	:	:	:	:	:	:	:	15	127	:	:
79 China	9	:	:	:	21x	3x	8x	41x	9	112	61	:
80 Saudi Arabia	7	:	:	:	:	:	:	:	:	121	:	:

Table A2: Nutrition continued

| | % of Infants with low birth weight 1990 | % of children (1986–92) who are: | | | % of children (1980–92) suffering from: | | | | Total goiter rate (6–11 years) (%) 1980–92 | Daily per capita calorie supply as a % of requirements 1988–90 | % share of total household consumption (1980–85) | |
		exclusively breastfed (0–3 months)	breastfed with complementary food (6–9 months)	still breast-feeding (20–23 months)	underweight (0–4 years) moderate & severe	severe	wasting (12–23 months) moderate & severe	stunting (24–59 months) moderate & severe			all food	cereals
81 Syrian Arab Rep.	11	..	..	..	..	..	..	..	73	126	..	..
82 Tunisia	8	21	53	25	10x	2x	4	23x	4	131	37	7
83 Moldova	..	..	..	..	..	..	..	..	..	..	..	..
84 Albania	7	..	..	..	..	..	..	..	41	107	..	..
85 Armenia	..	..	..	..	..	..	..	..	10	..	..	..
86 Paraguay	8	7	61	8	4	1	0	17	49	116	30	6
87 Korea, Dem. Peo. Rep.	..	..	..	..	..	..	..	..	..	121	..	..
88 Mexico	12	37	36	21	14	..	6x	22x	15	131	35	..
89 Thailand	13	4	69	34	26x	4x	10	28x	12	103	30	7
90 Russian Federation	..	..	..	..	..	..	..	..	..	..	..	..
91 Oman	10	..	..	..	23	5	11	22	..	..	..	..
92 Jordan	7	32	48	13	6	1	3	21	..	110	35	..
93 Georgia	..	..	..	..	..	..	..	..	20	..	..	..
94 Romania	7	..	..	..	..	..	..	..	10	116	..	..
95 Latvia	..	..	..	..	..	..	..	..	..	..	..	..
96 Ukraine	..	..	..	..	..	..	..	..	10	..	..	..
97 Argentina	8	..	..	..	..	..	..	..	8	131	35	4
98 Estonia	..	..	..	..	..	..	..	..	..	..	..	..
99 Mauritius	9	..	..	..	24	..	16x	22x	..	128	24	7
100 Venezuela	9	..	..	..	6	..	4	7	11	99	23	..

Table A2: Nutrition continued

Table A2: Nutrition continued

| | % of Infants with low birth weight 1990 | % of children (1986–92) who are | | | % of children (1980–92) suffering from: | | | | Total goiter rate (6–11 years) (%) 1980–92 | Daily per capita calorie supply as a % of requirements 1988–90 | % share of total household consumption (1980–85) | |
| | | exclusively breastfed (0–3 months) | breastfed with complementary food (6–9 months) | still breast-feeding (20–23 months) | underweight (0–4 years) | | wasting (12–23 months) moderate & severe | stunting (24–59 months) moderate & severe | | | all food | cereals |
					moderate & severe	severe						
101 Belarus	..	..	..	..	..	..	..	..	22	..	..	..
102 Trinidad and Tobago	10	10	39	16	7x	0x	5	4x	..	114	19	3
103 United Arab Emirates	6	..	..	26	..	..	..	..	..	..	..	..
104 Uruguay	8	..	..	..	7x	2x	..	16x	..	101	31	7
105 Yugoslavia (former)	..	..	..	..	..	..	..	..	5	140	27	4
106 Colombia	10	17	48	24	10x	2x	5	18x	10	106	29	..
107 Lithuania	..	..	..	..	..	..	..	..	..	..	..	..
108 Panama	10	..	..	..	16	..	7	24	13	98	38	7
109 Bulgaria	6	..	..	..	..	..	..	..	20	148	..	..
110 Sri Lanka	25	14	47	46	29x	2x	21x	39x	14	101	43	18
111 Malaysia	10	..	..	..	..	..	..	..	20	120	23	..
112 Chile	7	..	..	..	3x	0x	1	10x	9	102	29	7
113 Kuwait	7	..	..	..	6	..	2	14	..	..	..	..
114 Poland	..	..	..	..	..	..	..	..	10	131	29	4
115 Hungary	9	..	..	..	..	..	..	..	..	137	25	3
116 Costa Rica	6	..	..	..	6	..	3	8	3	121	33	8
117 Jamaica	11	..	..	..	7	1	6	7	..	114	36	14
118 Slovakia	..	..	..	..	..	..	..	..	..	..	..	..
119 Portugal	5	..	..	..	..	..	..	..	15	136	34	8
120 Czech Republic	..	..	..	..	..	..	..	..	..	..	..	..

Table A2: Nutrition continued

| | | % of Infants with low birth weight 1990 | % of children (1986–92) who are | | | % of children (1980–92) suffering from: | | | | | Total goiter rate (6–11 years) (%) 1980–92 | Daily per capita calorie supply as a % of requirements 1988–90 | % share of total household consumption (1980–85) | |
			exclusively breastfed (0–3 months)	breastfed with complementary food (6–9 months)	still breast-feeding (20–23 months)	underweight (0–4 years) moderate & severe	severe	wasting (12–23 months) moderate & severe	stunting (24–59 months) moderate & severe				all food	cereals
121	Cuba	8	:	:	:	:	:	1x	:		10	135	:	:
122	Israel	7	:	:	:	:	:	:	:		:	125	21	:
123	Belgium	6	:	:	:	:	:	:	:		5	149	15	2
124	USA	7	:	:	:	:	:	:	:		:	138	10	2
125	New Zealand	6	:	:	:	:	:	:	:		:	131	12	2
126	Italy	5	:	:	:	:	:	:	:		20	139	19	2
127	Spain	4	:	:	:	:	:	:	:		10	141	24	3
128	Greece	6	:	:	:	:	:	:	:		10	151	30	3
129	Korea, Rep. of	9	:	:	:	:	:	:	:		:	120	35	14
130	Austria	6	:	:	:	:	:	:	:		:	133	16	2
131	France	5	:	:	:	:	:	:	:		5	143	16	2
132	United Kingdom	7	:	:	:	:	:	:	:		:	130	12	2
133	Australia	6	:	:	:	:	:	:	:		:	124	13	2
134	Switzerland	5	:	:	:	:	:	:	:		:	130	17	:
135	Germany	:	:	:	:	:	:	:	:		10	:	12	2

197

Table A2: Nutrition continued

| | % of Infants with low birth weight 1990 | % of children (1986-92) who are | | | % of children (1980-92) suffering from: | | | | Total goiter rate (6-11 years) (%) 1980-92 | Daily per capita calorie supply as a % of requirements 1988-90 | % share of total household consumption (1980-85) | |
		exclusively breastfed (0-3 months)	breastfed with complementary food (6-9 months)	still breastfeeding (20-23 months)	underweight (0-4 years) moderate & severe	severe	wasting (12-23 months) moderate & severe	stunting (24-59 months) moderate & severe			all food	cereals
136 Canada	6	:	:	:	:	:	:	:	:	122	11	2
137 Denmark	6	:	:	:	:	:	:	:	5	135	13	2
138 Norway	4	:	:	:	:	:	:	:	:	120	15	2
139 Netherlands	:	:	:	:	:	:	:	:	3	114	13	2
140 Sweden	5	:	:	:	:	:	:	:	:	111	13	2
141 Hong Kong	8	:	:	:	:	:	:	:	:	125	12	1
142 Singapore	7	:	:	:	14x	:	:	:	:	136	19	:
143 Finland	4	:	:	:	:	:	:	:	:	113	16	3
144 Japan	6	:	:	:	:	:	:	:	:	125	17	4
145 Ireland	4	:	:	:	:	:	:	:	:	157	22	4

Countries listed in descending order of their 1992 under-five mortality rates (table 1).

Table A3: Health

		% of population with access to safe water 1988–91			% of population with access to adequate sanitation 1988–91			% of population with access to health services 1985–92			% fully immunized 1990–92 1-year-old children				pregnant women tetanus	ORT use rate 1987–92
		total	urban	rural	total	urban	rural	total	urban	rural	TB	DPT	polio	measles		
1	Niger	53	98	45	14	71	4	41	99	30	40	21	21	28	45	17
2	Angola	41	71	20	19	25	15	30x	:	:	27	12	13	26	8	48
3	Mozambique	22	44	17	20	61	11	39	100	30	64	53	53	60	32	30
4	Afghanistan	23	40	19		13		29	80	17	48	27	27	37	9	26
5	Sierra Leone	37	33	37	58	92	49	38	90	20	89	72	72	65	80	60
6	Guinea-Bissau	41	56	35	31	27	32	:	:	:	100	66	65	60	35	6
7	Guinea	53	87	56	21	84	5	75	100	55	65	52	52	50	70	65
8	Malawi	56x	97x	50x	84	100	81	80	:	:	99	86	84	82	66	14
9	Rwanda	66	75	62	58	77	56	80	:	:	94	85	85	81	88	26
10	Mali	41	53	38	24	81	10	35	:	:	70	34	34	41	8	41
11	Liberia	50	93	22	:	:	:	39	50	30	78	28	28	61	20	15
12	Somalia	37	50	29	18	44	5	27x	50x	15x	31x	18x	18x	30x	5x	78
13	Chad	57	25	70	:	:	:	30	:	:	43	17	17	41	5	15
14	Eritrea															
15	Ethiopia	25	91	19	19	97	7	46	:	:	21	13	13	10	7	68
16	Mauritania	66	67	65	.ª	34	:	45	72	33	73	34	34	39	40	54
17	Zambia	53	70	28	37	75	12	75x	100x	50x	83	57	59	56	20	90
18	Bhutan	34	60	30	13	50	7	65	:	:	81	79	77	82	43	85
19	Nigeria	36	81	30	35	40	30	66	85	62	50	31	30	36	25	80
20	Zaire	39	68	24	23	46	11	26	40	17	65x	32x	31x	31x	29x	45

Table A3: Health continued

		% of population with access to safe water 1988–91			% of population with access to adequate sanitation 1988–91			% of population with access to health services 1985–92			% fully immunized 1990–92 1-year-old children				pregnant women tetanus	ORT use rate 1987–92
		total	urban	rural	total	urban	rural	total	urban	rural	TB	DPT	polio	measles		
21	Uganda	33	60	30	32	63	28	61x	90x	57x	98	72	72	70	16	30
22	Cambodia	36	65	33	14	81	8	53	80	50	50	32	32	33	22	6
23	Burundi	57	99	54	49	71	47	80	100	79	91	80	80	70	56	49
24	Central African Rep.	24	19	26	46	45	46	45	:	:	94	77	77	62	87	24
25	Yemen	36	61	30	65	87	60	38	81	32	77	62	62	64	13	6
26	Tanzania, U. Rep. of	49	65	45	64	74	62	76x	99x	72x	99	84	83	82	15	83
27	Ghana	52	93	35	42	64	32	60	92	45	57	34	36	40	9	44
28	Madagascar	23	55	9	3	12	3	65	65	65	46	32	32	27	2	29
29	Sudan	48	55	43	75	89	65	51	90	40	75	67	67	66	14	28
30	Gabon	68	90	50	:	:	:	90x	:	:	96	78	78	76	86	25
31	Lesotho	47	59	45	22	14	23	80	:	:	59	58	58	80	40	78
32	Burkina Faso	68	44	72	10	35	5	49x	51x	48x	66	39	39	41	26	15
33	Benin	51	66	46	34	42	31	18	:	:	84	73	73	70	83	45
34	Senegal	48	84	26	55	85	36	40	:	:	65	47	47	43	26	27
35	Lao Peo. Dem. Rep.	36	54	33	21	97	8	67	:	:	39	23	25	55	19	30
36	Pakistan	56	80	45	24	55	10	55	99	35	91	78	78	76	42	34
37	Togo	60	77	53	23	56	10	61	:	:	74	53	47	29	81	33
38	Haiti	39	55	33	24	55	16	50	:	:	45	24	27	24	5	20
39	Nepal	42	67	39	6	52	3	:	:	:	82	72	72	64	18	14
40	Bangladesh	84	82	81	31	63	26	45	:	:	89	63	63	59	80	24

Table A3: Health continued

		% of population with access to safe water 1988–91			% of population with access to adequate sanitation 1988–91			% of population with access to health services 1985–92			% fully immunized 1990–92 1-year-old children				pregnant women tetanus	ORT use rate 1987–92
		total	urban	rural	total	urban	rural	total	urban	rural	TB	DPT	polio	measles		
41	Côte d'Ivoire	76	70	81	60	59	62	30x	61x	11x	47	47	47	51	35	16
42	India	85	87	85	16	53	2	..	..	..	96	89	89	85	77	37
43	Bolivia	52	77	27	26	40	13	63	90	36	86	77	84	80	52	63
44	Cameroon	48	100	27	74	100	64	41	44	39	52	37	37	37	7	84
45	Myanmar	32	37	..	36	39	35	48	..	..	80	73	73	71	72	19
46	Indonesia	51	68	43	44	64	36	80	..	..	95	91	91	89	60	44
47	Congo	38	92	2	..	..	..	83	97	70	88	74	74	64	60	67
48	Libyan Arab Jamahiriya	97	100	80	98	100	85	..	..	..	91	62	62	59	16	
49	Turkmenistan	..	..	..	..	..	..	..	..	..	97	84	91	76	..	80
50	Turkey	78x	95x	63x	..	..	..	..	..	..	65	76	76	72	22	..
51	Zimbabwe	84	95	80	40	95	22	85	96	80	79	73	73	72	60	77
52	Tajikistan	..	..	..	..	..	..	..	..	..	..	92	..	..	..	..
53	Iraq	77	93	41	..	96	..	93	97	78	79	63	64	68	45	70
54	Mongolia	80	100	58	74	100	47	95	..	..	85	84	84	86	..	65
55	Namibia	52	98	35	14	24	11	72	92	60	90	65	65	63	52	..
56	Papua New Guinea	33	94	20	..	57	..	96	..	..	67	61	61	66	52	46
57	Guatemala	62	92	43	60	72	52	34	47	25	56	65	69	58	18	24
58	Nicaragua	54	76	21	..	78	..	83	100	60	79	73	86	72	12	40
59	Kenya	49	74	43	43	69	35	77	..	40	93	85	85	81	37	69
60	Algeria	68x	85x	55x	57	80	40	88	100	80	97	89	89	82	27	27

Table A3: Health continued

		% of population with access to safe water 1988–91			% of population with access to adequate sanitation 1988–91			% of population with access to health services 1985–92			% fully immunized 1990–92, 1-year-old children				pregnant women tetanus	ORT use rate 1987–92
		total	urban	rural	total	urban	rural	total	urban	rural	TB	DPT	polio	measles		
61	South Africa	..	..	..	..	..	..	..	..	..	85	67	69	63	..	..
62	Uzbekistan	..	..	..	..	..	..	..	..	..	97	63	85	84	..	..
63	Brazil	87	95	61	72	84	32	75x	..	..	87	69	62	93	21	63
64	Peru	56	77	10	57	77	20	56	..	..	82	80	81	80	27	31
65	El Salvador	47	85	19	58	86	36	..	80	40	71	65	65	62	26	45
66	Morocco	56	100	18	..	100	..	70	100	50	93	87	81	81	80	13
67	Kyrgyzstan	..	..	..	..	..	..	..	..	..	96	88	91	94	..	..
68	Philippines	82	85	79	69	78	62	75	77	74	94	92	92	90	52	25
69	Ecuador	55	63	43	48	56	38	88	..	..	99	83	83	66	5	70
70	Botswana	90	100	88	88	100	85	89	100	85	71	82	82	65	46	64
71	Honduras	77	98	63	61	98	43	66	80	56	91	93	95	89	16	70
72	Iran, Islamic Rep. of	89	100	75	71	100	35	80	95	65	92	87	87	84	87	85
73	Egypt	90	95	86	50	80	26	..	..	..	92	89	89	89	70	34
74	Azerbaijan	..	..	..	..	..	..	..	..	..	53	69	70	50	..	..
75	Dominican Rep.	67	82	45	87	95	75	80	..	..	48	48	63	75	24	35
76	Kazakhstan	..	..	..	..	..	..	..	..	..	90	85	87	90	..	..
77	Viet Nam	24	39	21	17	34	13	91	100	80	91	88	89	90	42	52
78	Lebanon	92	95	85	..	..	..	95	98	85	4	85	85	51	..	45
79	China	72	87	68	79	68	81	90	100	88	94	94	95	94	3	22
80	Saudi Arabia	95	100	74	86	100	30	97	100x	88x	97	96	96	90	62	45

Table A3: Health continued

No.	Country	% of population with access to safe water 1988–91			% of population with access to adequate sanitation 1988–91			% of population with access to health services 1985–92			% fully immunized 1990–92 1-year-old children				pregnant women tetanus	ORT use rate 1987–92
		total	urban	rural	total	urban	rural	total	urban	rural	TB	DPT	polio	measles		
81	Syrian Arab Rep.	74	90	58	83	84	82	83	92	68	93	89	89	84	63	95
82	Tunisia	99	100	99	96	98	94	90x	100x	80x	80	95	95	87	44	22
83	Moldova	:	:	:	:	:	:	:	:	:	96	89	93	92	:	:
84	Albania	:	:	:	:	:	:	:	:	:	94	94	96	87	:	:
85	Armenia	:	:	:	:	:	:	:	:	:	:	:	:	:	:	:
86	Paraguay	35	50	24	62	56	67	61	:	:	99	85	87	86	54	52
87	Korea, Dem. Peo. Rep.	:	:	:	:	:	:	:	:	:	99	90	98	96	97	:
88	Mexico	76	81	68	50	70	17	78	80	60	95	91	92	91	42	72
89	Thailand	77	87	72	74	80	72	90	90	90	99	85	84	74	72	63
90	Russian Federation	:	:	:	:	:	:	:	:	:	88	73	69	83	:	65
91	Oman	84	91	77	71	75	40	95	100	95	97	97	97	97	97	19
92	Jordan	99	100	97	100	100	100	97	98	95	:	98	97	91	32	77
93	Georgia	:	:	:	:	:	:	:	:	:	63	45	45	58	:	:
94	Romania	:	:	:	:	:	:	:	:	:	99	97	90	92	:	:
95	Latvia	:	:	:	:	:	:	:	:	:	94	87	92	95	:	:
96	Ukraine	:	:	:	:	:	:	:	:	:	93	88	89	90	:	:
97	Argentina	65	73	17	69	75	35	71	80	21	99	78	83	89	:	70
98	Estonia	:	:	:	:	:	:	:	:	:	96	70	71	75	:	:
99	Mauritius	96	100	92	94	92	96	:	:	:	87	91	91	87	77	7
100	Venezuela	89	89	89	92	97	70	100	100	100	82	66	72	61	:	80

Table A3: Health continued

#		% of population with access to safe water 1988–91			% of population with access to adequate sanitation 1988–91			% of population with access to health services 1985–92			% fully immunized 1990–92 1-year-old children				pregnant women tetanus	ORT use rate 1987–92
		total	urban	rural	total	urban	rural	total	urban	rural	TB	DPT	polio	measles		
101	Belarus	97	:	:	:	:	:	:	:	:	94	90	90	94	:	:
102	Trinidad and Tobago	95	99	91	79	99	98	99	:	:	:	82	81	93	:	70
103	United Arab Emirates	75	85	5	77	93	22	99	:	:	98	86	86	85	:	81
104	Uruguay	:	:	:	61	60	65	82	:	:	99	93	93	93	13	96
105	Yugoslavia (former)	:	:	:	:	:	:	:	:	:	81	79	81	76	:	:
106	Colombia	86	87	82	64	84	18	60	:	:	86	77	84	74	40	40
107	Lithuania	:	:	:	:	:	:	:	:	:	94	78	88	89	:	:
108	Panama	83	100	66	84	100	68	80x	95x	64x	98	82	83	71	27	55
109	Bulgaria	:	:	:	:	:	:	:	:	:	100	99	99	97	:	:
110	Sri Lanka	60	80	55	50	68	45	93x	:	:	89	86	86	79	67	76
111	Malaysia	78	96	66	81	100	:	:	:	:	99	90	90	79	83	47
112	Chile	86	100	:	83	100	20	97	:	:	99	91	91	90	:	10
113	Kuwait	:	100	:	:	:	:	100	:	:	3	92	92	93	22	10
114	Poland	:	:	:	:	:	:	:	:	:	94	98	98	94	:	:
115	Hungary	:	:	:	:	:	:	:	:	:	99	100	98	100	:	:
116	Costa Rica	93	100	86	97	100	94	80x	100x	63x	92	90	90	84	68	78
117	Jamaica	100	100	100	89	100	80	90	:	:	85	84	74	63	50	10
118	Slovakia	:	:	:	:	:	:	:	:	:	91	99	99	96	:	:
119	Portugal	:	:	:	:	:	:	:	:	:	89	95	95	96	:	:
120	Czech Republic	:	:	:	:	:	:	:	:	:	98	99	98	97	:	:
121	Cuba	98	100	91	92	100	68	98	99	96	98	91	93	98	98	80
122	Israel	:	:	:	:	:	:	:	:	:	:	85x	89x	88x	:	:

Table A3: Health continued

	% of population with access to safe water 1988–91			% of population with access to adequate sanitation 1988–91			% of population with access to health services 1985–92			% fully immunized 1990–92, 1-year-old children				pregnant women tetanus	ORT use rate 1987–92
	total	urban	rural	total	urban	rural	total	urban	rural	TB	DPT	polio	measles		
123 Belgium	..	..	..	..	..	..	..	..	..	..	87	99	75	..	..
124 USA	..	100	..	..	..	..	..	..	..	..	58	74	77	..	..
125 New Zealand	97	..	82	..	..	..	..	..	..	20	81	68	82	..	..
126 Italy	..	..	..	..	..	..	..	..	..	6	95	85	50	..	..
127 Spain	..	..	..	..	..	..	..	..	..	..	93	94	97	..	..
128 Greece	..	..	..	..	..	..	100	..	..	56	54	96	76	..	..
129 Korea, Rep. of	97	97	96	100	100	100	..	100	100	76	80	79	96	..	..
130 Austria	..	..	..	..	..	..	..	..	..	97	90	90	60	..	..
131 France	..	..	..	..	..	..	..	..	..	80	95	85	71	..	..
132 United Kingdom	..	..	..	..	..	..	..	..	..	75	90	95	89	..	..
133 Australia	..	..	..	..	..	..	..	..	..	..	95	72	86	..	..
134 Switzerland	..	..	..	..	..	..	..	..	..	..	89	95	83	..	..
135 Germany	..	..	..	..	..	..	..	..	..	84	95	95	80	..	..
136 Canada	..	..	..	..	..	..	..	..	..	85x	85x	70x	85x	..	..
137 Denmark	..	..	..	..	..	..	..	..	..	..	99	99	86	..	..
138 Norway	..	..	..	..	..	..	..	..	..	95	91	86	90	..	..
139 Netherlands	..	..	..	..	..	..	..	..	..	..	97	97	94	..	..
140 Sweden	..	..	..	..	..	..	..	..	..	14	99	99	95	..	..
141 Hong Kong	100	100	96	88	90	50	99	..	..	94	90	90	42	..	..
142 Singapore	100	100	..	99	99	..	100	..	..	99	85	85	90	..	..
143 Finland	..	..	..	..	85	..	..	100	..	99	95	97	97	..	..
144 Japan	97	100	85	..	..	..	..	..	..	85	87	90	66	..	..
145 Ireland	..	..	..	..	..	..	..	..	..	..	65	81	78	..	..

Table A4: Education

| | Adult literacy rate | | | | No. of sets per 1000 population 1990 | | Primary school enrollment ratio | | | | | | % of grade 1 enrollment reaching final grade of primary school 1988 | Secondary school enrollment ratio 1986–91 (gross) | |
| | 1970 | | 1990 | | | | 1960 (gross) | | 1986–91 (gross) | | 1986–91 (net) | | | | |
	male	female	male	female	radio	television	male	female	male	female	male	female		male	female
1 Niger	6	2	40	17	60	5	8	3	37	21	31	19	75	9	4
2 Angola	16	7	56	29	54	6	30	14	98	91	..	..	..	..	..
3 Mozambique	29	14	45	21	42	3	71	43	68	48	45	37	39	9	5
4 Afghanistan	13	2	44	14	105	8	14	2	31	16	25	13	63	11	5
5 Sierra Leone	18	8	31	11	223	10	30	15	56	39	..	..	..	21	12
6 Guinea-Bissau	13	6	50	24	39	..	35	15	76	42	58	32	8	9	4
7 Guinea	21	7	35	13	42	7	27	9	50	24	34	17	44	15	5
8 Malawi	42	18	..	..	238	..	50	26	77	64	55	52	47	6	3
9 Rwanda	43	21	64	37	62	..	65	29	69	68	65	65	36	9	6
10 Mali	11	4	41	24	43	1	13	5	30	17	24	14	40	9	4
11 Liberia	27	8	50	29	225	18	40	13	51x	28x	..	..	..	31x	12x
12 Somalia	5	1	36	14	43	14	6	2	20x	10x	14x	8x	37	12x	7x
13 Chad	20	2	42	18	238	1	29	4	79	35	52	23	71	12	3
14 Eritrea	..	..	..	..	..	..	..	..	..	..	..	..	..	..	..
15 Ethiopia	8	..	33x	16x	191	2	9	3	46	30	32	24	44	17	12
16 Mauritania	..	..	47	21	144	23	12	3	60	42	..	..	68	22	10
17 Zambia	66	37	81	65	77	30	61	40	99	91	81	79	64	25	14
18 Bhutan	..	..	51	25	16	..	5	..	31	20	..	..	26	7	2
19 Nigeria	35	14	62	40	172	32	54	31	82	63	..	..	52	22	17
20 Zaire	61	22	84	61	103	1	89	32	89	67	67	53	73	32	16

206

Table 4: Education continued

| | | Adult literacy rate | | | | No. of sets per 1000 population 1990 | | Primary school enrollment ratio | | | | | | % of grade 1 enrollment reaching final grade of primary school 1988 | Secondary school enrollment ratio 1986–91 (gross) | |
| | | 1970 | | 1990 | | | | 1960 (gross) | | 1986–91 (gross) | | 1986–91 (net) | | | | |
		male	female	male	female	radio	television	male	female	male	female	male	female		male	female
21	Uganda	52	30	62	35	101	10	39	18	76	63	57	50	76x	16	8
22	Cambodia	:	23	48	22	113	9	:	:	:	:	:	:	50x	:	:
23	Burundi	29	10	61	40	58	1	33	10	79	64	55	46	83	6	4
24	Central African Rep.	26	6	52	25	66	4	50	11	83	51	66	43	48	17	6
25	Yemen	14	3	53	26	:	:	:	:	111	43	:	:	53	47	10
26	Tanzania, U. Rep. of	48	18	:	:	24	2	33	16	64	63	46	47	73	5	4
27	Ghana	43	18	70	51	266	15	58	31	82	67	:	:	87	48	31
28	Madagascar	56	43	88	73	200	20	74	57	94	90	64	63	32	20	18
29	Sudan	28	6	43	12	250	71	29	11	58x	41x	:	:	76	23x	17x
30	Gabon	43	22	74	49	141	37	:	:	:	:	:	:	44	:	:
31	Lesotho	49	74	:	:	70	6	73	109	99	115	64	76	50	21	31
32	Burkina Faso	13	3	28	9	26	5	12	5	45	28	36	23	64	9	5
33	Benin	23	8	32	16	90	5	39	15	87	44	69	36	40	16	6
34	Senegal	18	5	52	25	113	36	37	18	67	49	55	41	85	21	11
35	Lao Peo. Dem. Rep.	37	28	92x	76x	126	7	43	20	116	91	:	:	38x	31	21
36	Pakistan	30	11	47	21	87	17	39	11	47	26	:	:	51	29	13
37	Togo	27	7	56	31	211	6	64	25	126	80	85	58	46	33	10
38	Haiti	26x	17x	59	47	46	5	50	39	86	81	44	44	9	20	19
39	Nepal	23	3	38	13	34	2	19	3	112	57	84	43	:	42	17
40	Bangladesh	36	12	47	22	42	5	80	31	78	68	69	61	46	23	12

207

Table A4: Education continued

| | | Adult literacy rate | | | | No. of sets per 1000 population 1990 | | Primary school enrollment ratio | | | | | | % of grade 1 enrollment reaching final grade of primary school 1988 | Secondary school enrollment ratio 1986–91 (gross) | |
| | | 1970 | | 1990 | | | | 1960 (gross) | | 1986–91 (gross) | | 1986–91 (net) | | | | |
		male	female	male	female	radio	television	male	female	male	female	male	female		male	female
41	Cote d'Ivoire	26	10	67	40	142	61	62	22	88x	62x	:	:	73	27	12
42	India	47	20	62	34	79	32	83	44	109	83	:	:	53	54	33
43	Bolivia	68	46	85	71	599	163	70	43	87	78	83	75	50	37	31
44	Cameroon	47	19	67	43	139	29	77	37	108	93	80	69	68	31	21
45	Myanmar	85	57	89	72	82	2	60	53	106	100	:	:	:	25	23
46	Indonesia	66	42	88	75	147	60	78	58	119	114	100	96	79	49	41
47	Congo	50	19	70	44	110	6	:	:	:	:	:	:	62	37	14
48	Libyan Arab Jamahiriya	60	13	75	50	224	99	:	:	:	:	:	:	:	:	:
49	Turkmenistan	:	:	:	:	:	:	:	:	:	:	:	:	:	:	:
50	Turkey	69	34	90	71	161	175	90	58	114	105	:	:	97	66	42
51	Zimbabwe	63	47	74	60	85	31	82	65	118	116	:	:	75	54	46
52	Tajikistan	:	:	:	:	:	:	:	:	:	:	:	:	:	:	:
53	Iraq	50	18	70	49	205	69	94	36	104	87	:	:	58	58	37
54	Mongolia	87	74	:	:	132	41	80	80	96	100	90	78	:	87	96
55	Namibia	:	:	:	:	135	17	:	:	89	99	:	:	:	30	38
56	Papua New Guinea	39	24	65	38	72	2	24	15	77	65	79	67	61	15	10
57	Guatemala	51	37	63	47	65	52	48	39	82	70	:	:	36	20x	17x
58	Nicaragua	58	57	:	:	249	62	57	59	94	101	74	77	29	31	44
59	Kenya	44	19	80	59	125	9	62	29	96	92	92x	89x	62	27	19
60	Algeria	39	11	70	46	233	74	55	37	103	88	94	83	90	66	53

Table A4: Education continued

No.	Country	Adult literacy 1970 male	Adult literacy 1970 female	Adult literacy 1990 male	Adult literacy 1990 female	Sets/1000 1990 radio	Sets/1000 1990 television	Primary 1960 (gross) male	Primary 1960 (gross) female	Primary 1986–91 (gross) male	Primary 1986–91 (gross) female	Primary 1986–91 (net) male	Primary 1986–91 (net) female	% of grade 1 reaching final grade 1988	Secondary 1986–91 (gross) male	Secondary 1986–91 (gross) female
61	South Africa	:	:	78x	75x	326	105	:	:	:	:	:	:	:	:	:
62	Uzbekistan	:	:	:	:	:	:	:	:	101x	97x	:	:	:	31x	36x
63	Brazil	69	63	83	80	379	213	58	56	125x	120x	:	:	22	66x	60x
64	Peru	81	60	91	79	253	97	98	74	77	78	69	71	70x	26	26
65	El Salvador	61	53	76	70	:	:	59	56	:	:	:	:	27	:	:
66	Morocco	34	10	61	38	209	74	69	28	81	55	66	45	63	42	30
67	Kyrgyzstan	:	:	:	:	:	:	:	:	:	:	:	:	:	:	:
68	Philippines	84	81	90	89	138	48	98	93	111	110	100	98	71	72	75
69	Ecuador	75	68	88	84	315	83	82	75	118	117	:	:	63	55	57
70	Botswana	37	44	84	65	115	15	38	43	107	112	88	93	95	44	47
71	Honduras	55	50	75	71	385	72	68	67	108	109	89	94	43x	29x	30x
72	Iran, Islamic Rep. of	40	17	64	43	247	70	59	28	119	106	99	90	91	63	47
73	Egypt	50	20	63	34	324	109	79	52	105	90	:	:	95	92	71
74	Azerbaijan	:	:	:	:	:	:	:	:	:	:	:	:	:	:	:
75	Dominican Rep.	69	65	85	82	170	84	75	74	95	96	73	73	33	44x	57x
76	Kazakhstan	:	:	:	:	:	:	:	:	:	:	:	:	:	:	:
77	Viet Nam	79x	58x	92	84	108	39	103	74	105x	99x	:	:	57x	43x	40x
78	Lebanon	:	:	88	73	840	330	112	105	105x	95x	:	:	:	57x	56x
79	China	:	:	84	62	184	31	131	90	140	129	100	100	81	53	41
80	Saudi Arabia	15	2	73	48	318	283	32	3	83	72	69	56	90	55	41

Table A4: Education continued

		Adult literacy rate				No. of sets per 1000 population 1990		Primary school enrollment ratio						% of grade 1 enrollment reaching final grade of primary school 1988	Secondary school enrollment ratio 1986–91 (gross)	
		1970		1990				1960 (gross)		1986–91 (gross)		1986–91 (net)				
		male	female	male	female	radio	television	male	female	male	female	male	female		male	female
81	Syrian Arab Rep.	60	20	78	51	251	59	89	39	114	102	100	93	85	60	43
82	Tunisia	44	17	74	56	196	80	88	43	122	109	100	91	79	50	40
83	Moldova	:	:	:	:	:	:	:	:	:	:	:	:	:	:	:
84	Albania	:	:	:	:	176	86	102	86	98	98	:	:	91	85	74
85	Armenia	:	:	:	:	:	:	:	:	:	:	:	:	:	:	:
86	Paraguay	85x	75x	92	88	171	59	106	94	109	106	95	94	57	29	31
87	Korea, Dem. Peo. Rep.	:	:	:	:	119	15	:	:	110	103	:	:	:	:	:
88	Mexico	78	69	90	85	243	139	80	75	113	110	:	:	70	52	53
89	Thailand	86	72	96	90	185	112	97	88	86	85	:	:	59	33	32
90	Russian Federation	:	:	:	:	:	:	:	:	86	85	:	:	:	:	:
91	Oman	:	:	:	:	646	766	:	:	108	99	87	82	91	59	48
92	Jordan	64	29	89	70	254	81	:	:	105x	102x	94x	91x	95	79x	73x
93	Georgia	96	91	:	:	:	:	:	:	:	:	:	:	:	:	:
94	Romania	:	:	:	:	198	194	101	95	86	96	:	:	94	93	90
95	Latvia	:	:	:	:	:	:	:	:	:	:	:	:	:	:	:
96	Ukraine	94	92	:	:	794	327	:	:	:	:	:	:	:	:	:
97	Argentina	:	:	95	95	681	222	99	99	107	114	:	:	:	69	78
98	Estonia	:	:	100x	100x	:	:	:	:	:	:	:	:	:	:	:
99	Mauritius	77	59	:	:	356	215	96	90	102	104	92	94	98	53	53
100	Venezuela	79	71	87	90	436	167	98	99	94	94	60	62	70	30	41

Table A4: Education continued

		Adult literacy rate				No. of sets per 1000 population 1990		Primary school enrollment ratio						% of grade 1 enrollment reaching final grade of primary school 1988	Secondary school enrollment ratio 1986–91 (gross)	
		1970		1990				1960 (gross)		1986–91 (gross)		1986–91 (net)				
		male	female	male	female	radio	television	male	female	male	female	male	female		male	female
101	Belarus	95	..	..	..	306	268	111	108	..	..	..	..	..	..	..
102	Trinidad and Tobago	24	89	97x	93x	468	302	..	..	95	96	90	90	89	79	82
103	United Arab Emirates	93x	7	..	..	324	110	..	..	117	114	100	100	96	63	72
104	Uruguay	92	93x	97	96	603	233	117	117	107	106	80	79	93	61x	62x
105	Yugoslavia (former)		76	97	88	246	198	..	..	95	95	80	79	..	80	79
106	Colombia	79	76	87	86	170	115	74	74	109	111	..	..	56	48	57
107	Lithuania	..	..	99x	98x	..	..	..	..	..	..	..	..	..	..	..
108	Panama	81	81	88	88	223	165	89	86	109	105	91	92	79	57	62
109	Bulgaria	94	89	88	..	438	250	94	92	97	95	85	84	62	72	75
110	Sri Lanka	85	69	93	84	197	35	107	95	108	105	100	100	94	72	77
111	Malaysia	71	48	86	70	429	148	108	79	93	93	..	..	96	55	58
112	Chile	90	88	93	93	342	205	87	86	99	97	..	..	77	71	77
113	Kuwait	65	42	77	67	343	285	132	99	101	99	84	86	90	93	87
114	Poland	98	97	..	..	429	293	110	107	99	98	97	97	92	80	84
115	Hungary	98	98	99x	99x	595	410	103	100	94	94	90	91	94	78	79
116	Costa Rica	88	87	93	93	259	149	94	92	102	101	87	87	77	41	43
117	Jamaica	96	97	98	99	411	130	78	79	104	105	98	100	85	57	63
118	Slovakia	..	..	..	..	..	..	..	..	..	..	..	..	..	..	..
119	Portugal	78	65	89	81	218	177	132	129	121	117	99	100	..	58	59
120	Czech Republic	..	..	..	..	..	..	..	..	..	..	..	..	..	..	..
121	Cuba	86	87	95	93	345	207	109	110	105	100	96	95	88	84	94
122	Israel	93	83	95x	89x	471	266	99	97	92	95	..	..	78	79	86
123	Belgium	99	99	..	..	778	452	111	108	102	103	98	99	78	103	104

Table A4: Education continued

| | | Adult literacy rate | | | | No. of sets per 1000 population 1990 | | Primary school enrollment ratio | | | | | | % of grade 1 enrollment reaching final grade of primary school 1988 | Secondary school enrollment ratio 1986–91 (gross) | |
| | | 1970 | | 1990 | | | | 1960 (gross) | | 1986–91 (gross) | | 1986–91 (net) | | | | |
		male	female	male	female	radio	television	male	female	male	female	male	female		male	female
124	USA	99	99	..	..	2123	815	110	..	105	104	99	99	90	92	91
125	New Zealand	..	..	..	..	929	442	..	106	106	105	100	100	95	88	91
126	Italy	95	93	98	96	797	424	112	109	96	96	..	..	100	78	78
127	Spain	93	87	97	93	306	396	106	116	109	108	100	100	94	102	112
128	Greece	93	76	98	89	423	196	104	101	100	101	96	97	100	101	97
129	Korea, Rep.	94	81	99	94	1006	210	108	94	106	109	100	100	100	89	86
130	Austria	..	..	..	..	624	481	106	104	103	102	93	93	97	82	85
131	France	99	98	..	..	896	406	144	143	112	110	100	100	96	93	100
132	United Kingdom	..	..	..	..	1146	435	92	92	106	107	100	100	..	82	85
133	Australia	..	..	..	..	1280	486	103	103	105	105	97	97	99	82	85
134	Switzerland	..	..	..	..	855	407	118	118	..	..	89	..	..	..	..
135	Germany	..	..	..	..	952	514	..	..	105	105	..	90	..	99	96
136	Canada	..	..	..	..	1026	641	108	105	106	104	96	97	96	106	107
137	Denmark	..	..	..	..	1030	535	103	103	97	98	..	..	99	108	110
138	Norway	..	..	..	..	798	425	100	100	99	99	99	98	100	98	102
139	Netherlands	..	..	..	..	906	495	105	104	115	118	100	100	94	104	101
140	Sweden	..	..	..	..	888	474	95	96	106	107	100	100	100	89	93
141	Hong Kong	92	55	92x	74x	649	274	88	72	105	104	95x	95x	98	71	75
142	Singapore	..	..	..	..	643	376	120	101	111	109	100	100	100	68	71
143	Finland	99	99	..	..	998	497	100	95	100	99	..	..	100	104	124
144	Japan	99	..	..	..	907	620	103	102	101	101	100	100	100	94	97
145	Ireland	..	..	..	..	583	276	107	112	100	101	87	89	97	93	102

Countries listed in descending order of their 1992 under-five mortality rates (table 1).

Notes and References

1 Responsibility

1. Marc Miringoff and Sandra Opdycke, *The Index of Social Health: Monitoring the Social Well-Being of Children in Industrial Countries* (New York: Fordham Institute for Innovation in Social Policy, 1992), as reported in Peter Adamson, ed., *The Progress of Nations 1993* (New York: UNICEF, 1993), p. 45.
2. Adamson, ed., *The Progress of Nations* 1993, p. 4. This updates a similar statement in James P. Grant, *The State of the World's Children 1993* (New York: Oxford University Press, 1993).
3. Grant, *The State of the World's Children 1994* (New York: Oxford University Press, 1994), p. 1.
4. Grant, *The State of the World's Children 1994*, p. ii.
5. Michael Walzer, 'The Idea of Civil Society: A Path to Social Reconstruction', *Dissent*, Vol. 38, No. 2 (Spring 1991), pp. 293–304. Also see Jean Cohen and Andrew Arato, *Civil Society and Political Theory* (Cambridge, Massachusetts: MIT Press, 1992); David L. Blaney and Mustapha Kamal Pasha, 'Civil Society and Democracy in the Third World: Ambiguities and Historical Possibilities', *Studies in Comparative International Development*, Vol. 28, No. 1 (Spring 1993), pp. 3–24; Axel Honneth, 'Conceptions of "Civil Society",' *Radical Philosophy*, Vol. 64 (Summer 1993), pp. 19–22; Andrew Arato, *From Marxism to Democratic Theory: Essays on the Critical Theory of Soviet-Type Societies* (Armonk, New York: M. E. Sharpe, 1993).
6. James Garbarino, *Toward a Sustainable Society: An Economic, Social and Environmental Agenda for Our Children's Future* (Chicago: Noble Press, 1992), p. 104.
7. United Nations Development Programme, *Human Development Report 1992* (New York: Oxford University Press, 1993), p. 41. Data on the extent to which public expenditures are devoted to socially oriented programs and services may be found in the International Monetary Fund's *Government Finance Statistics Yearbook*. It is striking that, while most developed countries devote more than half of their public expenditures to social services, the United States devotes only about one quarter to this purpose, much less than the other developed countries.
8. As de Swaan puts it, 'there appears to be no familiar recipe for remedying this suffering with any certainty of effect. This is what causes the sense of tragedy and impotence so widespread in the Western discourse on poverty in the world periphery.' Abram de Swaan, *In Care of the State: Health Care, Education and Welfare in Europe and the USA in the Modern Era* (Cambridge, Massachusetts: MIT Press, 1988), p. 256.
9. Ronnie D. Lipschutz, 'Reconstructing World Politics: The Emergence of Global Civil Society,' *Millennium: Journal of International Studies*, Vol. 21, No. 3 (1992), pp. 389–420; Martin Shaw, 'Global Society and Global

Responsibility: The Theoretical, Historical and Political Limits of "International Society"', *Millennium: Journal of International Studies,* Vol. 21, No. 3 (1992), pp. 421–34; Paul Ghils, 'International Civil Society: International Non-Governmental Organizations in the International System,' *International Social Science Journal,* Vol. 133 (August 1992), pp. 417–29; Mihaly Simai, *The Future of Global Governance: Managing Risk and Change in the International System* (Washington, D.C: United States Institute of Peace, 1994).

10. Lipschutz, 'Reconstructing World Politics', p. 398.

2   The Global Economy

1. United Nations Development Programme, *Human Development Report 1992* (New York: Oxford University Press, 1992), p. 35.

2. United Nations Development Programme, *Human Development Report 1992,* p. 34.

3. United Nations Development Programme, *Human Development Report 1992,* pp. 40–1.

4. United Nations Development Programme, *Human Development Report 1992,* p. 57.

5. John Abraham, *Food and Development: The Political Economy of Hunger and the Modern Diet* (London: World Wide Fund for Nature and Kogan Page Ltd., 1991), p. 112.

6. George Kent, *The Political Economy of Hunger* (New York: Praeger, 1984), pp. 41–64.

7. Kent, *The Political Economy of Hunger,* p. 68.

8. United Nations Development Programme, *Human Development Report 1992,* p. 60.

9. United Nations Development Programme, *Human Development Report 1992,* p. 45.

10. United Nations Development Programme, *Human Development Report 1992,* pp. 44–5.

11. The literature is abundant. See, for example, Susan George, *A Fate Worse Than Debt: The World Financial Crisis and the Poor* (New York: Grove Press, 1988); World Bank, *World Development Report 1990* (New York: Oxford University Press, 1990); Bank Information Center, *Funding Ecological and Social Destruction: The World Bank and International Monetary Fund* (Washington, D.C.: BIC, 1990); J. De Jong, 'Ten Best Readings in … Structural Adjustment and Health,' *Health Policy and Planning,* Vol. 5 (1990), pp. 280–2; S. O. Alubo, 'Debt Crisis, Health, and Health Services in Africa,' *Social Science & Medicine,* Vol. 31 (1990), pp. 639–48; Danilo Türk, *The Realization of Economic, Social and Cultural Rights, Second Progress Report* (Geneva: Economic and Social Council, E/CN.4/Sub.2/1991/17, 1991); Susan George, *The Debt Boomerang: How Third World Debt Harms Us All* (London: Pluto Press, 1992). The United Nations Non-Governmental Liaison Service has published a 227-page directory of organizations concerned with these issues. See *Who's Who on Debt and Structural Adjustment: A Directory of NGOs Involved in Research, Information and Advocacy* (Geneva: UNNGLS, 1990).

12. James P. Grant, *The State of the World's Children 1989* (Oxford: Oxford University Press, 1989), pp. 16–7.
13. R. J. Vogel, 'Trends in Health Expenditures and Revenue Resources in Sub-Saharan Africa,' Draft. (Washington, D.C.: World Bank, 1989), as reported in Beth Ebel, *Patterns of Government Expenditure in Developing Countries During the 1980s: The Impact on Social Services* (Florence, Italy: UNICEF International Child Development Center, 1991), p. 41. Also see Ved P. Nanda, George W. Shepherd, Jr, and Eileen McCarthy-Arnolds, eds., *World Debt and the Human Condition: Structural Adjustment and the Right to Development* (Westport, Connecticut: Greenwood Press, 1993).
14. Richard Jolly and Giovanni Andrea Cornia, *The Impact of World Recession on Children* (Oxford: Pergamon Press, 1984); Giovanni Andrea Cornia, Richard Jolly, and Frances Stewart, eds., *Adjustment with a Human Face: Protecting the Vulnerable and Promoting Growth* (New York: Oxford University Press, 1987). A contrary view, arguing that debt's impact on children has been exaggerated, may be found in Nicholas Eberstadt, 'Is Third World Debt Killing Children?' *American Enterprise* (November/December 1990), pp. 57–63.
15. Stuart Gillespie and John Mason, *Nutrition-Relevant Actions: Some Experiences from the Eighties and Lessons for the Nineties* (Geneva: United Nations Administrative Committee on Coordination/Subcommittee on Nutrition, 1991), pp. 34–42.
16. Giovanni Andrea Cornia, Rolph van der Hoeven, and Thandika Mkandawire, eds., *Africa's Recovery in the 1990s: From Stagnation and Adjustment to Human Development* (New York: St. Martin's/UNICEF, 1992). Also see Carmelo Mesa-Lago, *Changing Social Security in Latin America: Toward Alleviating the Social Costs of Economic Reform* (Boulder, Colorado: Lynne Rienner, 1994).
17. Giovanni Andrea Cornia and Sándor Sipos, eds., *Children and the Transition to the Market Economy: Safety Nets and Social Policies in Central and Eastern Europe* (Aldershot: Avebury, 1991), p. 101.
18. UNICEF International Child Development Centre, *Central and Eastern Europe in Transition: Public Policy and Social Conditions* (Florence, Italy: ICDC, 1993).
19. Food and Agriculture Organization of the United Nations, *The State of Food and Agriculture 1974* (Rome: FAO, 1975), p. 110.
20. Basic data are from *World Development Report 1986* (New York: Oxford University, 1986), pp. 180–1.
21. World Bank, *World Development Report 1984* (New York: Oxford University Press, 1984), p. 60.
22. Paul R. Ehrlich and Anne H. Ehrlich, *Population, Resources, Environment: Issues in Human Ecology* (San Francisco: W. H. Freeman and Company, 1972), pp. 20–2.
23. Frances Moore Lappé and Rachel Schurman, *The Missing Piece in the Population Puzzle* (San Francisco: Food First Development Report No. 4, Institute for Food and Development Policy, 1988), p. 2.
24. World Bank, *World Development Report 1984*, p. 109.
25. Having children is a way of creating options when the opportunities are bleak psychologically as well as economically. See Leon Dash, *When*

Children Want Children: The Urban Crisis of Teenage Childbearing (New York: William Morrow and Company, 1989).

26. Garrett Hardin, 'The Tragedy of the Commons,' *Science*, Vol. 163 (December 13, 1968), pp. 1243–48. More recent perspectives are described in the emerging literature on 'common property' resources. See, for example, Panel on Common Property Resource Management, *Proceedings of the Conference on Common Property Resource Management* (Washington, D.C.: National Academy Press, 1986).

27. Lappé and Schurman, *The Missing Piece in the Population Puzzle*, pp. 20–21

28. Abdel R. Omran, 'The Epidemiologic Transition: A Theory of the Epidemiology of Population Change,' *Milbank Memorial Fund Quarterly*, Vol. 49, No. 4 (October 1971), Part I, pp. 509–38, at p. 511.

29. Lappé and Schurman, *The Missing Piece in the Population Puzzle*, p. 36.

30. Paul R. Ehrlich and Anne H. Ehrlich, 'Population, Plenty, and Poverty,' *National Geographic*, Vol. 174, No. 6 (December 1988), pp. 914–45.

31. Anastasia Toufexis, 'Overpopulation: Too Many Mouths,' *Time*, January 2, 1989, pp. 48–50.

32. Ehrlich and Ehrlich, 'Population, Plenty, and Poverty,' p. 922.

33. Rene Loewenson, *Modern Plantation Agriculture* (London: Zed, 1992).

34. Quoted in Werner Fornos, *Regional Powder Kegs: Charting U.S. Security in an Exploding World* (Washington, D.C.: The Population Institute, 1988), p. 4.

35. The World Bank's perspectives on poverty are articulated in its *World Development Report 1990*, its *Poverty Reduction Handbook* (1993) and its report, *Implementing the World Bank's Strategy to Reduce Poverty: Progress and Challenges* (1993).

36. United Nations Development Programme, *Human Development Report 1992*, p. 41. Data on the extent to which public expenditures are devoted to socially oriented programs and services may be found in the International Monetary Fund's *Government Finance Statistics Yearbook*. It is striking that, while most developed countries devote more than half of their public expenditures to social services, the United States devotes only about one quarter to this purpose, much less than the other developed countries.

37. James P. Grant, *The State of the World's Children 1993* (Oxford: Oxford University Press, 1993), pp. 1–2.

38. *UNICEF Annual Report 1993* (New York: UNICEF, 1993), p. 61.

39. James P. Grant, *The State of the World's Children 1994* (New York: Oxford University Press, 1994), p. 13.

40. The argument is made for the United States in Mary A. Jensen and Stacie G. Goffin, eds., *Visions of Entitlement: The Care and Education of America's Children* (Albany, New York: State University of New York Press, 1993).

3   Mortality

1. In James P. Grant, *The State of the World's Children* (New York: UNICEF, 1993), corrections were made, adjusting mortality figures that had been reported earlier to slightly lower levels. Adjustments were made partly on the basis of the new report, United Nations, *Child Mortality Since the 1960s: A Database for Developing Countries* (New York: United Nations, 1992).

2. This figure is obtained by summing the under-five deaths in the *Basic Indicators* table *of The State of the World's Children 1994*. That table is reproduced here, in the appendix, as Table A1.

3. Grant, *State of the World's Children*, 1987, p. 13.

4. Data on the distribution of deaths by age for the countries of the world may be found in United Nations, *Demographic Yearbook 1991* (New York: UN, 1992), Table 19, pp. 368–407.

5. World Bank, *World Development Report 1993: Investing in Health* (Washington, D.C.: World Bank, 1993), pp. 200–1.

6. United States House of Representatives, Select Committee on Children, Youth, and Families, *U.S. Children and their Families: Current Conditions and Recent Trends, 1989* (Washington, D.C.: U.S. Government Printing Office, 1989), p. 170.

7. Ruth Leger Sivard, *World Military and Social Expenditures (Washington, D.C.: World Priorities*, 1988), p. 28.

8. 'Wars and Peaces of 1991,' *COPRED Peace Chronicle*, Vol. 17, No. 1 (1992), p. 8.

9. Melvin J. Small and J. David Singer, *Resort to Arms: International and Civil War, 1816–1980* (Beverly Hills, California: Sage, 1982), p. 91.

10. Quincy Wright, *A Study of War*, Second edition (Chicago: University of Chicago Press, 1965), p. 1542.

11. R. J. Rummel, *Lethal Politics: Soviet Genocide and Mass Murder Since 1917* (New Brunswick, New Jersey: Transaction Books, 1990), p. xi.

12. Lloyd deMause, ed., *The History of Childhood: The Untold History of Child Abuse* (New York: Psychohistory Press, 1974 (republished in 1988 by Peter Bedrick Books); Maria W. Piers, *Infanticide* (New York: W. W. Norton, 1978); Lionel Rose, *The Massacre of the Innocents: Infanticide in Britain 1800–1939* (London: Routledge & Kegan Paul, 1986).

13. John Boswell, *The Kindness of Strangers: The Abandonment of Children in Western Europe from Late Antiquity to the Renaissance* (New York: Pantheon Books, 1988). He argues (pp. 42–5, 128–31) that although abandonment or 'exposure' was widespread in premodern times, it did not lead to death so often as many assume. 'The overwhelming belief in the ancient world was that abandoned children were picked up and reared by someone else (p. 131).' Exposure cannot be equated with infanticide.

14. Grant, *State of the World's Children 1993*, pp. 68–9.

15. Marietta Stanton, *Our Children Are Dying* (Buffalo, New York: Prometheus Books, 1990).

16. Ruth Leger Sivard, *World Military and Social Expenditures (Washington, D.C.: World Priorities*, 1991; United Nations Development Programme, *Human Development Report 1991* (New York: Oxford University Press, 1991).

17. Children's Defense Fund, *American Children in Poverty* (Washington, D.C.: CDF, 1984); Children's Defense Fund, *A Children's Defense Budget, FY 1988: An Analysis of Our Nation's Investment in Children* (Washington, D.C.: CDF, 1987); Children's Defense Fund, *The State of America's Children 1992* (Washington, D.C.: CDF, 1992).

18. Sharon Fass Yates, ed., *The Reader's Digest Legal Question & Answer Book* (Pleasantville, New York: The Reader's Digest Association, 1988), p. 601.

19. *DeShaney* v. *Winnebago County Department of Social Services.* United States Reports, 489 (Cases Adjudged in the Supreme Court at October Term, 1988), pp. 189–213.

20. 'Unnatural Acts,' *The Nation*, Vol. 252, No. 21 (June 3, 1991), pp. 723–74. Also see the letters responding to this editorial in the August 26/September 2, 1991 edition. The argument that 'natural' disasters are really not entirely natural or inevitable is elaborated in Anders Wijkman and Lloyd Timberlake, *Natural Disasters: Acts of God or Acts of Man?* (Washington, D.C.: International Institute for Environment and Development, 1984).

21. In *Infanticide* (pp. 15–19), Piers also speaks of 'infanticide by deliberate neglect.' She illustrates the concept by reference to a South American barrio in which 'the seventh or eighth child in a poor family was the one doomed to die. The means of killing were starvation and neglect.' There is a (disputed) concept in law of 'willful negligence,' defined as 'willful determination not to perform a known duty, or a reckless disregard of the safety or the rights of others, as manifested by the conscious and intentional omission of the care proper under the circumstances.' See Henry Campbell Black, *Black's Law Dictionary: Definition of the Terms and Phrases of American and English Jurisprudence, Ancient and Modern*, Fourth Edition (St. Paul, Minnesota: West Publishing Co., 1968), p. 1186.

22. Mark Ritchie, 'Challenging Global Monopolies: Citizen Movements take on Infant Formula Giants,' *Why Magazine*, Vol. 7, (1991), pp. 18–20.

23. Lloyd deMause, 'It's Time to Sacrifice … Our Children,' *Journal of Psychohistory*, Vol. 18, No. 2 (1990), p. 135–44. Also see Ashis Nandy, 'Reconstructing Childhood: A Critique of the Ideology of Adulthood,' *Alternatives*, Vol. X (Winter 1984–5), pp. 359–375; Bernard Flicker, 'Psychohistorical Roots of the War Against Children,' *Journal of Psychohistory*, Vol. 21, No. 1 (Summer 1993), pp. 69–78.

24. Israel Charny, 'Toward a Generic Definition of Genocide,' in George Andreopoulos, ed., *The Conceptual and Historical Dimensions of Genocide* (Philadelphia: University of Pennsylvania Press, 1994), pp. 64–94.

4   Child Labor

1. Abdelwahab Bouhdiba, *Exploitation of Child Labour* (New York: United Nations, 1982), pp. 2, 3, 11, 20.

2. Roger Sawyer,*Children Enslaved* (London: Routledge, 1988), p. 145. The book's frontispiece is a photograph of the child that clearly shows the chain on her leg.

3. See the editorial and several articles in *CHILDAsia*, No. 9 (1993).

4. International Labour Office, *World Labour Report 1993* (Geneva: ILO, 1993), p. 11. The ILO describes itself as the International Labour *Organization* and sometimes as the International Labour *Office.*

5. International Labour Office, *World Labour Report 1993*, pp. 12–3.

6. Data are provided in Children's Defense Fund, *The State of America's Children 1992* (Washington, D.C.: CDF, 1992), p. 126.

7. United States General Accounting Office, *Child Labor: Characteristics of Working Children* (Washington, D.C.: USGAO, 1991).

8. Marguerite Holloway, 'Hard Times: Occupational Injuries Among Children Are Increasing,' *Scientific American* (October 1993), pp. 14, 16.
9. International Labour Office, *World Labour Report 1993*, p. 18.
10. Bouhdiba, *Exploitation of Child Labour*, p. 6.
11. Victor Rialp, *Children and Hazardous Work in the Philippines*; S. W. E. Goonesekere, *Child Labour in Sri Lanka: Learning from the Past*; and Alec Fyfe, *Child Labour: A Guide to Project Design*. All three were published by the ILO in Geneva in 1993. Related ILO publications include *Child Labour: A Briefing Manual*; Assefa Bequele and Jo Boyden, eds., *Combating Child Labour* (Geneva: ILO, 1988); and William E. Myers, 'Urban Working Children: A Comparison of Four Surveys from South America,' *International Labour Review*, Vol. 128, No. 3 (1989), pp. 321–35.
12. At the World Conference on Human Rights held in Vienna in June 1993 the ILO distributed free copies of *Children in Shadow*, an elegant book full of color photographs illustrating case after case of children working under stressful conditions. It offered no insight as to what might be done about the problem.
13. Myron Weiner, *The Child and the State in India: Child Labor and Education Policy in Comparative Perspective* (Princeton, New Jersey: Princeton University Press, 1991).
14. United States Department of State, *Country Reports on Human Rights Practices for 1988* (Washington, D.C.: U.S. Government Printing Office, 1989), p. 946.
15. Centre for the Protection of Children's Rights, *A Just World for Our Future* (Bangkok: CPCR, 1989).
16. Sumanta Banerjee, *Child Labour in Thailand: A General Review* (London: Anti-Slavery Society, 1980), p. 30.
17. William E. Myers, ed., *Protecting Working Children* (London: Zed Books, 1991).
18. International Labour Office, *World Labour Report 1993*, p. 12.
19. Peter Dorman, *Worker Rights and U.S. Trade Policy: An Evaluation of Worker Rights Conditionality Under the General System of Preferences* (Washington, D.C.: U.S. Department of Labor, 1989).
20. Charles D. Gray and Robert A. Senser, 'Children Who Labor: The Tragedy of Child Workers Around the World,' *American Educator, Summer 1989*.
21. Generalized System of Preferences (GSP), Subcommittee of the Trade Policy Staff Committee, 1992 GSP Annual Review, *Workers Rights Review Summary, Case: 013-CP-92, Thailand* (Washington, D.C.: GSP Information Center, Office of the U.S. Trade Representative, 1993).
22. Letter received from Bureau of International Labor Affairs, Office of International Economic Affairs, U.S. Department of Labor, March 1994.
23. Bina Agarwal, 'Social Security and the Family: Coping with Seasonality and Calamity in Rural India,' in Ehtisham Ahmad, Jean Drèze, John Hills, and Amartya Sen, eds., *Social Security in Developing Countries* (Oxford: Clarendon Press, 1991), pp. 171–244; quotation is from pp. 231–2.
24. U.S. Congress. House. *Microenterprise Development. Hearing Before the Subcommittee on International Economic Policy of the Committee on Foreign Affairs* (Washington, D.C.: U.S. Government Printing Office, 1991), p. 4.

25. Alain Mingat and Jee-Peng Tan, 'Financing Public Higher Education in Developing Countries,' *Higher Education*, Vol. 15 (1986), pp. 283–97; Douglas Albrecht and Adrian Ziderman, 'Student Loans: An Effective Instrument for Cost Recovery in Higher Education?' *World Bank Research Observer*, Vol. 8, No. 1 (January 1993), pp. 71–90.

5   Child Prostitution

1. 'The Number of Prostitutes in Thailand,' *Bangkok Post, August 29, 1992;* reprinted in *ECPAT Newsletter*, No. 5 (October 1992), p. 7.

2. M. Lemineur, *Child Prostitution in Brazil*, as cited in Vitit Muntarbhorn, *Report of the Special Rapporteur, Mr. V. Muntarbhorn, pursuant to Commision on Human Rights resolution 1990/68, Addendum*, United Nations document E/CN.4/1992/55/Add.1 (11 February 1992), p. 9.

3. Kenneth J. Herrman, Jr. and Michael Jupp, 'International Sex Trade,' in Daniel S. Campagna and Donald L. Poffenberger, *The Sexual Trafficking in Children: An Investigation of the Child Sex Trade* (Dover, Massachusetts: Auburn House, 1988), p. 147. Judith Ennew, in *The Sexual Exploitation of Children* (Cambridge: Polity Press, 1986) suggests that much of the published information on child prostitution is exaggerated and sensationalized.

4. Yayori Matsui, *Women's Asia* (London: Zed Books, 1987), pp. 64–6.

5. Ove Narvesen, *The Sexual Exploitation of Children in Developing Countries* (Oslo: Redd Barna, 1989), p. 26.

6. Kathleen Barry, *Female Sexual Slavery* (New York: New York University Press, 1984), pp. 22, 24, 35.

7. Lai Ah Eng, *Peasants, Proletarians and Prostitutes: A Preliminary Investigation into the Work of Chinese Women in Colonial Malaya* (Singapore: Institute of Southeast Asian Studies, 1986), p. 28.

8. Noeleen Heyzer, *Working Women in South-East Asia: Development, Subordination and Emancipation* (Philadelphia: Open University Press, 1986), pp. 62–3.

9. Quoted in Edward J. Bristow, *Prostitution and Prejudice: The Jewish Fight Against White Slavery 1870–1939* (New York: Schocken Books, 1982), p. 1. For a time in central Europe the taint on the Jewish community was relieved by 'the requirement that Jewish women be baptized before being allowed to practice licensed prostitution (p. 16).'

10. Bristow, *Prostitution and Prejudice*, p. 2.

11. Barry, *Female Sexual Slavery*, p. 68.

12. 'Thai Report Highlights Child Slavery Problem,' *International Children's Rights Monitor*, Vol. 2, No. 1 (1985).

13. INTERPOL, *International Symposium on Traffic in Human Beings*, 21st-23rd September 1988, p. 10.

14. INTERPOL, *International Symposium . . .*, p. 9.

15. Herrman and Jupp, 'International Sex Trade,' p. 143.

16. Edward J. Bristow, *Vice and Vigilance: Purity Movements in Britain Since 1700* (Totowa, New Jersey: Rowman and Littlefield, 1977), p. 179.

17. Quoted in Ulla Ohse, *Forced Prostitution and Traffic in Women in West Germany* (Edinburgh, Scotland: Human Rights Group, 1984), p. 12.

18. Ramesh Menon, 'Child Prostitutes: Nobody's Children,' *India Today*, April 15, 1989, p. 126.
19. Herrman and Jupp, 'International Sex Trade,' p. 150.
20. Bristow, *Prostitution and Prejudice*, p. 98.
21. Quoted in *Restavek: Child Domestic Labor in Haiti* (Minneapolis, Minnesota: Minnesota Lawyers International Human Rights Committee, 1990), p. 22.
22 Tsukamoto Yumi, 'Trafficking in Women: Sex Tours Come Home to Japan,' in *Female Sexual Slavery and Economic Exploitation: Making Local and Global Connections*. Report of a Consultation Organized by the Non-Governmental Liaison Service (New York), San Francisco, California, October 25, 1984, pp. 57–9.
23. Sean O'Callaghan, *The Yellow Slave Trade: A Survey of the Traffic in Women and Children in the East* (London: Anthony Blond, 1968), p. 26.
24. Narvesen, *The Sexual Exploitation of Children in Developing Countries*, p. 46.
25. Narvesen, *The Sexual Exploitation of Children in Developing Countries*, pp. 46–7.
26. Nanya Pancharoen, 'Prostitution is a Lucrative Booming Industry in Thailand,' *The Nation*, February 27, 1989.
27. *Child Prostitution and Tourism: Philippines Country Report*, presented at the Ecumenical Consultation on Tourism and Child Prostitution, Chiang Mai, Thailand, May 1990, p. III:3.
28. 'Child Prostitution: An Unending Vortex,' *Thai Development Newsletter*, No. 17 (1989), p. 27.
29. Pico Iyer, *Video Night in Kathmandu: And Other Reports from the Not-So-Far-East* (New York: Knopf, 1988), p. 292.
30. *Pom Pom: Child and Youth Prostitution in the Philippines* (Quezon City, Philippines: Health Action Information Network), 1987, p. 27.
31. *Pom Pom*, p. 27.
32. *Pom Pom*, p. 28. The quotation is from *Spartacus Holiday Help Portfolio: Manila*, published in Amsterdam in 1980.
33. Narvesen, *The Sexual Exploitation of Children in Developing Countries*, p. 27.
34. Herrman and Jupp, 'International Sex Trade,' p. 143.
35. Anti-Slavery Society, 'Sexual Exploitation of Children,' *Response*, Vol. 8, No. 2 (Spring 1985), pp. 13–14.
36. Marlise Simons, 'The Sex Market: Scourge on the World's Children,' *New York Times*, April 9, 1993.
37. Aihwa Ong, 'Industrialization and Prostitution in Southeast Asia,' in *Female Sexual Slavery and Economic Exploitation*, pp. 13, 18.
38. *Time*, June 21, 1993, pp. 44–55.
39. Linda Hosek, 'Priest to Meet Navy Officials About Philippine Child Sex,' *Star-Bulletin* (Honolulu), August 29, 1989, p. A–7.
40. Brenda Stoltzfus, *Situationer on Prostitution in Olongapo* May 1987, p. 2.
41. Eva Arnvig, 'Child Prostitution in Cambodia: Did the UN Look Away?' *International Children's Rights Monitor*, Vol. 10, No. 3 (3rd Quarter 1993), pp. 4–6.

42. Lucy Komisar, 'In a Honduran Red-Light District,' *Utne Reader* (April/May 1985), p. 89.
43. Narvesen, *The Sexual Exploitation of Children in Developing Countries* p. 33.
44. *Child Prostitution and Tourism: Philippines Country Report*, presented at the Ecumenical Consultation on Tourism and Child Prostitution, Chiang Mai, Thailand, May 1990, p. II:1.
45. Seth Mydans, 'Philippine Town's Parents Battle Effort to Stop Their Children's Sex Trade,' *New York Times*, February 25, 1989, p. 3.
46. Paul Ehrlich, 'Asia's Shocking Secret,' *Reader's Digest* (October 1993), pp. 69–74.
47. Ron O'Grady, *Tourism in the Third World: Christian Reflections* (Maryknoll, New York: Orbis Books, 1982), p. 37.
48. Tim Bond, *Hello, What's Your Name, Then? Tourists, Boys, and Sri Lanka. The Results*, Geneva: Terre des Hommes, 1980.
49. *Sri Lanka National Report*, presented at the Ecumenical Consultation on Tourism and Child Prostitution, Chiang Mai, Thailand, May 1990, p. 3. For an interview with a 14-year old child prostitute in Sri Lanka, see 'My Best Customers are the Tourists,' *Child Workers in Asia*, Vol. 6, No. 2 (June 1990), pp. 16–7.
50. Jack Anderson, 'Bangkok's Kiddy Sex Market,' *San Francisco Chronicle*, June 1990.
51. A statement on NAMBLA's philosophy may be found in David Hechler, *The Battle and the Backlash: The Child Sexual Abuse War* (Lexington, Massachusetts: Lexington Books, 1988), pp. 293–9.
52. Bristow, *Prostitution and Prejudice*, pp. 2–3, 33–4.
53. Barry, *Female Sexual Slavery*, p. 70.
54. Bristow, *Prostitution and Prejudice*, p. 135.
55. Barry, *Female Sexual Slavery*, pp. 53–8.
56. Arthur Bonner, *Averting the Apocalypse: Social Movements in India Today* (Durham, North Carolina: Duke University Press, 1990), p. 45. Also see K. T. Suresh, *A Contextual View of Tourism and Child Prostitution in India*, presented at the Ecumenical Consultation on Tourism and Child Prostitution, Chiang Mai, Thailand, May 1990. Details may be found in M. Rita Rozario, *Trafficking in Women and Children in India: Sexual Exploitation and Sale* (New Delhi: Uppal Publishing House, 1988).
57. Quoted in Yumi, 'Trafficking in Women: Sex Tours Come Home to Japan,' in *Female Sexual Slavery and Economic Exploitation*, p. 57.
58. Simon Long, 'Chasing the Dragons of the Flesh Trade,' *The Sunday Correspondent* (London), January 14, 1990.
59. Matsui, *Women's Asia*, pp. 70–1.
60. Park Sun Ai, in Ron O'Grady, *The Child and the Tourist* (Bangkok: End Child Prostitution in Asian Tourism, 1991).
61. M. L. Tan, 'An Overview of Pedophilia and Child Prostitution in the Philippines,' in *Pom Pom*, pp. 12–3.
62. Erik Cohen, 'Thai Girls and Farang Men: The Edge of Ambiguity,' *Annals of Tourism Research*, Vol. 9 (1982), p. 409.
63. Anita Dahiya, 'Problems of Prostitution with Special Reference to Girl Child: A Legal Perspective,' paper C-1 in proceedings of the *International Conference Hosted by the Indian Law Institute on the Theme: Shaping the*

Future by Law: Children, Environment and Human Health (New Delhi: Indian Law Institute, 1994).

64. *Sexual Exploitation of Children: Hearings on H.R. 4571 Before the Subcommittee on Crime of the House Committee on the Judiciary*, 95th Contress, 1st Session (1977), p. 347.

65. Children's Defense Fund, *The State of America's Children 1992* (Washington, D.C.: CDF, 1992), p. x.

66. An overview of legislation in the United States relating to juvenile prostitution is provided in D. Kelly Weisberg, *Children of the Night: A Study of Adolescent Prostitution* (Lexington, Massachusetts: Lexington Books, 1985). An appendix charts the main features of the state statutes. A journalistic account describing the impacts of enforcement attempts may be found in Elaine Landau, *On the Streets: The Lives of Adolescent Prostitutes* (New York: Julian Messner/Simon & Schuster, 1987).

67. Weisberg, *Children of the Ni*ght, p. 206.

68. Prostitution is not mentioned in the exhaustive compendium by Robert H. Mnookin and D. Kelly Weisberg, *Child, Family and State: Problems and Materials on Children and the Law*, Second Edition (Boston: Little Brown, 1988). The 1979–89 Cumulative Index for the *Children's Legal Rights Journal* does not mention prostitution.

69. Howard Davidson, 'The New United Nations Convention on the Rights of the Child: A Preliminary Assessment of Legal Isssues Related to U.S. Ratification,' *Children's Legal Rights Journal*, Vol. 11, No. 1 (Spring 1990), pp. 8–12.

70. Weisberg, *Children of the Night*, p. 216.

71. Weisberg, *Children of the Night*, p. 234.

72. Weisberg, *Children of the Night*, p. 209.

73. Michael Fooner, *Interpol: Issues in World Crime and International Criminal Justice* (New York: Plenum Press, 1989); Malcolm Anderson, *Policing the World: Interpol and the Politics of International Police Cooperation* (Oxford: Clarendon Press, 1989).

74. Barry, *Female Sexual Slavery*, pp. 283–98.

75. For a report on the 1989 meeting see Commission on Human Rights, Sub-Commission on Prevention of Discrimination and Protection of Minorities, Forty-First Session, *Slavery and Slavery-Like Practices: Question of Slavery and the Slave Trade in All Their Practices and Manifestations, Including the Slavery-Like Practice of Apartheid and Colonialism, Report of the Working Group on Contemporary Forms of Slavery on its Fourteenth Session*, United Nations document E/CN.4/Sub.2/1989/39 (28 August 1989).

76. Department of International Economic and Social Affairs, *Activities for the Advancement of Women: Equality, Development and Peace; Report of Jean Fernand-Laurent, Special Rapporteur on the Suppression of the Traffic in Persons and the Exploitation of the Prostitution of Others* (New York: United Nations, 1985).

77. Muntarbhorn, *Sale of Children*, United Nations document E/CN.4/1991/51 (28 January 1991), and Vitit Muntarbhorn, *Sale of Children*, United Nations document E/CN.4/1992/55 (22 January 1992). Also see Vitit Muntarbhorn, *Report of the Special Rapporteur, Mr. V. Muntarbhorn, pursuant*

to *Commision on Human Rights resolution 1990/68, Addendum Visit by the Special Rapporteur to Brazil*, United Nations document E/CN.4/1992/55/Add.1 (11 February 1992). Earlier work of the Commission on Human Rights on child prostitution is reported in *Slavery and Slavery-Like Practices: Question of Slavery and the Slave Trade in All Their Practices and Manifestations, including the Slavery-Like Practice of Apartheid and Colonialism*, E/CN.4/Sub.2/1989/39 (28 August 1989).

78. *International Children's Rights Monitor*, Vol. 2, No. 1 (1985).
79. Barry, *Female Sexual Slavery*, pp. 23–4.
80. Kathleen Barry, Charlotte Bunch, and Shirley Castley, eds., *International Feminism: Networking Against Female Sexual Slavery* (New York: International Women's Tribune Center, 1983).
81. *Female Sexual Slavery and Economic Exploitation: Making Local and Global Connections*. Report of a Consultation Organized by the Non-Governmental Liaison Service (New York), San Francisco, California, October 25, 1984.
82. ECPAT can be reachby mai at 328 Phayatai Road, Bangkok, Thailand, 10400, by phone at 662 215 3388, or by fax at 662 215 8272.
83. Barry, *Female Sexual Slavery*, pp. 32–3.
84. M. L. Tan, 'Preface,' in *Pom Pom*, p. 1.
85. Simons, 'The Sex Market'. Vitit Muntarbhorn, in *Sale of Children* (E/CN.4/1992/55), pp. 27–8 also observed that 'customers are opting more and more for younger prostitutes, particularly virgins, in the belief that they will protect themselves from the threat of AIDS. The market is spiralling towards the very young ...'

6 Armed Conflict

1. Ron Arias, 'Agonies of the Innocents,' *People Weekly*, February 29, 1988, pp. 46–53.
2. Anne Elizabeth Nixon, *The Status of Palestinian Children During the Uprising in the Occupied Territories* (Stockholm: Rädda Barnen, 1990).
3. James P. Grant, *The State of the World's Children 1994* (New York: Oxford University Press, 1994), p.4.
4. Jane Green Schaller and Elena O. Nightingale, 'Children and Childhoods: Hidden Casualties of War and Civil Unrest,' *Journal of the American Medical Associaton*, Vol. 268, No. 5 (August 5, 1992), pp. 642–4. The El Mozote massacre is described in detail in *The New Yorker* of December 6, 1993. The killing of children is described on pp. 84–8.
5. Neil Boothby, 'Children and War,' *Cultural Survival Quarterly*, Vol. 10, No. 4 (1986), pp. 28–30.
6. 'Children Under Attack By Governments,' *Amnesty Action*, January/February 1988, p. 2.
7. Michael Jupp, 'Apartheid: Violence Against Children,' *Cultural Survival Quarterly*, Vol. 10, No. 4 (1986), pp. 34–7.
8. Rémi Russbach, 'Casualties of Conflicts and Mine Warfare,' in Kevin M. Cahill, ed., *A Framework for Survival: Health, Human Rights, and Humanitarian Assistance in Conflicts and Disasters* (New York: Basic

Books/Council on Foreign Relations, 1993), pp. 121–37. Also see Susan Ruel, *The Scourge of Land Mines: UN Tackles Hidden Peacetime Killers* in the United Nations Department of Public Information series, *United Nations Focus*, in October 1993.

9. 'A Time for Decision,' *International Review of the Red Cross*, No. 297 (November–December 1993), pp. 471–3. UNICEF has published a report on its *UNICEF Mine Awareness Project in El Salvador*. See 'Making People Aware of Mines in El Salvador,' *First Call for Children*, No. 1 (January–March 1994), p. 2.

10. Boothby, 'Children and War.'

11. Boothby, 'Children and War.'

12. *International Children's Rights Monitor*, Vol. 5, No. 1 (1988), p. 21.

13. *International Children's Rights Monitor*, Vol. 5, No. 1 (1988), p. 23.

14. Dominique Leveille, 'Children Used by the Guerrilla in Mozambique: Younger than the War Itself,' *International Children's Rights Monitor*, Vol. 5, No. 1 (1988), p. 24.

15. Cole P. Dodge, 'Child Soldiers of Uganda: What Does the Future Hold?' *Cultural Survival Quarterly*, Vol. 10, No. 4 (1986), pp. 31–3.

16. The estimate was made in a 1987 paper on *Children's Military Training and Service: Instances of Extra-Legal Conscription and Conditions of Service and Training and Employment* by Dorothea Woods. Dr. Woods maintained this 200 000 estimate in personal correspondence in late 1991.

17. Dorothea Woods, *Children at War: Some Developments 1991–1993* (June 1993). Ms. Woods' reports are distributed by the Quaker United Nations Office–Geneva, Quaker House, Avenue du Mervelet 13, 1209 Geneva, Switzerland.

18. Meng Try Ea, 'War and Famine: The Example of Kampuchea,' in Bruce Currey and Graeme Hugo, eds., *Famine as a Geographical Phenomenon* (Dordrecht, Holland: D. Reidel Publishing Company, 1984), pp. 33–47.

19. *Children on the Front Line: The Impact of Apartheid, Destabilization and Warfare on Children in Southern and South Africa* (New York: UNICEF, 1987).

20. Francis M. Deng and Larry Minear, *The Challenges of Famine Relief: Emergency Operations in the Sudan* (Washington, D.C.: The Brookings Institution, 1992); Thomas G. Weiss and Larry Minear, eds., *Humanitarianism Across Borders: Sustaining Civilians in Times of War* (Boulder, Colorado: Lynne Rienner, 1993).

21. 'One Fourth of Somalia Tots Dead,' *Honolulu Star-Bulletin*, August 18, 1992, p. A-8.

22. Jean Mayer, 'International Agreements in the Food and Health Fields,' in Alan K. Henrikson, ed., *Negotiating World Order: The Artisanship and Architecture of Global Diplomacy* (Wilmington, Delaware: Scholarly Resources, Inc., 1986), pp. 3–17.

23. Robert Conquest, *The Harvest of Sorrow: Soviet Collectivization and the Terror -- Famine* (New York: Oxford University Press, 1986), p. 297.

24. Dan Jacobs, *The Brutality of Nations* (New York: Alfred A. Knopf, 1987).

25. Beth Osborne Daponte, 'A Case Study in Estimating Casualties from War and Its Aftermath: the 1991 Persian Gulf War,' *PSR Quarterly* (Physicians for Social Responsibility), Vol. 3, No. 2 (June 1993), pp. 57–66.

26.   Richard Reid, 'Lifelines to the Innocent: Children Caught in War,' in Cahill, *A Framework for Survival*, pp. 275–92, at 276. Also see Ellen Messer, 'Food Wars: Hunger as a Weapon of War in 1993,' in Peter Uvin, ed., *The Hunger Report: 1993* (Providence, Rhode Island: World Hunger Program, Program University/Gordon and Breach, 1994), pp. 43–69.

27.   See, for example, Anna Freud and Dorothy T. Burlingham, *War and Children* (New York: Medical War Books, 1943); Alice Cobb, *War's Unconquered Children Speak* (Boston: Beacon Press, 1953).

28.   Alison Acker, *Children of the Volcano* (Westport, Connecticut: Lawrence Hill & Co., 1986), pp. 24–5.

29.   William Vornberger, ed., *Fire From the Sky: Salvadoran Children's Drawings* (New York: Writers and Readers Publishing Cooperative, 1986).

30.   Arata Osada, *Children of the A-Bomb: The Testament of the Boys and Girls of Hiroshima* (Tokyo: Uchida Rokakuho, 1959); Child Study Association of America, *Children and the Threat of Nuclear War* (New York: Duell, Sloan and Pearce, 1964); Florence Weiner, *Peace is You and Me: Children's Writings and Paintings on Love and Peace* (New York: Avon, 1971); Children of Hiroshima (London: Taylor & Francis, 1981); Helen Caldicott, *Missile Envy: The Arms Race and Nuclear War* (Toronto: Bantam Books, 1986), pp. 251–6; Phyllis La Farge, *The Strangelove Legacy: Children, Parents, and Teachers in the Nuclear Age* (New York: Harper & Row, 1987).

31.   Jeremy Harbison and Joan Harbison, *A Society Under Stress: Children and Young People in Northern Ireland* (Somerset, England: Open Books, 1980).

32.   Jennifer W. Bryce, *Cries of Children in Lebanon: As Voiced by Their Mothers* (Amman, Jordan: UNICEF Regional Office for the Middle East and North Africa, 1986).

33.   Cole P. Dodge and Magne Raundalen, eds., *War, Violence and Children in Uganda* (Oslo: Norwegian University Press, 1987). Also see Cole P. Dodge and Paul D. Wiebe, eds., *Crisis in Uganda: The Breakdown of Health Services* (New York: Pergamon Press, 1985).

34.   Ivanka Zivcic, 'Emotional Reactions of Children to War Stress in Croatia,' *Journal of the American Academy of Child and Adolescent Psychiatry*, Vol. 32, No. 4 (July 1993), pp. 709–13. The diary of a young girl suffering through the war in Sarajevo, reminiscent of Anne Frank's famous diary, was published in the U.S. in 1994. See Zlata Filipovic, *Zlata's Diary: A Child's Life in Sarajevo* (New York: Viking Penguin, 1994).

35.   Howard Tolley, Jr., *Children and War: Political Socialization to International Conflict* (New York: Teachers College Press, 1973).

36.   An overview of such studies may be found in Peter S. Jensen and John Shaw, 'Children as Victims of War: Current Knowledge and Future Research Needs,' *Journal of the American Academy of Child and Adolescent Psychiatry*, Vol. 32, No. 4 (July 1993), pp. 697–708.

37.   James P. Grant, *The State of the World's Children 1986* (New York: Oxford University Press, 1986), p. 72.

38.   Grant, *The State of the World's Children 1987*, p. 17.

39.   Grant, *The State of the World's Children 1987*, p. 9. The impact of defense spending on children is examined systematically in Saadet Deger and

Somnath Sen, *Arms and the Child* (New York: Oxford University Press, 1993).

40. John C. Caldwell, *Children of Calamity* (New York: John Day Company, 1957).
41. *International Children's Rights Monitor*, Vol. 5, No. 2/3 (1988), p. 10.
42. John A. Shade, *America's Forgotten Children: The Amerasians* (Perkasie, Pennsylvania: Pearl S. Buck Foundation, Inc., 1981).
43. Beverly Creamer, 'Children of the Dust: Hoping for New Lives in America,' *Honolulu Advertiser*, May 9, 1988, p. B-1.
44. 'Filipino Amerasians to File Class Action Suit,' *Sunday Star-Bulletin and Advertiser* (Honolulu), February 28, 1993, p. A19; S. L. Bachman, 'Life Around U.S. Bases Abroad May Change,' *Honolulu Advertiser*, March 14, 1993, p. B-1; 'Amerasian Children: Claim in US Courts,' *International Children's Rights Monitor*, Vol. 10, No. 4 (4th quarter, 1993), p. 29.
45. '300 Babies Reported Abandoned,' *New York Times*, January 27, 1993, p. A3.
46. Susan Brownmiller, *Against Our Will: Men, Women, and Rape* (New York: Simon and Schuster, 1975); Shana Swiss and Joan E. Giller, 'Rape as a Crime of War: A Medical Perspective,' *JAMA (Journal of the American Medical Association)*, Vol. 270, No. 5 (August 4, 1993), pp. 612–5.
47. Maggie Black, *The Children and the Nations: The Story of Unicef* (New York: UNICEF, 1986).
48. Everett M. Ressler, Neil Boothby, and Daniel J. Steinbock, *Unaccompanied Children: Care and Protection in Wars, Natural Disasters, and Refugee Movements* (New York: Oxford University Press, 1988).
49. Everett Ressler, *Evacuation of Children from Conflict Areas: Considerations and Guidelines* (Geneva: UNHCR and UNICEF, 1992).
50. *A Children's Defense Budget, FY 1988: An Analysis of Our Nation's Investment in Children* (Washington, D.C.: Children's Defense Fund, 1987). Also see Stephen Coats, *Military Spending and World Hunger: Let Them Eat Missiles* (Washington, D.C.: Bread for the World Background Paper No. 62, 1982); Marian Wright Edelman, 'How the Military Budget Hurts America's Children,' *Food Monitor*, No. 41 (Summer 1987), pp. 3–5, 23.
51. See, for example, Lester Brown, 'Redefining National Security' in Lester Brown *et al., State of the World 1986* (Washington, D.C.: Worldwatch Institute, 1986), pp. 195–211.
52. Muzammel Huq, 'The Structure of Hunger,' *Unesco Courier*, September 1980, p. 16.
53. *International Review of the Red Cross*, No. 294 (May–June 1993), p. 256. The numbers are regularly updated in each issue of the *Review*.
54. The application of the Geneva conventions and the protocols to children is analyzed in Denise Plattner, 'Protection of Children in International Humanitarian Law,' *International Review of the Red Cross* (May–June 1984) and Sandra Singer, 'The Protection of Children During Armed Conflict Situations,' *International Review of the Red Cross* (May–June 1986), pp. 133–68. Also see M. Ressler, *Unaccompanied Children*, pp. 246–61.
55. Several countries made reservations or declarations in which they indicated their preference for prohibiting recruitment of any child up to the age of 18. See the texts for Argentina, Colombia, Ecuador, Poland, Spain, and

Uruguay in *Reservations, Declarations and Objections Relating to the Convention on the Rights of the Child*, CRC/C/2, 22 August 1991.

56. 'Child-Rights Treaty Ready, But Debate Over It Goes On,' *New York Times*, December 11, 1988, p. 15.

57. I am indebted to Dorothea Woods for providing this paraphase of and comment on an article by Serge Marti, 'Les Nations Unies ont adopté à l'unanimité la convention sur les droits de l'enfant' *Le Monde*, November 21, 1989. On May 17, 1991 the *Times* of London reported that a parliamentary inquiry had called for a ban on troops being sent to fight abroad after it was learned that 200 minors had been deployed to the Gulf. Two soldiers aged 17 were among the 34 British casualties in the Gulf war.

58. *World Declaration on the Survival, Protection and Development of Children and Plan of Action for Implementing the World Declaration on the Survival, Protection and Development of Children in the 1990s* (New York: United Nations, 1990).

59. Neil Boothby, 'Children and War,' *Cultural Survival Quarterly*, Vol. 10, No. 4 (1986), pp. 28–30.

60. Neil Boothby, in United States Senate, *Children of War: Victims of Conflict and Dislocation*. Hearing before the Subcommittee on Children, Family, Drugs and Alcoholism of the Committee on Labor and Human Resources (Washington, D.C.: U.S. Government Printing Office, 1990), p. 45.

61. Maurice Flagg, in United States Senate, *Children of War*, pp. 110–11.

62. See 'ICRC Protection and Assistance Activities in Situations Not Covered by International Humanitarian Law,' *International Review of the Red Cross*, January–February 1988.

63. Plattner, 'Protection of Children in International Humanitarian Law,' p. 140.

64. *ICRC and Children in Situations of Armed Conflict* (Geneva: International Committee of the Red Cross, July 1987), p. 13.

65. Peter T. White, 'A Little Humanity Amid the Horrors of War,' *National Geographic*, Vol. 170, No. 5 (November 1986), pp. 647–79.

66. Maria Teresa Dutli, 'National Measures for Implementation of National Humanitarian Law, *Dissemination*, No. 13 (May 1990), pp. 8–10. Also see Frits Kalshoven and Yves Sandoz, *The Implementation of International Humanitarian Law* (Boston: Nijhoff, 1989).

67. *Children in Situations of Armed Conflict* (New York: UNICEF E/ICEF/1986/CRP.2, 1986); *Overview: Children in Especially Difficult Circumstances* (New York: UNICEF E/ICEF/1986/L.6, 1986).

68. 'Protection Urged for Children in Armed Conflict,' *UNICEF Intercom*, No. 46 (October 1987), p. 17.

69. Varindra Tarzie Vittachi, *Between the Guns: Children as a Zone of Peace* (London: Hodder & Stoughton, 1993).

70. Ernesto Attias and Ilene Cohn, *Children and War: Report on 'The Psychosocial Impact of Violence on Children in Central America'* (Guatemala: UNICEF Area Office for Central America and Panama, 1990).

71. Everett M. Ressler, Joanne Marie Tortorici, and Alex Marcelino, *Children in War: A Guide to the Provision of Services* (New York: UNICEF, 1993).

72. Boothby, 'Children and War.'

73. This proposal was included among the final recommendations in *Children of War: Report from the Conference on Children of War Organized by*

Swedish Red Cross, Swedish Save the Children and Raoul Wallenberg
Institute, Stockholm 31 May–2 June 1991 (Lund: Raoul Wallenberg Institute
of Human Rights and Humanitarian Law, Report No. 10, 1991).

7 Malnutrition

1. James E. Austin, *Confronting Urban Malnutrition: The Design of Nutrition
    Programs* (Baltimore: Johns Hopkins University Press/World Bank, 1980),
    p. 10.
2. D. S. McLaren, 'The Great Protein Fiasco,' *Lancet*, Vol. 2 (1974), pp. 93–6.
3. Urban Jonsson, *Nutrition and the United Nations Convention on the Rights
    of the Child* (Florence, Italy: International Child Develpment Centre, 1993).
4. See, for example, C. S. Wilson, 'Food Taboos of Childbirth: The Malay
    Example,' *Ecology of Food and Nutrition*, Vol. 2 (1973), pp. 267–74; C.
    Laderman, 'Food Ideology and Eating Behavior: Contributions from Malay
    Studies,' *Social Science & Medicine*, Vol. 19, No. 5 (1984), pp. 547–59; K.
    A. Dettwyler, 'Infant Feeding in Mali: Variations in Belief and Practice,'
    Social Science & Medicine, Vol. 23 (1986), pp. 651–64.
5. See the Special Issue on *Household Food Distribution* of *Food and
    Nutrition Bulletin*, Vol. 5, No. 4 (December 1983). This journal regularly
    carries articles on the distribution of food within the household.
6. United Nations, Administrative Committee on Coordination/Subcommittee
    on Nutrition, *Second Report …*, p. viii.
7. United Nations Children's Fund, *Food, Health and Care: The UNICEF
    Vision and Strategy for a World Free From Hunger and Malnutrition* (New
    York: UNICEF, 1993).
8. Amartya Sen, *Poverty and Famines: An Essay on Entitlements* (New York:
    Oxford, 1981); Jean Drèze and Amartya Sen, *Hunger and Public Action*
    (Oxford: Clarendon Press, 1989); Jean Drèze and Amartya Sen, eds., *The
    Political Economy of Hunger*, Vols. I–III (New York: Oxford, 1990).
9. Drèze and Sen, *Hunger and Public Action*, pp. 9, 22.
10. Sen and his colleagues have provided an overview of ways in which social
    service programs can be structured, but did not argue that the needy should
    have rights to some services under some conditions. See Ehtisham Ahmad,
    Jean Drèze, John Hills, and Amartya Sen, eds., *Social Security in
    Developing Countries* (Oxford: Clarendon Press, 1991).
11. *Child Survival and Development in Indonesia 1985–1989* (Jakarta:
    Government of Indonesia and UNICEF, 1985), p. 1.
12. Arnfried A. Kielman and Colin McCord, 'Weight-for-Age as an Index of
    Risk of Death in Children,' *Lancet*, Vol. 1, No. 8076 (June 10, 1978),
    pp. 1247–50.
13. Lincoln C. Chen, A. K. M. A. Chowdhury, and Sandra L. Huffman,
    'Anthropometric Assessment of Energy-Protein Malnutrition and
    Subsequent Risk of Mortality Among Preschool Aged Children,' *American
    Journal of Clinical Nutrition*, Vol. 33, No. 8 (August 1980), pp. 1836–45.
    Also see World Bank, *World Development Report 1993* (New York: Oxford
    University Press, 1993), p. 77.
14. S. W. R. de A. Samarasinghe, 'Sri Lanka: A Case Study from the Third
    World,' in David E. Bell and Michael R. Reich, eds., *Health, Nutrition, and*

Economic Crises: Approaches to Policy in the Third World (Dover, Massachusetts: Auburn House, 1988), pp. 39–80, especially p. 75.

15. C. R. Soman, 'Inter-Relationship between Fertility, Mortality and Nutrition–The Kerala Experience,' in P. V. Sukhatme, ed., *Newer Concepts in Nutrition and Their Implications for Policy* (Pune, India: Maharashtra Association for the Cultivation of Science, 1982); T. N. Krishnan, 'Infant Mortality in Kerala State, India,' *Assignment Children*, Vol. 65/68 (1984), pp. 293–308.

16. The linkage between mild and moderate (rather than severe) malnutrition and children's mortality is explored in Reynaldo Martorell and Teresa J. Ho, 'Malnutrition, Morbidity, and Mortality,' in W. Henry Mosley and Lincoln C. Chen, eds, *Child Survival: Strategies for Research* (Cambridge: Cambridge University Press, 1984), pp. 49–68.

17. In UNICEF's *The Progress of Nations 1994* (New York: UNICEF, 1994), Urban Jonsson says 'about 55% of the 13 million under-five deaths in the world each year are the deaths of children who were malnourished. And of those 7 million nutrition-related deaths, some 80 % are the deaths of children who were only mildly or moderately malnourished (p. 7).' He carefully speaks of *nutrition-related* deaths, and stops short of suggesting they were entirely due to malnutrition. In October 1994 the *Journal of Nutrition* published a special supplement on 'The Relationship between Anthropometry and Mortality in Developing Countries.'

18. W. Henry Mosley and Lincoln C. Chen, 'An Analytic Framework for the Study of Child Survival in Developing Countries,' in Mosley and Chen, *Child Survival*, pp. 25–45.

19. Leonard Sagan, *The Health of Nations: True Causes of Sickness and Well-Being* (New York: Basic Books, 1987), pp. 100–02.

20. James P. Grant, *The State of the World's Children 1987* (New York: Oxford University Press, 1987), p. 65.

21. G. H. Beaton and H. Ghassemi, 'Supplementary Feeding Programs for Young Children in Developing Countries,' *American Journal of Clinical Nutrition*, Vol. 35 (1982), pp. 864–916.

22. United Nations, Administrative Committee on Coordination/Subcommittee on Nutrition, *Second Report on the World Nutrition Situation* (Geneva: ACC/SCN, 1992), p. 7. Also see Michael C. Latham, 'Growth Monitoring and Promotion' and other articles in John H. Himes, ed., *Anthropometric Assessment of Nutritional Status* (New York: Wiley-Liss, 1991), and J. Cervinkas, N. M. Gerein, and Sabu George, *Growth Promotion and Development: Proceedings of a Colloquium held in Nyeri, Kenya, 12–13 May 1992* (Ottawa: International Development Research Centre, 1993). There are computer programs that can be used to help analyze the data. *EPINUT* is an analytical program for nutritional anthropometry that is included in *EpiInfo*, a multipurpose computer system for dealing with epidemiological statistics. Version 6 was released in mid-1994 by USD, Incorporated, 2075-A West Park Place, Stone Mountain, Georgia 30087 (fax: 404 469-0681).

23. Michael C. Latham, 'Protein-Energy Malnutrition–Its Epidemiology and Control,' *JEPTO (Journal of Environmental Pathology, Toxicology, and Oncology)*, Vol. 10, No. 4–5 (July–October 1990), pp. 168–80.

24. John B. Mason, 'Nutrition and Food Aid,' *SCN News*, No. 10 (Late 1993), pp. 1–8.
25. This conforms with recent findings that public expenditure on children generally yields far better results when focused on very small children. See Carnegie Task Force on Meeting the Needs of Young Children, *Starting Points: Meeting the Needs of Young Children* (New York: Carnegie Corporation of New York, 1994).
26. Food and Agriculture Organization of the United Nations, *The Fifth World Food Survey* (Rome: FAO, 1985), p. 24.
27. World Bank, *Poverty and Hunger: Issues and Options for Food Security in Developing Countries* (Washington, D.C.: WB, 1986), p. 1.
28. Physician Task Force on Hunger in America, *Hunger in America: The Growing Epidemic* (Boston: Harvard University School of Public Health, 1985); J. Larry Brown, 'Hunger in the U.S.' *Scientific American*, Vol. 256, No. 2 (February 1987), pp. 36–41; J. Larry Brown and H. F. Pizer, *Living Hungry in America* (New York: Macmillan Library, 1987). Contrary views are presented in several articles in *Insight*, Vol. 4, No. 26 (June 27, 1988), pp. 8–15.
29. United Nations, Administrative Committee on Coordination/Subcommittee on Nutrition, *Second Report ...*, p. 1.
30. United Nations, Administrative Committee on Coordination/Subcommittee on Nutrition, *Second Report ...*, p. 10.
31. United Nations, Administrative Committee on Coordination/Subcommittee on Nutrition, *Second Report ...*, p. 9.

8 Nutrition Rights

1. Addeke H. Boerma, *A Right to Food* (Rome: Food and Agriculture Organization of the United Nations, 1976) p. 153. Despite the title of this collection of Boerma's speeches, the idea of a right to food is not elaborated. A critical analysis of FAO's role in relation to the right to food may be found in Julianne Cartwright Taylor, 'FAO and the Right to Food,' in Asbjørn Eide, Wenche Barth Eide, Susantha Goonatilake, Joan Gussow, and Omawale, eds., *Food as Human Right* (Tokyo: United Nations University, 1984), pp. 187–212.
2. Richard Jolly, 'Foreword,' in Beverley A. Carlson and Tessa M. Wardlaw, *A Global, Regional and Country Assessment of Child Malnutrition* (New York: UNICEF, 1990), p. 9.
3. The history of international recognition of a right to food is only sketched here. For more thorough accounts see Eide, et al., *Food as Human Right*; Philip Alston and Katarina Tomaševski, eds., *The Right to Food* (Dordrecht, Netherlands: Martinus Nijhoff, 1984); Katarina Tomaševski, ed., *The Right to Food: Guide Through Applicable International Law* (Dordrecht, Netherlands: Martinus Nijhoff, 1986); *Right to Adequate Food as a Human Right* (New York: United Nations, 1989); and Asbjørn Eide, Arne Oshaug, and Wenche Barth Eide, 'Food Security and the Right to Food in International Law and Development,' *Transnational Law & Contemporary Problems*, Vol. 1, No. 2 (Fall 1991), pp. 415–67. Also see the articles from the symposium on International Law and World Hunger in the *Iowa Law*

Review, Vol. 70 (1985) and another similar symposium in the *Howard Law Journal*, Vol. 30 (Spring 1987).

4.   S. Y. Krishnaswamy, ed., *Man's Right to Freedom From Hunger: A Report of a Special Assembly held at the Headquarters of the Food and Agriculture Organization of the United Nations, Rome, Italy, 14 March 1963* (Rome: FAO, 1963).

5.   United States Congress. House. *The Right to Food Resolution. Hearings Before the Subcommittee on International Resources, House of Representatives, 94th Congress, 2nd Session* (Washington, D.C.: United States Government Printing Office, 1976).

6.   U.S. Congress. House. *Decades of Disasters: The United Nations Response.* Hearing Before the Select Committee on Hunger, July 30, 1991 (Washington, D. C.: U.S. Government Printing Office, 1991). On pp. 122–58 this hearing report reproduces a useful overview by the International Law Association's International Committee on the Right to Food.

7.   *Right to Adequate Food as a Human Right*, p. 21.

8.   U.S. Congress. House. *Decades of Disasters*, pp. 22, 71.

9.   Alston and Tomaševski, *The Right to Food*, pp. 7, 9.

10. Jean-Philippe Platteau, 'Traditional Systems of Social Security and Hunger Insurance: Past Achievements and Modern Challenges,' in Ehtisham Ahmad, Jean Drèze, John Hills, and Amartya Sen, eds., *Social Security in Developing Countries* (Oxford: Clarendon Press, 1991), pp. 161–2. The historical evolution of social welfare programs is analyzed in Abram de Swaan, *In Care of the State: Health Care, Education and Welfare in Europe and the USA in the Modern Era* (Cambridge: Polity Press, 1988). The study gives special attention to the ways in which welfare programs serve the interests of the powerful. Also see Claus Offe, *Contradictions of the Welfare State* (Cambridge, Massachusetts: MIT Press, 1984).

11. Ehtisham Ahmad and Athar Hussain, 'Social Security in China: A Historical Perspective,' in Ahmad et al., *Social Security in Developing Countries*, pp. 247–304.

12. Cheryl Christensen, *The Right to Food: How to Guarantee* (New York: World Order Models Project, Working Paper Number Six, Institute for World Order, 1978), p. 33.

13. Lloyd Timberlake and Laura Thomas, *When the Bough Breaks ... Our Children, Our Environment* (London: Earthscan Publications, 1990), p. 248.

14. The *Limburg Principles*, published in United Nations document E/CN.4/1987/17, Annex, were reprinted in the special Symposium issue on *The Implementation of the International Covenant on Economic, Social and Cultural Rights* of the *Human Rights Quarterly*, Vol. 9, No. 2 (1987).

15. Eide, *Right to Adequate Food as a Human Right*, para. 170, 175, 180.

16. Asbjørn Eide, Arne Oshaug, and Wenche Barth Eide, 'Human Rights: A Normative Basis for Food and Nutrition-Relevant Policies,' *Food Policy*, Vol. 19, No. 6 (December 1994).

17. See, for example, my article 'Nutrition Education as an Instrument of Empowerment,' *Journal of Nutrition Education*, Vol. 20, No. 4 (July/August 1988), pp. 193–5.

18. The concern is elaborated in Peter G. Peterson and Neil Howe, *On Borrowed Time: How the Growth in Entitlement Spending Threatens America's Future* (San Francisco: ICS Press, 1988). But 'the major entitlement programs – Medicare, Social Security, farm aid – give huge subsidies to retirees and farmers who earn more than $100,000' in what can be described as 'federal welfare spending for the wealthy.' See 'A Time for Leadership,' *Time*, December 9, 1991, pp. 22–4.

19. Peter Adamson, *The Progress of Nations* (New York: UNICEF, 1993), p. 3.

20. James Weill, 'Assuring an Adequate Standard of Living for the Child,' in Cynthia Price Cohen and Howard A. Davidson, eds., *Children's Rights in America: U.N. Convention on the Rights of the Child Compared with United States Law* (Washington, D.C.: American Bar Association and Defense for Children International-USA, 1990), pp. 197–217; quoted from p. 213.

21. Department of Health and Human Services and Department of Agriculture, 'Ten-Year Comprehensive Plan for the National Nutrition Monitoring and Related Research Program,' *Federal Register*, Vol. 56, No. 209 (Tuesday, October 29, 1991), pp. 55716–34.

22. World Bank, *World Development Report 1993: Investing in Health* (Washington, D.C.: World Bank, 1993), p. 80.

23. Also see James R. Himes, *Implementing the United Nations Convention on the Rights of the Child: Resource Mobilization and the Obligations of the States Parties* (Florence, Italy: International Child Development Centre, 1992). Himes speaks of the importance of planning, management, and monitoring of child rights work by objectives, but does not take the further step of suggesting that nutrition rights themselves might be concretized as objectives.

24. Still more specifically, this could be 'as analyzed with the EpiNut software' that was described in a footnote in Chapter 7.

25. For example, the strategy could be one of empowerment, based on facilitation of local efforts to systematically assess, analyze, and act on the malnutrition problem. See UNICEF, *Strategy for Improved Nutrition of Children and Women in Developing Countries* (New York: UNICEF, 1990), and Urban Jonsson, *Nutrition and the United Nations Convention on the Rights of the Child* (Florence, Italy: International Child Development Centre, 1993).

26. WANAHR's newsletter and other information can be obtained from the Secretariat at the Norwegian Institute of Human Rights, Gensen 18, N-0159 Oslo, Norway (Phone: 47 22 42 13 60; Fax: 47 22 42 25 42).

27. Eide, Oshaug, and Eide, 'Food Security'.

28. Information about FIAN, and its magazine, *Hungry for What is Right*, may be obtained from FIAN International, P.O. Box 102243, D-69012, Heidelberg, Germany (Phone: 49 6221 830 620; Fax: 49 6221 830 545).

9 Children's Rights

1. On the evolution of children's rights see Philip E. Veerman, *The Rights of the Child and the Changing Image of Childhood* (Dordrecht, The Netherlands: Martinus Nijhoff, 1992).

2. See Maria Enrica Agostinelli, *On Wings of Love: The United Nations Declaration of the Rights of the Child* (New York: Collins, 1979) for an interpretation and illustration of the principles designed for children.

3. Rebecca J. Cook, 'Human Rights and Infant Survival: A Case for Priorities,' *Columbia Human Rights Law Review*, Vol. 18, No. 1 (Fall/Winter 1986/87), pp. 1–41.

4. World Campaign for Human Rights, *The Rights of the Child* (Geneva: United Nations Centre for Human Rights, 1992); Sharon Detrick, ed., *The United Nations Convention on the Rights of the Child: A Guide to the 'Travaux Préparatoires'* (Dordrecht, The Netherlands: Martinus Nijhoff, 1992); Kay Castelle, *In the Child's Best Interest: A Primer on the U.N. Convention on the Rights of the Child*, New Edition (East Greenwich, Rhode Island: Foster Parents Plan International and Defence for Children International, 1989); Special issue on *The Rights of the Child of the Bulletin of Human Rights*, 91/2, published by the United Nations Centre for Human Rights in Geneva in 1992. Useful background information may be found in articles on the rights of the child in the *American Psychologist* of January 1991.

5. In the United Nations system human rights are the responsibility of the Economic and Social Council of the United Nations, and particularly ECOSOC's subsidiary Commission on Human Rights. A number of committees address specific issues such as the Committee on the Elimination of Racial Discrimination, the Human Rights Committee, the Committee on Economic, Social, and Cultural Rights, the Committee on the Elimination of Discrimination against Women, and the Committee against Torture, and now also the Committee on the Rights of the Child.

6. *World Declaration on the Survival, Protection and Development of Children and Plan of Action for Implementing the World Declaration on the Survival, Protection and Development of Children in the 1990s* (New York: United Nations, 1990).

7. P. Prakash, 'India: Advertising of Infant Foods to be Restricted,' *Lancet*, Vol. 340 (1992), pp. 962–963.

8. Målfrid Grude Flekkøy, *A Voice for Children: Speaking Out as Their Ombudsman* (London: UNICEF/Jessica Kingsley Publishers, 1991).

9. Bernard Rosen, *Holding Government Bureaucracies Accountable*, Second Edition (New York: Praeger, 1989); Paul C. Light, *Monitoring Government: Inspectors General and the Search for Accountability* (Washington, D.C.: Brookings, 1993).

10. Peter Adamson, ed., *The Progress of Nations* (New York: UNICEF, 1993), p. 4. This annual publication from UNICEF is itself designed for this purpose.

11. A proposal for systematic management of data for the full range of rights in the convention is described in Cynthia Price Cohen, Stuart N. Hart, and Susan M. Kosloske, 'The U. N. Convention on the Rights of the Child: Developing an *Information Model* to Computerize the Monitoring of Treaty Compliance,' *Human Rights Quarterly*, Vol. 14, No. 2 (1992), pp. 216–31.

12. See, for example, Herbert F. Spirer and Louise Spirer, *Data Analysis for Monitoring Human Rights* (Washington, D.C.: American Association for the Advancement of Science, 1993).

13. Other dimensions on which nutrition service programs can be assessed are discussed in Joan Jennings, Stuart Gillespie, John Mason, Mahshid Lofti, and Tom Scialfa, eds., *Managing Successful Nutrition Programs* (Geneva: United Nations Administrative Committee on Coordination/Subcommittee on Nutrition, 1991).

10   International Children's Rights

1. Francis M. Deng and Larry Minear, *The Challenges of Famine Relief: Emergency Operations in the Sudan* (Washington, D.C.: The Brookings Institution, 1992); Thomas G. Weiss and Larry Minear, eds., *Humanitarianism Across Borders: Sustaining Civilians in Times of War* (Boulder, Colorado: Lynne Rienner, 1993).

2. Frances Moore Lappé, Joseph Collins, and David Kinley, *Aid as Obstacle: Twenty Questions About Our Foreign Aid and the Hungry* (San Francisco: Institute for Food and Development Policy, 1980); Independent Commission on International Humanitarian Issues, *Famine: A Man-Made Disaster?* (New York: Vintage, 1985); Graham Hancock, *Lords of Poverty: The Free-Wheeling Lifestyles, Power, Prestige and Corruption of the Multi-Million Dollar Aid Business* (London: Macmillan, 1989).

3. To convey the idea that we are concerned with compassionate assistance regardless of whether it is a conflict situation, we could devise an encompassing term such as *humane assistance.* Jean Pictet says that 'while humanitarian law is only applicable in cases of armed conflict, human rights are operative above all in times of peace ... the two systems are related but distinct ... If we were to bring them together under one all-embracing title, we might think of the term 'humane law', which would be defined as follows: humane law consists of all international legal provisions ensuring respect for and full development of the human being.' United Nations Educational, Scientific and Cultural Organization, *International Dimensions of Humanitarian Law* (Geneva: Henry Dunant Institute, 1988), p. xxi.

4. Mary Glendon, *Rights Talk: The Impoverishment of Political Discourse* (New York: Free Press, 1991), pp. 76–108.

5. Glendon, *Rights Talk*, pp. 89–90.

6. Glendon, *Rights Talk*, p. 77.

7. On the developing doctrine of humanitarian intervention, see Fernando R. Tesón, *Humanitarian Intervention: An Inquiry into Law and Morality.* (Dobbs Ferry, New York: Transnational Publishers, 1988); Richard B. Lillich, *International Human Rights: Problems of Law, Policy and Practice,* Second Edition (Boston: Little, Brown, 1991), pp. 372-441; David J. Schefer; Richard N. Gardner; and Gerald B. Helman, *Post-Gulf War Challenges to the UN Collective Security System: Three Views on the Issue of Humanitarian Intervention* (Washington, D.C.: United States Institute of Peace, 1992); Yves Beigbeder, *The Role and Status of International Humanitarian Volunteers and Organizations: The Right and Duty to Humanitarian Assistance* (Dordrecht, Holland: Martinus Nijhoff, 1991), pp. 353–84. There also have been numerous articles in the law journals.

8. Varindra Tarzie Vittachi, *Between the Guns: Children as a Zone of Peace* (London: Hodder & Stoughton, 1993).
9. David Binder and Barbara Crossette, 'As Ethnic Wars Multiply, U.S. Strives for a Policy,' *New York Times*, February 7, 1993, pp. 1, 12.
10. Kenneth B. Noble, 'Tens of Thousands Flee Ethnic Violence in Zaire,' *New York Times*, March 21, 1993, p. 3.
11. Leo Kuper, *Genocide: Its Political Use in the Twentieth Century* (New Haven: Yale University Press, 1981); Israel W. Charny, ed., *Genocide: A Critical Bibliographic Review*, Volumes 1 and 2 (New York: Facts of File, 1988 and 1991); George A. Lopez and Michael Stohl, *Dependence, Development, and State Repression* (New York: Greenwood Press, 1989); R. J. Rummel, *Lethal Politics: Soviet Genocides and Mass Murders Since 1917* (New Brunswick, New Jersey: Transaction, 1990); R. J. Rummel, *China's Bloody Century: Genocide and Mass Murder Since 1900* (New Brunswick, New Jersey: Transaction, 1991); R. J. Rummel, *Democide: Nazi Genocide and Mass Murder* (New Brunswick, New Jersey: Transaction, 1992).
12. However, see the three papers by Sandoz, Plattner, and Torrelli in *International Review of the Red Cross*, No. 288 (May–June 1992). They speak of a duty to assist civilian victims of armed conflict under international humanitarian law. Despite Torrelli's argument, that duty is not strongly grounded in the victims' right to assistance. Those rights are not well articulated in international humanitarian law.
13. To illustrate, see 'Guiding Principles on the Right to Humanitarian Assistance,' *International Review of the Red Cross*, No. 297 (November–December 1993), pp. 519–25.
14. In 1988 the French proposed a General Assembly resolution for disaster relief based on explicit recognition of the rights of the needy to receive assistance. That aspect disappeared by the time Res. 43/131 of December 8, 1988 was finalized. See Beigbeder, *The Role and Status of International Humanitarian Volunteers and Organizations*, pp. 354, 380–3.
15. Jan Eliasson, 'A Message from the Under Secretary-General for Humanitarian Affairs,' *UNDRO News* (March–April 1992), pp. 2–4. Also see Jan Eliasson, 'The World Response to Humanitarian Emergencies,' in Kevin M. Cahill, ed., *A Framework for Survival: Health, Human Rights, and Humanitarian Assistance in Conflicts and Disasters* (New York: Council on Foreign Relations/Basic Books, 1993), pp. 308–18.
16. Larry Minear, 'Making the Humanitarian System Work Better,' in Cahill, ed., *A Framework for Survival*, pp. 234–56.
17. Peter Macalister-Smith, *International Humanitarian Assistance: Disaster Relief Actions in International Law and Organization* (Dordrecht, Holland: Martinus Nijhoff, 1985), p. x.
18. Ruben Banerjee, 'Children on Sale for Rs 20,' *India Today*, February 15, 1993, pp. 80–1.
19. United Nations Development Programme, *Human Development Report 1992* (New York: Oxford University Press, 1992), pp. 44–5.
20. Kofi N. Awoonor, 'The Concerns of Recipient Nations,' in Cahill, ed., *A Framework for Survival*, pp. 63–81.

21. James P. Grant, *The State of the World's Children 1994* (New York: Oxford University Press, 1994), p. 21

22. David H. Lumsdaine, *Moral Vision in International Politics: The Foreign Aid Regime, 1949–1989* (Princeton, New Jersey: Princeton University Press, 1993), p. 97.

23. William Ryan, *Blaming the Victim, Revised*, updated edition (New York: Vintage Books, 1976).

24. Macalister-Smith, *International Humanitarian Assistance*, p. 56.

25. Macalister-Smith, *International Humanitarian Assistance*, pp. 109–10.

26. Peter Macalister-Smith, 'Protection of the Civilian Population and the Prohibition of Starvation as a Method of Warfare,' *International Review of the Red Cross*, No. 284 (September–October 1991), pp. 440–59.

27. Brian Urquhart and Erskine Childers, 'Strengthening International Responses to Humanitarian Emergencies,' in *Towards a More Effective United Nations*, special issue of *Development Dialogue* (Uppsala, Sweden: Dag Hammarskjold Foundation, 1991), pp. 41–85, at pp. 79–80

28. This argument should be placed in the context of the ongoing discussion of whether international assistance of different kinds should be provided conditionally to advance specific policies relating to human rights, economic ideologies, nutrition, or other considerations. See, for example, Mark W. Charlton, *The Making of Canadian Food Aid Policy* (Montreal: McGill-Queen's University Press, 1992); Edward Clay and Olav Stokke, eds., *Food Aid Reconsidered: Assessing the Impact on Third World Countries* (London: Frank Cass, 1991); Francis M. Deng and Larry Minear, *The Challenges of Famine Relief: Emergency Operations in the Sudan* (Washington, D.C.: The Brookings Institution, 1992); Rachel Garst and Tom Barry, *Feeding the Crisis: U.S. Food Aid and Farm Policy in Central America* (Lincoln: University of Nebraska Press, 1990); Tony Jackson, *Against the Grain: The Dilemma of Project Food Aid* (Oxford: OXFAM, 1982); Larry Minear, *Humanitarianism Under Siege: A Critical Review of Operation Lifeline Sudan* (Trenton, New Jersey: Red Sea Press/Bread for the World, 1991); Lars Adam Rehof and Claus Gulmann, *Human Rights and Domestic Law and Development Assistance Policies of the Nordic Countries* (Dordrecht, Netherlands: Martinus Nijhoff, 1989); Paul B. Thompson, *The Ethics of Aid and Trade: U.S. Food Policy, Foreign Competition, and the Social Contract* (Cambridge: Cambridge University Press, 1992); Katarina Tomaševski, *Development Aid and Human Rights* (New York: St. Martin's Press, 1989); Steven L. Varnis, *Reluctant Aid or Aiding the Reluctant? U.S. Food Aid Policy and Ethiopian Famine Relief* (New Brunswick, New Jersey: Transaction, 1990).

29. Food and Agriculture Organization of the United Nations, *World Food Security Compact* (Rome: FAO, 1986).

30. It is curious that the role of international nongovernmental organizations in global civil society has been studied while the role of international governmental organizations has been ignored. See Paul Ghils, 'International Civil Society: International Non-governmental Organizations in the International System,' *International Social Science Journal*, Vol. 44, No. 33 (August 1992), pp. 417–31.

31. Garrett Hardin, 'The Tragedy of the Commons,' *Science*, CLXII (December 13, 1968), pp. 1243–8.
32. Martin Shaw, 'Global Society and Global Responsibility: The Theoretical, Historical and Political Limits of "International Society,"' *Millennium: Journal of International Studies*, Vol. 21, No. 3 (1992), pp. 421–34, at p. 431.

Select Bibliography

Acker, Alison, *Children of the Volcano* (Westport, Connecticut: Lawrence Hill & Co., 1986).

Adamson, Peter, ed., *The Progress of Nations 1993* (New York: UNICEF, 1993).

Agostinelli, Maria Enrica, *On Wings of Love: The United Nations Declaration of the Rights of the Child* (New York: Collins, 1979).

Ahlström, Christer and Nordquist, Kjell-Åke, *Casualties of Conflict: Report for the Campaign for the Protecton of Victims of War* (Uppsala: Department of Peace and Conflict Research, Uppsala University, Sweden, 1991).

Alston, Philip; Parker, Stephen; and Seymour, John, eds., *Children, Rights, and the Law* (New York: Oxford University Press, 1992).

Alston, Philip and Tomaševski, Katarina, eds., *The Right to Food* (Dordrecht, The Netherlands: Martinus Nijhoff, 1984).

Antonovsky, A. and Bornsten, J., 'Social Class and Infant Mortality,' *Social Science & Medicine*, Vol. 11 (1977), pp. 454–70.

Aries, Philippe, *Centuries of Childhood: A Social History of Family Life* (New York: Alfred A. Knopf, 1962).

Arnvig, Eva, 'Child Prostitution in Cambodia: Did the UN Look Away?', *International Children's Rights Monitor*, Vol. 10, No. 3 (3rd Quarter 1993), pp. 4–6.

Attias, Ernesto and Cohn, Ilene, *Children and War: Report on 'The Psychosocial Impact of Violence on Children in Central America* (Guatemala: UNICEF Area Office for Central America and Panama, 1990).

Bell, David E. and Reich, Michael R., eds., *Health, Nutrition, and Economic Crises: Approaches to Policy in the Third World* (Dover, Massachusetts: Auburn House, 1988).

Black, Maggie, *The Children and the Nations: The Story of Unicef* (New York: UNICEF, 1986).

Boothby, Neil, 'Children and War,' *Cultural Survival Quarterly*, Vol. 10, No. 4 (1986), pp. 28–30.

Boothby, Neil, 'Khmer Children: Alone at the Border,' *Indochina Issue*, Vol. 32 (December 1982).

Boswell, John, *The Kindness of Strangers: The Abandonment of Children in Western Europe from Late Antiquity to the Renaissance* (New York: Pantheon Books, 1988).

Bouhdiba, Abdelwahab, *Exploitation of Child Labour* (New York: United Nations, 1982).

Boulding, Elise, *Children's Rights and the Wheel of Life* (New Brunswick, New Jersey: Transaction Books, 1979).

Bristow, Edward J., *Prostitution and Prejudice: The Jewish Fight Against White Slavery 1870–1939* (New York: Schocken Books, 1982).

Brown, J. Larry and Pizer, Hank, *Living Hungry in America* (New York: Macmillan, 1987).

Bryce, Jennifer W., *Cries of Children in Lebanon: As Voiced by Their Mothers* (Amman, Jordan: UNICEF Regional Office for the Middle East and North Africa, 1986).

Cahill, Kevin M., ed., *A Framework for Survival: Health, Human Rights, and Humanitarian Assistance in Conflicts and Disasters* (New York: Council on Foreign Relations/Basic Books, 1993).

Caldwell, John C. 'Routes to Low Mortality in Poor Countries,' *Population and Development Review*, Vol. 12, No. 2 (June 1986), pp. 171–220.

Caldwell, John C., *Children of Calamity* (New York: John Day Company, 1957).

Campagna, Daniel S. and Poffenberger, Donald L., *The Sexual Trafficking in Children: An Investigation of the Child Sex Trade* (Dover, Massachusetts: Auburn House, 1988).

Carlson, Beverley A. and Wardlaw, Tessa M., *A Global, Regional and Country Assessment of Child Malnutrition* (New York: UNICEF, 1990).

Carnegie Task Force on Meeting the Needs of Young Children, *Starting Points: Meeting the Needs of Young Children* (New York: Carnegie Corporation of New York, 1994).

Cash, Richard; Keusch, Gerald; and Ramstein, Joel, eds., *Child Health and Child Survival: UNICEF's GOBI-FFF* (London: Croom & Helm, 1987).

Castelle, Kay, *In the Child's Best Interest: A Primer on the U.N. Convention on the Rights of the Child*, New Edition (East Greenwich, Rhode Island: Foster Parents Plan International and Defence for Children International, 1989).

Child Study Association of America, *Children and the Threat of Nuclear War* (New York: Duell, Sloan and Pearce, 1964).

Children and the Environment (New York and Nairobi: UNICEF and UNEP, 1990).

Children in Situations of Armed Conflict (New York: UNICEF E/ICEF/1986/CRP.2, 1986).

Children in Situations of Armed Conflict in Africa (Nairobi, Kenya: African Network on Prevention and Protection Against Child Abuse and Neglect, 1988).

Children of Hiroshima (London: Taylor & Francis, 1981).

Children on the Front Line: The Impact of Apartheid, Destabilization and Warfare on Children in Southern and South Africa (New York: UNICEF, 1987).

Children's Defense Fund, *The State of America's Children 1992* (Washington, D.C.: CDF, 1992).

Children's Defense Fund, *American Children in Poverty* (Washington, D.C.: CDF, 1984).

Children's Defense Fund, *A Children's Defense Budget, FY 1988: An Analysis of Our Nation's Investment in Children* (Washington, D.C.: CDF, 1987).

Christensen, Cheryl, *The Right to Food: How to Guarantee* (New York: World Order Models Project, Working Paper Number Six, Institute for World Order, 1978), p. 33.

Cobb, Alice, *War's Unconquered Children Speak* (Boston: Beacon Press, 1953).

Cohen, Cynthia Price and Davidson, Howard A., eds., *Children's Rights in America: U.N. Convention on the Rights of the Child Compared with United States Law* (Washington, D.C.: American Bar Association and Defense for Children International–USA, 1990).

Cohen, Cynthia Price; Hart, Stuart N.; and Kosloske, Susan M., 'The U. N. Convention on the Rights of the Child: Developing an Information Model to Computerize the Monitoring of Treaty Compliance,' *Human Rights Quarterly*, Vol. 14, No. 2 (1992), pp. 216–31.

Cohen, Ilene, 'The Convention on the Rights of the Child: What it Means for Children in War,' *International Journal of Refugee Law*, Vol. 3, No. 1 (1991), pp. 100–9.

Cook, Rebecca J., 'Human Rights and Infant Survival: A Case for Priorities,' *Columbia Human Rights Law Review*, Vol. 18, No. 1 (Fall/Winter 1986/87), pp. 1–41.

Cornia, Giovanni Andrea, 'A Survey of Cross-Sectional and Time-Series Literature on Factors Affecting Child Welfare,' *World Development*, Vol. 12, No. 3 (March 1984), pp. 187–202.

Cornia, Giovanni Andrea; Jolly, Richard; and Stewart, Frances, *Adjustment with a Human Face: Protecting the Vulnerable and Promoting Growth* (New York: Oxford, 1987).

Cornia, Giovanni Andrea and Sipos, Sándor, *Children and the Transition to the Market Economy: Safety Nets and Social Policies in Central and Eastern Europe* (Aldershot: Avebury/UNICEF, 1991).

Deger, Saadet and Sen, Somnath, *Arms and Child* (New York: Oxford University Press, 1993).

deMause, Lloyd, ed., *The History of Childhood: The Untold History of Child Abuse* (New York: Psychohistory Press, 1974 (republished in 1988 by Peter Bedrick Books)).

Detrick, Sharon, ed., *The United Nations Convention on the Rights of the Child: A Guide to the 'Travaux Préparatoires'* (Dordrecht, The Netherlands: Martinus Nijhoff, 1992).

Dodge, Cole P., 'Child Soldiers of Uganda: What Does the Future Hold,' *Cultural Survival Quarterly*, Vol. 10, No. 4 (1986), pp. 31–3.

Dodge, Cole P. and Wiebe, Paul D. eds., *Crisis in Uganda: The Breakdown of Health Services* (New York: Pergamon Press, 1985).

Dodge, Cole, *War, Violence and Children in Uganda* (New York: Oxford University Press, 1987).

Drèze, Jean and Sen, Amartya, *Hunger and Public Action* (Oxford: Clarendon Press, 1989).

Drèze, Jean and Sen, Amartya, eds., *The Political Economy of Hunger*, Vols. I–III (New York: Oxford, 1990).

Edelman, Marian Wright, *Families in Peril: An Agenda for Social Change* (Cambridge, Massachusetts: Harvard University Press, 1987).

Eide, Asbjørn; Eide, Wenche Barth; Goonatilake, Susantha; Gussow, Joan; and Omawale, eds., *Food as Human Right* (Tokyo: United Nations University, 1984).

Eide, Asbjørn; Oshaug, Arne; and Eide, Wenche Barth, 'Food Security and the Right to Food in International Law and Development,' *Transnational Law & Contemporary Problems*, Vol. 1, No. 2 (Fall 1991), pp. 415–67.

Ennew, Judith and Milne, Brian, *The Next Generation: Lives of Third World Children* (Philadelphia: New Society Publishers, 1990).

Ennew, Judith, *The Sexual Exploitation of Children* (Cambridge: Polity Press, 1986).

Flekkøy, Målfrid Grude, *A Voice for Children: Speaking Out as Their Ombudsman* (London: UNICEF/Jessica Kingsley Publishers, 1991).

Food, Health, and Care: The UNICEF Vision and Strategy for a World Free from Hunger and Malnutrition (New York: UNICEF, 1992).

Freeman, Michael and Veerman, Philip, eds., *The Ideologies of Children's Rights* (Dordrecht, The Netherlands: Martinus Nijhoff, 1992).

Freud, Anna and Burlingham, Dorothy T., *War and Children* (New York: Medical War Books, 1943).

Galway, Katrina; Wolff, Brent; and Sturgis, Richard, *Child Survival: Risks and the Road to Health* (Columbia, Maryland: Institute for Resource Development/Westinghouse/USAID, 1987).

Garbarino, James; Kostelny, Kathleeen; and Dubrow, Nancy, *No Place to Be A Child: Growing Up in a War Zone* (Lexington, Massachusetts: Lexington Books, 1991).

Garbarino, James, *Toward a Sustainable Society: An Economic, Social and Environmental Agenda for Our Children's Future* (Chicago: Noble Press, 1992).

George, Susan, *A Fate Worse Than Debt: The World Financial Crisis and the Poor* (New York: Grove Press, 1988).

Gooneskekere, S. W. E., *Child Labour in Sri Lanka: Learning from the Past* (Geneva: International Labour Office, 1993).

Grant, James P., *The State of the World's Children* (New York: Oxford University Press/UNICEF, annual).

Gustafsson, Lars H.; Lindkvist, Agneta; and Böhm, Birgitta, *Krigens Barn* (Oslo: Kommuneforlaget, 1989).

Gutman, W. E. 'State-supported Executions of Children,' *Omni*, November 1991.

Gwatkin, Davidson R. and Brandel, Sarah, *Reducing Infant and Child Mortality in the Developing World* (Washington, D.C.: Overseas Development Council, 1981).

Gwatkin, Davidson R., *Signs of Change in Developing Country Mortality Trends: The End of an Era?* (Washington, D.C.: Overseas Development Council, 1981).

Gwatkin, Davidson R.; Wilcox, Janet R.; and Wray, Joe D., *Can Health and Nutrition Interventions Make a Difference?* (Washington, D.C.: Overseas Development Council, 1980).

Hancock, Graham, *Lords of Poverty: The Power, Prestige, and Corruption of the International Aid Business* (New York: Atlantic Monthly Press, 1989).

Harbison, Jeremy and Harbison, Joan, *A Society Under Stress: Children and Young People in Northern Ireland* (Somerset, England: Open Books, 1980).

Health Action Information Network, *Pom Pom: Child and Youth Prostitution in the Philippines* (Quezon City, Philippines: HAIN, 1987).

Himes, John H., ed., *Anthropometric Assessment of Nutritional Status* (New York: Wiley-Liss, 1991).

Hobcraft, J. N.; McDonald, J. W.; and Rutstein, S. O., 'Socio-Economic Factors in Infant and Child Mortality: A Cross-national Comparison,' *Population Studies*, Vol. 36 (1984), pp. 193–223.

Hughes, Dana; Johnson, Kay; Rosenbaum, Sara; Simons, Janet; and Butler, Elizabeth, *The Health of America's Children: Maternal and Child Health Data Book* (Washington, D.C.: Children's Defense Fund, 1987).

ICRC and Children in Situations of Armed Conflicts (Geneva: International Committee of the Red Cross, 1987).

International Children's Rights Monitor (Geneva: Defence for Children International, quarterly)

Jennings, Joan; Gillespie, Stuart; Mason, John; Lofti, Mahshid; and Scialfa, Tom, eds., *Managing Successful Nutrition Programs* (Geneva: United Nations Administrative Committee on Coordination/Subcommittee on Nutrition, 1991).

Jensen, Mary A. and Goffin, Stacie G., eds., *Visions of Entitlement: The Care and Education of America's Children* (Albany, New York: State University of New York Press, 1993).

Jolly, Richard and Cornia, Giovanni Andrea, *The Impact of World Recession on Children* (Oxford: Pergamon Press, 1984).

Jonsson, Urban, *Nutrition and the United Nations Convention on the Rights of the Child* (Florence, Italy: International Child Development Centre, 1993).

Jupp, Michael et al., *The Children's Clarion: Database on the Rights of the Child* (New York: Defense for Children International–USA, 1987).

Jupp, Michael, 'Apartheid: Violence Against Children,' *Cultural Survival Quarterly*, Vol. 10, No. 4 (1986), pp. 34–7.

Jupp, Michael, *Children Under Apartheid* (New York: Defense for Children International–USA, 1987).

Jupp, Michael, 'The Human Rights of Children,' *International Health News*, Vol. 8, No. 1 (January 1987), p. 1.

Kahn, A. J.; Kamerman, S. B.; and McGowan, B. G., *Child Advocacy: Report on a National Baseline Study* (New York: Columbia University School of Social Work, 1972).

Kent, George, 'Children as Human Capital?,' *Food and Nutrition Bulletin*, Vol. 10, No. 4 (December 1988), pp. 54–8.

Kent, George, 'Children's Right to Adequate Nutrition,' *International Journal of Children's Rights*, Vol. 1, No. 2 (1993), pp. 133–54.

Kent, George, 'The Denial of Children's Mortality,' *Internet on the Holocaust and Genocide*, No. 44–6 (September 1993), pp. 18, 20.

Kent, George, 'The Massive Mortality of Children,' in Israel W. Charny, ed., *The Widening Circle of Genocide* (New Brunswick, New Jersey: Transaction Books, 1994).

Kent, George, 'Empowering Non-governmental Organizations,' *CHILDAsia*, No. 5 (March–April 1992), pp. 9–11.

Kent, George, 'Nutrition Education as an Instrument of Empowerment,' *Journal of Nutrition Education*, Vol. 20, No. 4 (July/August 1988), pp. 193–5.

Kent, George, 'Who Would Not Save Their Own Children? The Impact of Powerlessness on Child Survival,' *Development Forum*, Vol. 16, No. 6 (November–December 1988), p. 11.

Kent, George, *The Political Economy of Hunger: The Silent Holocaust* (New York: Praeger, 1984).

Kent, George, *The Politics of Children's Survival* (New York: Praeger, 1991).

Kent, George, *War and Children's Survival* (Honolulu: Spark M. Matsunaga Institute for Peace, 1990).

Kent, George, 'Little Foreign Bodies: International Dimensions of Child Prostitution,' in Michael Freeman and Philip Veerman, eds., *The Ideologies of Children's Rights* (Dordrecht, The Netherlands: Martinus Nijhoff, 1992), pp. 323–46.

Kimmich, Madeleine H., *America's Children: Who Cares? Growing Needs and Declining Assistance in the Reagan Era* (Washington, D.C.: Urban Institute Press, 1985).

Köhler, Lennart and Jakobsson, Gunborg, *Children's Health and Well-Being in the Nordic Countries* (London: Mac Keith Press, 1987).

Krill, Françoise, 'The Protection of Children in Armed Conflicts,' in Michael Freeman and Philip Veerman, eds., *The Ideologies of Children's Rights* (Dordrecht, The Netherlands: Martinus Nijhoff, 1992), pp. 347–56.

La Farge, Phyllis, *The Strangelove Legacy: Children, Parents, and Teachers in the Nuclear Age* (New York: Harper & Row, 1987).

Lenzer, Jeanne, 'Youth Liberation – A Call to Action,' *Z Magazine*, Vol. 6, No. 2 (February 1993), p. 49–52.

Leowski, Jerzy, 'Mortality from Acute Respiratory Infections in Children Under 5 Years of Age,' *World Health Statistics*, Vol. 39, No. 2 (1986), pp. 138–44.

Lillich, Richard B., *International Human Rights: Problems of Law, Policy and Practice*, Second Edition (Boston: Little, Brown, 1991), pp. 372–441.

Lipschutz, Ronnie D., 'Reconstructing World Politics: The Emergence of Global Civil Society,' *Millennium: Journal of International Studies*, Vol. 21, No. 3 (1992), pp. 389–420,

Lumsdaine, David Halloran, *Moral Vision in International Politics: The Foreign Aid Regime, 1949–1989* (Princeton, New Jersey: Princeton University Press, 1993).

Matsui, Yayori, *Women's Asia* (London: Zed Books, 1987).

Messer, Ellen, 'Food Wars: Hunger as a Weapon of War in 1993,' in Peter Uvin, ed., *The Hunger Report: 1993* (Providence, Rhode Island: World Hunger Program, Program University/Gordon and Breach, 1994), pp. 43–69.

Miller, C. Arden, 'Infant Mortality in the U.S.,' *Scientific American*, Vol. 253, No. 1 (July 1985), pp. 31–7.

Minear, Larry, *Humanitarianism Under Siege: A Critical Review of Operation Lifeline Sudan* (Trenton, New Jersey: Red Sea Press/Bread for the World, 1991).

Minear, Larry; Weiss, Thomas G.; and Campbell, Kurt M., *Humanitarianism and War: Learning the Lessons from Recent Armed Conflicts* (Providence, Rhode Island: Watson Institute for International Studies, Brown University, 1991).

Mosley, W. Henry and Chen, Lincoln C., eds., *Child Survival: Strategies for Research* (Cambridge: Cambridge University Press, 1984).

Muntarbhorn, Vitit, *Sale of Children*, United Nations document E/CN.4/1991/51 (28 January 1991), and Vitit Muntarbhorn, *Sale of Children*, United Nations document E/CN.4/1992/55 (22 January 1992).

Muntarbhorn, Vitit, *Report of the Special Rapporteur, Mr. V. Muntarbhorn, pursuant to Commision on Human Rights resolution 1990/68, Addendum Visit by the Special Rapporteur to Brazil*, United Nations document E/CN.4/1992/55/Add.1 (11 February 1992).

Murray, Christopher J. L., 'A Critical Review of International Mortality Data,' *Social Science & Medicine*, Vol. 25, No. 7 (1987), pp. 773–81.

Myers, William E., ed., *Protecting Working Children* (London: Zed Books, 1991).

Narvesen, Ove, *The Sexual Exploitation of Children in Developing Countries* (Oslo: Redd Barna, 1989.)

National Commission to Prevent Infant Mortality, *Death Before Life: The Tragedy of Infant Mortality* (Washington, D.C.: NCPIM, 1988).

Nixon, Anne Elizabeth, *The Status of Palestinian Children During the Uprising in the Occupied Territories* (Stockholm: Rädda Barnen, 1990).

Osada, Arata, *Children of the A-Bomb: The Testament of the Boys and Girls of Hiroshima* (Tokyo: Uchida Rokakuho, 1959).

Overview: Children in Especially Difficult Circumstances (New York: UNICEF E/ICEF/1986/L.6, 1986).

Piers, Maria W., *Infanticide* (New York: W. W. Norton, 1978).

Plattner, Denise, 'Protection of Children in International Humanitarian Law,' *International Review of the Red Cross* (May–June 1984), pp. 140–52.

Puffer, R. R. and Serrano, C. V., *Patterns of Mortality in Childhood*, Scientific Publication, No. 262 (Washington, D.C.: Pan American Health Organization, 1973).

Report on Child Victims of Armed Conflict, Radda Barnen, NGO Forum, Rome, April 28, 1984.

Ressler, Everett M.; Boothby, Neil; and Steinbock, Daniel J., *Unaccompanied Children: Care and Protection in Wars, Natural Disasters, and Refugee Movements* (New York: Oxford University Press, 1988).

Ressler, Everett, *Evacuation of Children from Conflict Areas: Considerations and Guidelines* (Geneva: UNHCR and UNICEF, 1992).

Ressler, Everett M.; Tortorici, Joanne Marie; and Marcelino, Alex. *Children in War: A Guide to the Provision of Services* (New York: UNICEF, 1993).

Rialp, Victor, *Children and Hazardous Work in the Philippines* (Geneva: International Labour Office, 1993).

Richart, David W. and Bing, Stephen, *Fairness is a Kid's Game* (Louisville: Kentucky Youth Advocates, Inc., 1989).

Right to Adequate Food as a Human Right (New York: United Nations, 1989).

Rohde, Jon E., 'Why the Other Half Dies: The Science and Politics of Child Mortality in the Third World,' *Assignment Children*, Vol. 61/62, No. 1 (1983), pp. 35–67.

Rose, Lionel, *The Massacre of the Innocents: Infanticide in Britain 1800–1939* (London: Routledge & Kegan Paul, 1986).

Rosenblatt, Roger, *Children of War* (Garden City, New York: Doubleday, 1983).

Rozario, M. Rita, *Trafficking in Women and Children in India: Sexual Exploitation and Sale* (New Delhi: Uppal Publishing House, 1988).

Sagan, Leonard, *The Health of Nations: True Causes of Sickness and Well-Being* (New York: Basic Books, 1987).

Sawyer, Roger, *Children Enslaved* (London: Routledge, 1988).

Sen, Amartya, *Poverty and Famines: An Essay on Entitlements* (New York: Oxford, 1981).

Shade, John A., *America's Forgotten Children: The Amerasians* (Perkasie, Pennsylvania: Pearl S. Buck Foundation, Inc., 1981).

Singer, Sandra, 'The Protection of Children During Armed Conflict Situations,' *International Review of the Red Cross* (May–June 1986), pp. 133–68.

Sivard, Ruth Leger, *World Military and Social Expenditures 1987–88*, 12th Edition (Washington, D.C.: World Priorities, 1987).

Stanton, Marietta, *Our Children Are Dying* (Buffalo, New York: Prometheus Books, 1990).

Suarez-Orozco, Marcelo M., 'The Treatment of Children in the "Dirty War": Ideology, State Terrorism and the Abuse of Children in Argentina,' in Nancy Scheper-Hughes, ed., *Child Survival: Anthropological Perspectives on the Treatment and Maltreatment of Children* (Dordrecht, The Netherlands: D. Reidel, 1987), pp. 227–46.

Tesón, Fernando R., *Humanitarian Intervention: An Inquiry into Law and Morality* (Dobbs Ferry, New York: Transnational Publishers, 1988).

Tolley, Howard, Jr., *Children and War: Political Socialization to International Conflict* (New York: Teachers College Press, 1973).

Underwood, Barbara, ed., *Nutrition Intervention Strategies in National Development* (New York: Academic Press, 1983).

United Nations, Administrative Committee on Coordination/Subcommittee on Nutrition, *Second Report on the World Nutrition Situation* (Geneva: ACC/SCN, 1992).

United Nations, *Child Mortality Since the 1960s: A Database for Developing Countries* (New York: United Nations, 1992).

United Nations Children's Fund, *Food, Health and Care: The UNICEF Vision and Strategy for a World Free From Hunger and Malnutrition* (New York: UNICEF, 1993).

United Nations, Department of International Economic and Social Affairs, *Activities for the Advancement of Women, Equality, Development and Peace; Report of Jean Fernand-Laurent, Special Rapporteur on the Suppression of the Traffic in Persons and the Exploitation of the Prostitution of Others* (New York: United Nations, 1985).

United Nations, Department of International Economic and Social Affairs, *Demographic Yearbook* (New York: United Nations, annual).

United Nations, Department of International Economic and Social Affairs, *Socio-Economic Differentials in Child Mortality in Developing Countries* (New York: United Nations, 1985).

United States Agency for International Development, *Child Survival: A Second Report to Congress on the AID Program* (Washington, D.C.: USAID, 1988).

United States Congress House, *The Right to Food Resolution. Hearings Before the Subcommittee on International Resources, House of Representatives, 94th Congress, 2nd Session* (Washington, D.C.: United States Government Printing Office, 1976).

United States General Accounting Office, *Child Labor: Characteristics of Working Children* (Washington, D.C.: USGAO, 1991).

United States House of Representatives, Select Committee on Children, Youth, and Families, *U.S. Children and their Families: Current Conditions and Recent Trends, 1989* (Washington, D.C.: U.S. Government Printing Office., 1989).

United States Senate, *Children of War: Victims of Conflict and Dislocation. Hearing before the Subcommittee on Children, Family, Drugs and Alcoholism of the Committee on Labor and Human Resources* (Washington, D.C.: U.S. Government Printing Office, 1990).

Urquhart, Brian and Childers, Erskine, 'Strengthening International Responses to Humanitarian Emergencies,' in *Towards a More Effective United Nations*, special issue of *Development Dialogue* (Uppsala, Sweden: Dag Hammarskjold Foundation, 1991), pp. 41–85.

Veerman, Philip E., *The Rights of the Child and the Changing Image of Childhood* (Dordrecht, The Netherlands: Martinus Nijhoff, 1992).

Vittachi, Varindra Tarzie, *Between the Guns: Children as a Zone of Peace* (London: Hodder & Stoughton, 1993).

Vornberger, William, ed., *Fire From the Sky: Salvadoran Children's Drawings* (New York: Writers and Readers Publishing Cooperative, 1986).

Weiner, Myron, *The Child and the State in India: Child Labor and Education Policy in Comparative Perspective* (Princeton, New Jersey: Princeton University Press, 1991).

Weisberg, D. Kelly, *Children of the Night: A Study of Adolescent Prostitution* (Lexington, Massachusetts: Lexington Books, 1985).

Wilson, Francis and Ramphele, Mamphela, 'Children in South Africa,' in *Children on the Front Line: The Impact of Apartheid, Destabilization and Warfare on Children in Southern and South Africa* (New York: UNICEF, 1987), pp. 39–67.

Woodbury, Marda, *Childhood Information Resources* (Arlington, Virginia: Information Resources Press, 1985).

World Campaign for Human Rights, *The Rights of the Child* (Geneva: United Nations Centre for Human Rights, 1992).

World Declaration on the Survival, Protection and Development of Children and Plan of Action for Implementing the World Declaration on the Survival, Protection and Development of Children in the 1990s (New York: United Nations, 1990).

World Health Organization, *World Health Statistics Annual* (Geneva: WHO, annual).

Zeitlin, Marian; Ghassemi, Hossein; and Mansour, Mohammed, *Positive Deviance in Child Nutrition: With Emphasis on Psychosocial and Behavioural Aspects and Implications for Development* (Tokyo: United Nations University, 1989).

Index

accountability   145–8
  assessing accountability mechanisms
    154–5
  nutrition rights   127–8, 136, 154–5
Acker, Alison   87–8
adjustment, economic   16–18
Administrative Committee on
    Coordination/Subcommittee on
    Nutrition (ACC/SCN)   110, 111,
    112, 113, 173
adoption   59–60
advocacy   35–6
  armed conflict   98–102
  nutrition rights   137–9
Afghanistan   182, 190, 198, 205
  armed conflict   83, 84
AFL–CIO   50
Africa   16, 17
  see also under names of individual
    countries
Aga Khan, Prince Sadruddin   166
age
  median at death   31
  minimum for employment   48
agency, question of   98–102
Agenda for Consultations and Possible
    Action to Deal with Acute and
    Large-scale Food Shortages
    (1981)   176
aid (development assistance)   16,
    167–9
AIDS   31, 37, 82, 224
Albania   186, 194, 202, 209
Algeria   184, 192, 200, 207
Alston, Philip   119–20
Amnesty International   84
Andersen, Jack   71
anemias, nutritional   103
Angola   86, 182, 190, 198, 205
anthropometric measures of
    malnutrition   107–9
Anti-Slavery International   46, 47–8,
    77
Apocalypse Now (film)   69

Argentina   72, 186, 194, 202, 209
armed conflicts   33, 83–102
  fatalities   32, 83, 86
  defense expenditures   90–2
  humanitarian assistance   160–1,
    163, 165, 166, 236
  international humanitarian law
    92–6; implementation 96–8
  nutrition rights   86–7, 171
  question of agency   98–102
  ways in which children are harmed
    83–90
Armenia   186, 194, 202, 209
Asian Regional Seminar on Children in
    Bondage   51
assistance   *see* development assistance;
    humanitarian assistance
auctions, of girls   72
Australia   188, 196, 204, 211
Austria   188, 196, 204, 211
Azerbaijan   185, 193, 201, 208

Bahay Tuluyan program   66–7
Bangladesh   106, 183, 191, 199, 206
  flood and cyclone deaths (1991)   38
  Grameen Bank micro-loans   52–3
  prostitution   72
bar ownership   68
bargaining power   15, 19
basic indicators   182–9
basic needs   121–2
'beach boys'   70
Belarus   187, 195, 203, 210
Belgium   188, 196, 204, 210
Benin   183, 191, 199, 206
Bhutan   182, 190, 198, 205
birth rates   182–9
  population and the economy   20–4
Boerma, Addeke H.   117, 231
Bolivia   184, 192, 200, 207
bonded labor   46
  see also labor
Bonded Labour Liberation Front   49,
    51

Boothby, Neil   83–4, 86, 96, 97, 101
Bosnia   83, 84, 90, 159, 160
   see also Yugoslavia (former)
Boswell, John   217
Botswana   185, 193, 201, 208
Bouhdiba, Abdelwahab   218
Brazil   185, 193, 201, 208
   children's rights   142–3
   prostitution   57
   rich–poor divide   13
breastfeeding   190–7
Bristow, Edward J.   220
Buenos Aires   72
Bulgaria   187, 195, 203, 210
Burkina Faso   183, 191, 199, 206
Burma   59
Burundi   183, 191, 199, 206
Butler, Josephine   77

calorie supply per capita   190–7
Cambodia   69, 183, 191, 199, 206
   see also Kampuchea
Cameroon   184, 192, 200, 207
Canada   189, 197, 204, 211
capping entitlements   129–30
'catalog' brides   60
Central African Republic   183, 191,
   199, 206
Centre for the Protection of Children's
   Rights   64
Chad   182, 190, 198, 205
Charny, Israel   42
Chen, Lincoln   107
child labor   *see* labor
child prostitution   *see* prostitution
Children's Defense Fund   36, 90
Children's Ombudsman   146
children's rights   43, 141–56
   accountability   145–8
   international monitoring   155–6
   monitoring and reporting on
      148–55
   soft vs. hard rights   142–4
   see also humanitarian assistance;
      nutrition rights
Children's Rights Coalition   146
Chile   187, 195, 203, 210
China   185, 193, 201, 208
   children and earning income   25

economic reforms   121
   prostitution   58, 59, 72
chronic conditions   166–7
civil society   5–8, 10, 144
   global   8–10, 10, 176–7
class   92
Clinton, President Bill   168
Colombia   187, 195, 203, 210
Committee on Economic, Social and
   Cultural Rights (CESCR)   138,
   149–50, 155
Committee on the Rights of the Child
   101, 142, 155
'commons, tragedy of the'   22–3
community   122
   nutrition rights   123, 129
   responsibility   6–7
compassionate assistance   *see*
   humanitarian assistance
complaint procedure   147, 155
compliance monitoring   *see*
   monitoring
compulsory humanitarian intervention
   171
concentration of wealth/power   18–19
conditions, children's   3–5
Congo   184, 192, 200, 207
consent, assistance and   159–63
contracts, social   147–8, 151, 158
*Convention on the Elimination of All
   Forms of Discrimination Against
   Women*   9, 81
Convention on the Law of the Sea
   95–6
*Convention on the Prevention and
   Punishment of the Crime of
   Genocide*   41
Convention on the Rights of the Child
   (1989/90)   101, 141–2, 149
   armed conflict   93–5;
      implementation of Article   38
      97–8
   child labor   48
   child prostitution   79–80, 82
   cultural relativism   81
   international rights   170
   nutrition   118, 120, 144
Costa Rica   3, 188, 195, 203, 210
Côte d'Ivoire   184, 192, 200, 207

coverage of service programs 153–4
crises, humanitarian 9
    see also humanitarian assistance
Cuba 119, 188, 196, 203, 210
Cullen, Father Shay 68
cultural relativism 80–2
customers, prostitutes' traveling
    62–71
Czech Republic 188, 195, 203, 210
Czechoslovakia 83

De Swaan, Abram 213, 232
death squads 84
debt 16–18
*Declaration on the Protection of
    Women and Children in
    Emergencies and Armed Conflicts*
    93
Declaration of the Rights of the Child
    (1924) 141
Declaration of the Rights of the Child
    (1959) 28, 48, 141
Defence for Children International
    (DCI) 36, 77
defense expenditures 88–9, 90–2
deliberate neglect 38–9, 40–1, 218
deMause, Lloyd 40
demographic transition 20–2
denial 36–7
Denmark 189, 197, 204, 211
Department of Humanitarian Affairs
    165
DeShaney v. *Winnebago County
    Department of Social Services*
    38
developing countries
    humanitarian intervention 162
    malnutrition 110–12
    see also under individual names
development, socioeconomic 24
development assistance (aid) 16,
    167–9
diarrhea 33, 104
    see also ORT
distance 36
distribution
    children's conditions and 3–4
    population and economy 23–6,
    roots of poverty 18–19

division of labor 13–15
domestic service 61–2
Dominican Republic 185, 193, 201,
    208
DPT immunization 180, 198–204
Drèze, Jean 105, 125, 229
duties *see* obligations
Dyer, Alfred 77

Eastern Europe 67
    see also under individual countries
Eberstadt, N. 215
Eckhardt, William 32
economic efficiency 121
economic growth 19, 47
    see also gross national product
Economic and Social Council of the
    UN (ECOSOC) 76–7, 149, 234
Ecuador 185, 193, 201, 208
Edelman, Marian Wright 39–40
education
    indicators 3, 179–80, 182–9,
    205–11
    private vocational schooling
    51–5
effectiveness of service programs 153
efficiency, economic 121
Egypt 185, 193, 201, 208
Eide, Asbjørn 138
Eide, Wenche Barth 138
Eisenhower, Dwight D. 88
El Mozote massacre 83, 224
El Salvador 83, 185, 193, 201, 208
    armed conflict 97
Eliasson, Jan 165
Elizabeth Saunders Home for Mixed-
    blood Children 89
emergencies 122
    food supplies 171–2
empowerment 125, 233
End Child Prostitution in Asian
    Tourism (ECPAT) 78, 224
England 21
    see also United Kingdom
Ennew, Judith 220
enrollment ratios
    primary 3, 179–80, 182–9, 205–11
    secondary 179–80, 205–11

entitlements   105–6, 125
    capping   129–30
environment   24–5
EPINUT   230
Eritrea   182, 190, 198, 205
Estonia   186, 194, 202, 209
Ethiopia   182, 190, 198, 205
    famine   86, 166
events orientation   36–7
exploitation   73, 81
    see also labor; prostitution
'exposure'   33, 217

fake marriages   60–1
family
    police reluctance to intervene   160
    responsibility   6–7
family planning programs   24, 26
farmland   22–3
fertility   *see* birth rates
Filipovic, Zlata   226
Finland   189, 197, 204, 211
food
    access to and distribution within
        household   104
    armed conflicts and supply   86–7
    calorie supply per capita   190–7
    emergency supplies   171–2
    trade   14–15
    see also malnutrition; nutrition
        goals; nutrition programs;
        nutrition rights
Food and Agriculture Organization
    (FAO)   109, 173, 174
Foodfirst Information and Action
    Network (FIAN)   138, 233
Foreign Bodies (film)   80
France   188, 196, 204, 211
Frank, Anne   42
funding   128

Gabon   183, 191, 199, 206
Generalized System of Preferences
    (GSP)   50–1
Geneva Conventions   93
genocide   41–3
    see also mass murder
Genovese, Kitty   158–9
Georgia   186, 194, 202, 209

Germany   60, 188, 196, 204, 211
Ghana   183, 191, 199, 206
Glendon, Mary   158
Global Action Plan   174–6
global civil society   8–10, 10, 176–7
global economy   13–28
    debt and structural adjustment
        16–18
    division of labor   13–15
    international obligations   27–8
    population   20–7
    roots of poverty   18–20
    goals as rights   133–7
goiter   103, 180, 190–7
Gomez scale of expected weight
    107
government(s)/state
    murder by   32
    obligations and children's rights
        148
    obligations and nutrition rights
        121–3; assessing government
        service programs   152–4
    policy's role in mortality   34–43;
        priorities and poverty   34–6
    and prostitution   63, 80
    responsibility   6–7, 7–8, 99
    see also local government
Grameen Bank   52–3
Grant, James P.   33, 179, 216
Greece   188, 196, 204, 211
gross national product (GNP)   19
    per capita   26, 179, 182–9
    underweight children and   111–12,
        113
growth, economic   19, 47
    see also gross national product
growth measurement (physical)
    107–9
Guatemala   184, 192, 200, 207
Guinea   182, 190, 198, 205
Guinea-Bissau   182, 190, 198, 205
Gulf War   87, 95, 228

Haiti   62, 183, 191, 199, 206
hard rights   142–4
Hardin, Garrett   22–3, 37, 177
hatred, indifference or   39–41
Hawaii   146

health
  access to health services 180,
    198–204
  armed conflict's impact on health
    care 86–7
  expenditures 17
  indicators 198–204
higher education 53
Himes, James R. 233
Ho, T. J. 230
homicide 37–8
  see also genocide; infanticide; mass
    murder
Honduras 69, 185, 193, 201, 208
Hong Kong 189, 197, 204, 211
  prostitution 62–3
hostages 84
humane law 235
humanitarian assistance 157–77, 235
  chronic conditions 166–7
  consent 159–63
  development assistance vs 167–9
  Global Action Plan 174–6
  global civil society 8–10, 176–7
  international principle 169–71
  progressive realization 163–6
  rights to 158–9
  see also nutrition rights
humanitarian intervention 159–63,
    171
humanitarian law, international 92–6,
    157, 235
  implementation 96–8
Hungary 187, 195, 203, 210
hunger
  defense budgets and 90–2
  as instrument of warfare 86–7,
    171
  see also malnutrition; nutrition
    rights
Huq, Muzammel 91, 227

immunization 180, 198–204
incentives 127–8
income share 180, 182–9
income transfer programs 27
indenturing, international 61–2
India 184, 192, 200, 207
  child labor 45–6, 46, 48

child prostitution 57, 58, 60, 72,
    74
children's rights 143
malnutrition 106
nutrition programs 131–2
population and poverty 26
starvation and sales of children 166
indifference, hatred or 39–41
Indonesia 106, 184, 192, 200, 207
infant formula 143
  intentionality and harmful effects
    39
  malnutrition 104–5
infant mortality rate 31–2, 179,
    182–9
  see also mortality
infanticide 33, 217
inflation 19–20, 66
intentionality 37–9
International Abolitionist Federation
    (IAF) 77–8, 81
International Catholic Child Bureau
    78
international children's rights *see*
    humanitarian assistance; nutrition
    rights
International Committee for the Red
    Cross (ICRC) 98, 99–100, 101,
    160–1
International Conference on Children
    in Situations of Armed Conflict in
    Africa (1987) 100–1
International Conference on Nutrition
    (1992) 174–5, 176
  goals 134, 152
  humanitarian intervention 162
  nutrition rights 118–19, 134
*International Covenant on Civil and
    Political Rights* 141
*International Covenant on Economic,
    Social and Cultural Rights* (1966)
    117–18, 141, 149, 170
  Limburg Principles 122, 135
  Optional Protocol 138
International Criminal Police
    Organization (INTERPOL) 76
International Decade for Natural
    Disaster Reduction (IDNDR)
    163, 164

International Emergency Food Reserve (IEFR) 172
International Federation Terre des Hommes 78
International Feminist Network Against Female Sexual Slavery (IFN) 78
International Fund for Agricultural Development (IFAD) 173
international governmental organizations (IGOs)
  child prostitution 76–7
  implementation of international nutrition rights 173–6
  responsibility 7, 9
  see also under individual names
International Labour Office/Organization (ILO) 46, 47, 76, 218
  Child Labour Collection 48
  Children in Shadow 219
  Convention 138–48
international law
  child prostitution 78–80
  hard and soft 144
  humanitarian 92–6, 157, 235; implementation 96–8
  universal minimum human rights 82
International Medical Congress (1871) 79
International Monetary Fund (IMF) 213, 216
international nongovernmental organizations (INGOs)
  child prostitution 77–8
  nutrition rights 138–9, 175
  responsibility 7, 9
  see also under individual names
international obligations 27–8
International Red Cross and Red Crescent Museum, Geneva 100
International Save the Children Alliance 36, 78
intervention, humanitarian 159–63, 171
Iran 85, 185, 193, 201, 208
Iraq 184, 192, 200, 207
  execution of children 84

Gulf War 87
  humanitarian assistance for Kurds 157, 159, 160, 164
Ireland 189, 197, 204, 211
Islam 81
Israel 83, 188, 196, 203, 210
Italy 188, 196, 204, 211

Jamaica 188, 195, 203, 210
Japan 62, 189, 197, 204, 211
  sex tourism 73
Jews 39, 59, 220
John Paul II, Pope 118–19, 171
Jolly, Richard 117
Jonsson, Urban 230
Jordan 186, 194, 202, 209

Kampuchea 86
  see also Cambodia
Kashmir 45–6
Kazakhstan 185, 193, 201, 208
Kenya 184, 192, 200, 207
Korea, Democratic People's Republic of 186, 194, 202, 209
Korea, Republic of 188, 196, 204, 211
kulaks 87
Kurds in Iraq 157, 159, 164
Kuwait 187, 195, 203, 210
Kyrgyzstan 185, 193, 201, 208

labor, child 45–55
  business-like schooling 51–5
  remedies 47–51
  see also prostitution
labor, division of 13–15
land 22–3
Landau, Elaine 223
Lao, People's Democratic Republic of 183, 191, 199, 206
Lappé, Frances Moore 22
Latvia 186, 194, 202, 209
law/legislation
  child labor 48–9
  child prostitution: domestic law 74–5; international law 78–80
  global civil society 177
  international *see* international law
  legal recourse 147, 155
  legal systems 144

monitoring and reporting on rights 150–2
nutrition rights 124, 129–30
soft and hard rights 142–4
Lebanon 88, 185, 193, 201, 208
Lesotho 183, 191, 199, 206
Lewis Carroll Collector's Guild 71
Lexington, Kentucky, Exploited and Missing Child Unit 75
Liaison Group on Children in Armed Conflict, proposed 102
Liberia 182, 190, 198, 205
Libyan Arab Jamahiriya 184, 192, 200, 207
Lidice massacre 83
life expectancy 179, 182–9
Limburg Principles on the Implementation of the International Covenant on Economic, Social and Cultural Rights 122, 135
literacy rate, adult 179, 182–9, 205–11
Lithuania 187, 195, 203, 210
loan programs, tuition 52–4
local government 6–7, 126
low birth weight 3, 180, 190–7

Madagascar 183, 191, 199, 206
Mahbub-ul-Haq 89
'mail order' brides 60
malaria 33
Malawi 166, 182, 190, 198, 205
Malaya 58
Malaysia 187, 195, 203, 210
Mali 182, 190, 198, 205
malnutrition 103–13, 117, 120, 156, 230
  causes 103–6; basic (societal) 105–6; clinical (immediate) 104; underlying (household level) 104–5
  extent 109–13
  growth measurement 107–9
  international children's rights 166–77
  low priority due to events orientation 36–7
  and mortality 106–7

protection from 123–4
  see also nutrition rights
mandate 154
Manifesto Against Hunger (1981) 41
Manila 70
Man's Right to Freedom from Hunger (1963) 117
marriage 60–1
Martorell, Reynaldo 230
mass murder 161–2
  see also genocide
Matsui, Yayori 73
Mauritania 182, 190, 198, 205
Mauritius 186, 194, 202, 209
Mayer, Jean 86–7
measles 4, 33
  immunization 198–204
Mexico 162, 186, 194, 202, 209
micro-loan programs 52–4
Middle East 63–4
migration
  child prostitution 59–62, 66
  global economy 14
military travelers 67–9
mines, leftover 84
mixed-race children 89–90
Moldova 186, 194, 202, 209
Mongolia 184, 192, 200, 207
monitoring, compliance 145, 148–55
Moro, Arthur 59
Morocco 185, 193, 201, 208
mortality 3, 31–43
  armed conflicts 32, 83, 86
  causes 33
  denial 36–7
  genocide 41–3
  hatred or indifference 39–41
  infant mortality rate 31–2, 179, 182–9
  intentionality 37–9
  malnutrition and 106–7
  population and economy 20–3
  priority, not policy 34–6
  rates 179, 182–9
Mosley, W. Henry 107
Mozambique 86, 182, 190, 198, 205
Mozambique National Resistance (MNR/Renamo) 85
Mui Tsai system 58

multi-layering   125–6, 135
multinational corporations (MNCs)
    67, 74
Muntarbhorn, Vitit   77, 224
Myanmar   184, 192, 200, 207

Namibia   184, 192, 200, 207
Nanda, Ved   119
national government/state   *see*
    government(s)/state
National Plans of Action   120, 134
nationalism   36
Nazism   39
needs, basic   121–2
neglect   38–9, 42
    deliberate   38–9, 40–1, 218
Nepal   72, 183, 191, 199, 206
Netherlands   189, 197, 204, 211
New Zealand   188, 196, 204, 211
Nicaragua   83, 184, 192, 200, 207
Niger   182, 190, 198, 205
Nigeria   182, 190, 198, 205
    armed conflict   86, 87
nongovernmental organizations   127,
    145, 175
    international   *see* international
        nongovernmental organizations
noon meal program   131–2
North American Man-Boy Love
    Association (NAMBLA)   71
Northern Ireland   88
Norway   189, 197, 204, 211
nutrition goals   152
nutrition indicators   190–7
nutrition programs   123
    assessing government's   152–4
    funding   128
    using existing   124–5, 130–3, 137
nutrition rights   117–39
    advocacy   137–9
    capping entitlements   129–30
    fulfillment   122, 152
    funding   128
    goals as rights   133–7
    history   117–20
    incentives   127–8
    international   170–6; Global Action
        Plan   174–6; implementation
        173–4; monitoring   155–6

monitoring and reporting on
    50–5; accountability
    mechanisms   154–5;
    government's service programs
    152–4; the law   150–2;
    mandate 154; nutrition
    problems   150
multi-layering   125–6, 135
principle   121–5
protection of   122, 123–4, 152
reason for focus on children
    120–1
respect for   122, 152
soft and hard rights   143–4
using existing programs   124–5,
    130–3, 137
'Nutrition Rights Corporation',
    proposed   137

obligations
    civil society   7–8; global civil
        society   177
    humanitarian assistance   158–9,
        163, 236
    international   27–8
    nutrition rights   122–3, 138, 170–1
    social contracts   148
Office of Foreign Disaster Assistance
    (OFDA)   164
Olongapo City   68
Oman   186, 194, 202, 209
Ombudsman, Children's   146
*Optional Protocol to the International
    Covenant on Civil and Political
    Rights*   141
*Optional Protocol to the International
    Covenant on Economic, Social
    and Cultural Rights*   138
ORT (oral rehydration treatment) use
    181, 198–204
Oshaug, Arne   138

Paedo Alert News   71
Pakistan   183, 191, 199, 206
    child labor   46, 49, 51
PAN magazine   71
Panama   187, 195, 203, 210
Pangsanjan   69–70, 80
Papua New Guinea   184, 192, 200, 207

Paraguay 59, 186, 194, 202, 209
parasitic diseases 104
parents 6–7
Park Sun Ai 73, 222
pay/wages 15, 26
peace, zones of 101, 161
Pearl S. Buck Foundation 89
pedophiles 67, 69–71
pertussis (whooping cough) 33
  immunization 180, 198–204
Peru 66, 185, 193, 201, 208
  children as soldiers 85
Philippines 185, 193, 201, 208
  child prostitution 57, 58, 67, 73,
    80; bar ownership 68;
    customers 64, 66–7, 67–8, 69,
    69–70; government policy 63
  mixed-race children 89–90
Pictet, Jean 235
*Plan of Action for Implementing the
  World Declaration on the
  Survival, Protection and
  Development of Children (1990)*
  96, 133–4, 142
Plan of Action for Nutrition (1992)
  119, 120, 174–5, 176
Plan of Action on World Food Security
  (1979) 176
plantations 26, 74
Platteau, Jean-Philippe 121
Poland 187, 195, 203, 210
polio immunization 198–204
population 20–7
Portugal 188, 195, 203, 210
poverty
  development assistance 167–8
  government priorities and mortality
    34–6
  international obligations 27
  population growth and 22–4
  roots of 18–20
power
  concentration of 18–19
  empowerment 125, 233
  exploitation and 73
pregnant women, tetanus 198–204
primary education
  children reaching final grade 181,
    205–11

enrollment ratios 3, 179–80,
    182–9, 205–11
private vocational schooling 51–5
privatization, semi- 137
progressive social policy 4–5
prostitutes' children 69
prostitution 57–82
  domestic law 74–5
  economic pressures 71–4
  international control 76–82;
    cultural relativism 80–2;
    IGOs 76–7; INGOs 77–8;
    international legislation
    78–80
  trafficking 58–62, 72
  traveling customers 62–71
protein-energy malnutrition (PEM)
  103, 107–13
  see also malnutrition
protein sparing 103
provinces 126
psychological damage 87–8

racism 36
Rädda Barnen 96
radio sets 205–11
Rajivan, Anuradha Khati 132
rape 90
Red Cross
  International Committee for The
    (ICRC) 98, 99–100, 101,
    160–1
  national societies 98, 165
refugee camps 126
Refugee Policy Group 165
relativism, cultural 80–2
relief corridors 163
reporting on rights 148–55
rescue, rights of 158–9
responsibility 3–11, 171
  children's conditions 3–5
  civil society 5–8
  global civil society 8–10
rich–poor divide 13
  see also global economy
ritual marriages 60
Romania 186, 194, 202, 209
Rousseau, Jean Jacques 147–8
Rummel, R. J. 32

Index

runaway shelters   75
Russian Federation   67, 186, 194, 202, 209
Rwanda   182, 190, 198, 205

safe water, access to   198–204
sales of children   72, 166
sanitation   198–204
Saudi Arabia   185, 193, 201, 208
Save the Children   36, 78
Sawyer, Roger   218
schooling   *see* education
Schurman, Rachel   22
secondary school enrollment   179–80, 205–11
security
    defense expenditure and human welfare   90–2
    having children and   22, 215
self-sufficiency   168–9
semi-privatization   137
Sen, Amartya   105, 125, 229
'Sendoro Luminoso' ('Shining Path')   85
Senegal   183, 191, 199, 206
service, domestic   61–2
service programs   *see* nutrition programs; social services
sex tours, organized   65
Sierra Leone   182, 190, 198, 205
Singapore   189, 197, 204, 211
Sivard, Ruth Leger   90
skills   51–5
Slovakia   188, 195, 203, 210
social contracts   147–8, 151, 158
social policy, progressive   4–5
social services
    accountability   145–6
    capping entitlements   129–30, 232–3
    development assistance and self-sufficiency   168
    expenditure on   8, 17, 27, 130, 213, 216; under-weight children   111–12
    responsibility   122
    transitional economies   18
    see also nutrition programs
social support mechanisms   54

socially-oriented adjustment programs   17
socioeconomic development   24
soft rights   142–4
soldiers, children as   85–6, 94–5, 96–7, 97
    see also military travelers
Somalia   182, 190, 198, 205
    famine   86, 166
    humanitarian assistance   157, 159, 160, 164
South Africa   185, 193, 201, 208
    imprisonment and torture of children   84
sovereignty   160, 162, 176–7
Spain   188, 196, 204, 211
Spartacus Gay Guide   71
Sri Lanka   106, 187, 195, 203, 210
    child prostitution   67, 70
starvation   *see* hunger
state   *see* government(s)/state
street children   33, 65, 84
structural adjustment   16–18
stunting   108–9, 180, 190–7
sub-Saharan Africa   16
    see also under individual countries
subsistence rights   121–2
Sudan   183, 191, 199, 206
    civil war and famine   86, 166
Sweden   33–4, 189, 197, 204, 211
Swedish Red Cross   165
Suriname   84
Switzerland   188, 196, 204, 211
Syrian Arab Republic   186, 194, 202, 209

Tajikistan   184, 192, 200, 207
Tamilnadu Integrated Nutrition Program (TINP)   131–2
Tan, M. L.   73, 222
Tanzania   72, 183, 191, 199, 206
Task Force on Children's Nutrition Rights   139
Task Force on Monitoring and Implementation of the Right to Food   138
Task Force on the Use of Food as a Weapon of War or for Political Purposes   138

television sets   205–11
terrorism   83–4
tetanus
  immunization   180, 198–204
  neonatal   33
  pregnant women   198–204
Thailand   186, 194, 202, 209
  child labor   45, 46, 47, 49, 50
  child prostitution   57, 58, 60, 64,
    74, 80; pedophiles   67, 71; sex
    tours   65; US military bases
    68
Thomas J. Watson Jr. Institute for
  International Studies   165
Timberlake, Lloyd   218
Time magazine   67
Togo   183, 191, 199, 206
Tokyo   72
Tomaševski, Katarina   119
Tomorrow Will There Be a Rainbow
  (film)   64
tourism, prostitution and   62–7
trade, international
  and child labor   49–51
  division of labor   14–15
trafficking, prostitution and   58–62,
  72
'tragedy of the commons'   22–3
transitional economies   17–18
traveling customers, prostitutes'
  62–71
triage   37, 168
Trinidad and Tobago   187, 195, 203,
  210
tuberculosis (TB) immunization
  198–204
tuition loan programs   52–4
Tunisia   186, 194, 202, 209
Turkey   184, 192, 200, 207
Turkmenistan   184, 192, 200, 207

Uganda   183, 191, 199, 206
armed conflict   85, 88
Ukraine   186, 194, 202, 209
  'de-kulakization'   87
unaccompanied children   90
underweight   3, 180, 190–7
  measure of malnutrition   108–9,
    111, 111–12, 113

United Arab Emirates   187, 195, 203,
  210
United Kingdom (UK)   4, 188, 196,
  204, 211
  children as soldiers   95, 228
  Contagious Diseases Acts   79
  see also England
United Nations (UN)
  ACC/SCN   110, 111, 112, 113, 173
  Centre for Human Rights   169–70
  CESCR   138, 149–50, 155
  conventions on child prostitution
    and exploitation of women   79
  Department of Humanitarian Affairs
    165
  ECOSOC   76–7, 149, 234
  FAO   109, 173, 174
  international nutrition monitoring
    149, 156
  peacekeeping forces and prostitution
    68–9
  progressive realization of rights to
    humanitarian assistance   163–5
  Resolution   46/182 162, 164,
    164–5
  United Nations Children's Fund
    (UNICEF)   36, 142, 169–70,
    173, 174
  adjustment policy   17
  annual budget   27
  armed conflict   89, 90, 100–1;
    zones of peace   161
  child prostitution   76
  Children in War studies   101
  children's conditions   3, 4
  development assistance   167, 169
  malnutrition   108
United Nations Development
  Programme (UNDP)   15, 167,
  214
United Nations Disaster Relief
  Coordinator (UNDRO)   163,
  164, 165
United Nations High Commissioner for
  Refugees (UNHCR)   101
United States (US)   4, 188, 196, 204,
  211
  accountability   127, 146, 146–7

Aid to Families with Dependent
	Children (AFDC)	131
Amerasian Act	89–90
United States (US)	(*cont.*)
	armed conflict	93, 95; mixed-race
		children	89–90
	child labor	47, 48;	GSP 50–1
	child prostitution	74–5; military
		bases	67–8
	Children's Defense Fund	36, 90
	development assistance	167
	entitlement programs	232–3
	humanitarian assistance	157, 164
	infant mortality rate	31–2, 35,
		188
	Law of the Sea	95–6
	malnutrition	109
	Mann Act (1910)	79
	Medford Declaration to End Hunger
		131
	no-duty-to-rescue principle	158–9
	nutrition rights	118, 130–1;
		monitoring	131
	poverty	18
	Runaway and Homeless Youth Act
		75
	social services expenditure	216
	Special Supplemental Food Program
		for Women, Infants and
		Children (WIC)	131
	White House Task Force on
		Combating Terrorism	26
United States Agency for International
	Development (USAID)	169
	Office of Foreign Disaster
		Assistance	164
*Universal Declaration on the
	Eradication of Hunger and
	Malnutrition* (1974)	118
*Universal Declaration of Human
	Rights* (1948)	117, 141, 143, 147
Uruguay	187, 195, 203, 210
Uzbekistan	185, 193, 201, 208

venereal disease	68
Venezuela	186, 194, 202, 209
Viet Nam	67, 185, 193, 201, 208
violence against children	83–5
	see also armed conflicts

vocational schools, private	51–5

wages/pay	15, 26
Wannsee Conference (1942)	39
war	*see* armed conflicts
wasting	108–9, 180, 190–7
water, access to safe	198–204
Weisberg, D. Kelly	75, 223
welfare programs	*see* nutrition
	programs; social services
Wijkman, Anders	218
willful negligence	218
Woods, Dorothea	96–7, 225
Working Group of Experts on
	Contemporary Forms of Slavery
	76
World Alliance for Nutrition and
	Human Rights (WANAHR)
	138, 233
World Bank	27, 109, 216
	Social Dimensions of Adjustment
		17
World Conference on Human Rights
	(1993)	49–50
World Declaration on Nutrition (1992)
	119, 120, 162, 174–5, 176
World Food Assembly	118
World Food Council (WFC)	118,
	173
World Food Programme (WFP)	123,
	169, 172, 173
World Food Security Compact (1985)
	176
World Health Organization (WHO)
	103, 173, 174
World Summit for Children (1990)
	120, 133, 134, 142, 152
World War II	32, 90

xerophthalmia	103

Yemen	183, 191, 199, 206
Yugoslavia (former)	187, 195, 203,
	210
	humanitarian assistance	157, 159,
		160

Zaire	182, 190, 198, 205
	armed conflict	161